Chicken Soup for the Soul

My Dog's Life

D0047878

Chicken Soup for the Soul: My Dog's Life
101 Stories about All the Ages and Stages of Our Canine Companions
Jack Canfield, Mark Victor Hansen, Jennifer Quasha. Foreword by Wendy Diamond.

Published by Chicken Soup for the Soul Publishing, LLC   www.chickensoup.com
The publisher gratefully acknowledges the many publishers and individuals who granted Chicken Soup for the Soul permission to reprint the cited material.

Front cover photo courtesy of Getty Images/Stone Collection, © GK Hart/Vikki Hart. Wendy Diamond photo on back cover courtesy of Wendy Diamond. Back cover photo courtesy of iStockphoto.com/Eriklam (© Erik Lam). Interior photos courtesy of iStockphoto.com/PaulTessier (© Paul Tessier), /Malven (©Michelle Malven), /JP Schrage (© Jan Paul Schrage), /nojustice (© Joseph C. Justice Jr.).

Cover and Interior Design & Layout by Pneuma Books, LLC
For more info on Pneuma Books, visit www.pneumabooks.com

Distributed to the booktrade by Simon & Schuster. SAN: 200-2442

Publisher's Cataloging-in-Publication Data
(Prepared by The Donohue Group)

Chicken soup for the soul : my dog's life : 101 stories about all the ages and stages of our canine companions / [compiled by] Jack Canfield, Mark Victor Hansen, [and] Jennifer Quasha ; foreword by Wendy Diamond.

p. ; cm.

Summary: A collection of 101 true stories from people about all the ages and stages of living with their dogs. Stories are personal anecdotes, ranging from funny to sad, dealing with issues of life, love, family, perseverance, joy in life, death, friendship, and other human emotions.
ISBN: 978-1-935096-65-8

1. Dogs--Literary collections. 2. Dogs--Anecdotes. 3. Dog owners--Literary collections. 4. Dog owners--Anecdotes. 5. Human-animal relationships--Literary collections. 6. Human-animal relationships--Anecdotes. I. Canfield, Jack, 1944- II. Hansen, Mark Victor. III. Quasha, Jennifer. IV. Diamond, Wendy. V. Title: My dog's life

PN6071.D6 C456 2011
810.8/02/03629772   2010938812

PRINTED IN THE UNITED STATES OF AMERICA
on acid∞free paper
20 19 18 17 16 15 14 13 12 11   02 03 04 05 06 07 08 09 10

Chicken Soup for the Soul® My Dog's Life

101 Stories about
All the Ages and Stages of
Our Canine Companions

Jack Canfield
Mark Victor Hansen
Jennifer Quasha
Foreword by Wendy Diamond

Chicken Soup for the Soul Publishing, LLC
Cos Cob, CT

www.chickensoup.com

Contents

❸
~Who's the Boss?~

❹
~It's a Ruff Life~

❺
~For the Love of Dog~

❻

~Leader of the Pack~

❼

~These Old Bones~

❽

~A Walk Down Memory Lane~

❾

~Over the Rainbow~

⑩
~I'll Always Love You~

Foreword

hat's your favorite stage of dog parenthood? Is it when you first bring home your new dog and he looks up at you with those innocent, loving puppy eyes—and then chews up your favorite pair of pumps? We've all been there. Or is it when he turns into a "teenager" and his full-sized, often-naughty personality pushes your buttons—until he collapses exhausted next to you needing a snuggle—with those sleepy eyes you can't resist and that gentle snore that doesn't seem to bother you at all? Maybe it's when your dog has hit her prime and settled into adulthood. Both you and she have a good sense of each other and your daily rhythms have adapted into a peaceful routine. Or is it the senior stage when your best friend has slowed down, and you can be quiet together and simply enjoy each other's company? And then there are the twilight years, when, as pet parents, we feel so needed. We realize that those tables are turned, and that we need to pay our best friends back for all those years of licks and unconditional love.

How can we choose our favorite stage? Well, we don't have to! We all know that every age and stage is special in its own way, and this book has unforgettable stories about every one of those special ages and stages.

Since I rescued Lucky as a puppy some ten years ago, and though she does not discuss her exact age, we have been through a lot of wonderful ages and stages together. Like many of us who get a dog for the first time, it's fair to say that adopting Lucky changed my life. I had never felt unconditional love like that before. And after I saw how bad many animal shelters were, and how much love I felt for her, I knew I had to do something. Since then I have been truly blessed—I'd go so far as to say *lucky*—to be able to serve as an advocate for homeless animals.

What I do every day stems from that day I found Lucky. But as every dog parent knows, we are all lucky, and this book illustrates so well the many blessings we have been given by our dogs. Every story in this *Chicken Soup for the Soul* book reminds us how our dogs have changed and positively contributed to our lives. The stories also remind us of the great gift it is to have our dogs in our lives, the friendship we share, and how the human-animal bond makes us better people every day.

I promise you that in every chapter of this book you will love the stories. Imagine reading about a woman who adopts a puppy to find out a couple of years later that it is a coyote pup! After years of trying to get her puppy to bond with her and her family, author Andrea Peebles realizes that her "pet" is a wild animal—a wild animal that teaches her a lot. I love Meg Stragier's story about how her husband forgot to close the back door after she left the water on in her rose garden. Their Newfie puppy goes out to play and then comes back in unnoticed. Their entire house is covered with mud! Meg employs "instant forgiveness" toward their puppy, she and her husband laugh it off, and the two of them spend hours cleaning up together. Talk about inspiring! In Shirley M. Corder's piece, she recounts the stressful evening when she found out that her puppy had eaten toxic fly-killing powder. From training mishaps to delinquent obedience school "students"—every story embodies the essence of dog parenthood.

Then the teenage dog stories remind us of how sometimes our four-legged teens are kind of similar to the two-legged variety! Like some teenagers, dogs don't understand that their crazy antics have consequences! Co-author Jennifer Quasha tells the story of her dog, a naughty teenage Bichon Frise, who eats a corncob... whole. J.J. Kay tells her story about trying to rein in her eager teenage dog in an effort to become a therapy dog. Like so many overactive young pooches, his kindness and kisses are so effusive they can knock people down.

One of my favorite stories is written by new mother Michelle Sedas. She shares her heart-wrenching story about almost giving up her beloved dog when he was a teenager because she was overwhelmed by his unruly behavior. She tells us how she and her family were able to solve this unfortunately very common problem.

In our adult dog chapters you will read stories about how our dogs help us: to love, to exercise, to be heard, to be strong, and to laugh. Chicken Soup for the Soul editors have selected amazing stories, such as Robbie Iobst's story of their family dog, Scooby, who realizes her son is having an asthma attack and alerts her. You'll find a story about a dog named Rudy, who on a walk hears a strange noise that his pet parent can't hear and leads her to a house where an elderly woman had fallen and broken her leg. On the lighter side you will read about Sam, a Black Lab who loves to play jokes on his pet parents, but who himself can't stand being laughed at. There's also a great story about a service dog for a blind woman who leads his pet parent down the pet food aisle in the supermarket because he can't resist smelling the dog food!

In our senior dogs and twilight years chapters you will read stories which will prove to you why older dogs really can make the best friends and why you should definitely consider adopting an older dog from a shelter next time you are in the market for a new friend. Dawn M. Hesse adopts a senior dog and then wonders why on earth she chose to adopt him — until he breaks through two doors to save her when their house catches on fire. In a story by Saralee Perel you'll read about how she lives with a spinal cord injury and is grateful to her aging Shepherd/Collie mix, who still acts as her protector. You'll love the wonderful story from Rachel Neumeier about an old agility dog who is deaf but ends up winning a competition since he is the only contestant not bothered by the noise of a thunderstorm raging outside!

Lastly, I promise, the stories on grieving and recovery will not depress you! They will inspire and empower you during a time that every pet parent dreads, the death and subsequent recovery from the passing of a beloved dog. Read about how, the day after Kathe

Campbell's beloved Keeshond died, she randomly picked up a newspaper and saw an ad placed by a hard-to-find Keeshond breeder in another state with one last puppy. Learn about how the Birnsteel family decides to deal with their dog's death. They hold a wake and invite friends over to share their memories and funny stories. And, lastly, amazing animal communicator Dawn E. Hayman shares with us her incredible story about her beloved dog who tells her how he will come back in a new body.

As you can see, so many wonderful writers have opened their hearts and shared their stories with us about their beloved dogs. So whatever your favorite stage of dog parenthood is, one thing is for sure: dogs don't go off to college, get married or fly the coop so it's important to be the best dog parent you can be at all times. Relish every moment of pet parenting and relish these magnificent stories as I did. Each one is a reminder of how powerful, magical and life-changing being a pet parent really is.

~Wendy Diamond

My Dog's Life

A Bundle of Fur

Not Your Typical Puppy

Any glimpse into the life of an animal quickens our own and makes it so much the larger and better in every way.
~John Muir

Upon returning from a week's vacation we found our two-year-old Doberman Pinscher sitting outside his dog-house growling. When I looked inside I saw the ugliest puppy that I had ever seen. She was scrawny, bloated and wormy, with mangy sprigs of wiry rust-colored fur that stuck straight up all over. Though she looked to be no more than six or eight weeks old, when I reached in to pull her out she snarled and snapped like a badger. I assumed abuse and neglect were to blame for her bad attitude. I decided to feed her and leave her alone, and when she calmed down she would come out on her own.

Three days later she was still cowering in the back corner of the doghouse, so I decided to try again so I could bring her to the vet. Slowly I pulled her out, but as soon as I started to lift her up she snarled and snapped again. I put a towel over her and picked her up. At the vet's office, I warned them that even though she was small and frail she was a Tasmanian devil in disguise. They gave her the first dose of treatment for worms and mange, and sent a second and third dose home with me. As she began to feel better and calm down, I managed, without losing any fingers, to slip a small collar around her neck.

Several weeks later, as my husband held her by her collar to sponge on the final dose of her mange treatment, something spooked her and she began to jump wildly. She flipped, causing her collar—with my husband's hand on it—to tighten around her neck. In a panic, she bit his hand, down to the bone, in four different places before he could get untangled and out of her reach. We had tried to be patient with her, but for him, that was the last straw. Bleeding and angry, he said we were going to have to put her down.

"We cannot have a vicious dog like this around kids," he said. "She is dangerous and she's only a puppy. Imagine what may happen when she has size to back up that temper."

I understood his concern but felt that the only reason she bit him was because she thought he was choking her when his hand got twisted up in her collar. If I promised to keep kids away from her, would he give me a chance to try something else first? Maybe I could call someone in authority to come and get her? He agreed.

The next morning I called the Department of Natural Resources, explained the problem, and asked if they could please send someone to remove her and take her to an animal refuge. The man on the phone laughed and said, "Lady, are you living in a Disney movie? We are going to put that dog down. And that is all we are going to do with her."

Kill her or keep her. Those were our choices. When the bleeding had stopped and the scars were healing my husband agreed that she could stay, for a while. Before her arrival we had huge catfish in our lake that used to eat from my hand, hummingbirds that let me hold the feeder while they zoomed inches from my head, and feral cats that I had loved into family pets. I was certain that with a little patience I could have this ugly little dog sleeping at the foot of the bed. It had become a personal challenge to win her over.

Before I knew it, a year had come and gone, and I had lost all hope and most of my patience. A.J. wouldn't love us, but she wouldn't leave us either. As long as we never tried to bother her, she never bit or even growled, and seemed timid and docile. Like a teenager, it just wasn't in her to express love, affection or appreciation for her never-empty bowl.

When we came home from work our Doberman and our little Pekingese mix were always excited to see us, wagging their tails, jumping and vying for our attention. A.J. stood back, bewildered. She had no idea why they would be so happy to see people. A.J. liked the dogs, but they did not like her. They never wanted anything to do with her. A.J. just sadly followed along behind them while they shunned her. Even as a puppy A.J. was different. She didn't want to play, she never went through the "chewing stage," and although well fed, much to my dismay, she killed every small animal that happened to appear—squirrels, possums, raccoons—anything that moved.

After two long years of trying to win her over I had finally given up. She had made very little progress. She would let us pet her on the head for about two minutes, she would very cautiously eat treats from my hand, and she followed us everywhere we went—although always at a safe distance. But unlike our other dogs she displayed no love, loyalty, or affection.

One afternoon while I was walking with A.J. at her usual ten paces behind, I ran into one of our neighbors who made a comment about my pretty "red dog." I began to relay some of my frustration with trying to get her to bond with us.

"I bet she's one of those coyote pups that the old man up the road found in the woods behind his house," she said. "He said he had found the mother dead and heard whimpering nearby. And in a little dug out hole there were four reddish brown cubs that he thought might have been part dog." When my neighbor had asked him what he had done with the cubs, she said he laughed and told her that he had "found them all homes."

"I knew he meant that he had dropped those pups at neighboring farms," she added.

Suddenly, it began to make sense: A.J. wouldn't bond with us, the other dogs didn't like her, and she showed no affection. No wonder she bit like a crocodile and wouldn't play or act like a dog. She wasn't a dog. She was a wild animal. Instantly, my frustration with her melted into complete wonder as I realized that what had looked like two years of zero progress with a bad-tempered, stubborn dog was in fact a near miracle with an animal that was doing exactly what she was designed to do. I no longer saw her as an ungrateful, unloving dog but as a wild animal that had grown to love us as much as she was capable of and showed more trust and affection than she was ever supposed to. The problem all along had been with my perception. When I began to see and accept her for what she was, instead of what I expected her to be, I was amazed at the things we had accomplished, not what we had not.

We lost A.J. this year and buried her in the woods behind our barn alongside our other beloved family pets. Although she wasn't your typical "pet," she was a very real part of our family, and I still catch myself waiting for her as I go on my daily walk. In the ten years we shared our life with her I learned a little bit about living with a coyote and a whole lot about living, period. I was able to look past my own expectations and accept her for the truly amazing creature that she was.

~Andrea Peebles

"Yes, you're adopted. But there's more..."

Never Tuckered Out

There is no hope unmingled with fear, and no fear unmingled with hope.
~Baruch Spinoza

"D on't worry," said Dee, tickling Tucker's smooth pink belly. "We're going to have a good time; you go do the same." She winked confidently at me.

Three months into our puppy parenting, my husband announced that he and I were going on a business trip. Finding a place for my nine-year-old daughter, Zoe, to stay the weekend was easy, but finding a place for our nine-month-old, four-pound Yorkie was a different story. Tucker had never been away from us and I hated the thought of putting her in a kennel, so when I heard that my husband's receptionist had doggie-sat another Yorkie for six months, I was relieved. Dee was great with Tucker and as much as a mom could feel "comfortable" handing over her baby, I felt confident that she would be safe.

After the first nervous night of checking in with Dee, I finally relaxed and enjoyed my carefree morning at the hotel while my husband went off to business meetings. I'd just returned from a beach walk and was ready to shower when my cell phone rang.

"Tucker's gone," Dee sobbed. "She got out the front door and we've been looking for her. She's been gone about an hour," she said, trying to compose herself. "My daughter's looking everywhere."

"I'm on my way," I said frantically, and grabbed my car keys.

I sped along the freeway with my heart pounding as I gripped the steering wheel repeating the mantra. "I'm gonna find you Tucker. I'm gonna find you Tucker."

Memories flooded my mind on that hour drive. I hadn't willingly become a dog owner. I'd been worn down by eight years of Zoe's begging. My mind wandered to the first day we took our puppy home.

"Tucker," said Zoe from the back seat of the car. "Let's call her Tucker."

"Cute," I said turning around to see the little black ball of fluff nuzzled protectively in her arms, "but everyone will think she's a boy."

"Mom, it's like *Tuck Everlasting*," she said definitively. "She's going to be with me forever, plus look—I can 'tuck'er' under my arms."

"Oh, that is sweet," I said. "Okay, Tucker it is."

Despite weeks of nighttime howling, many potty-training mistakes, and one chewed cell phone charger cord, Tucker and I became inseparable buddies. She'd dive under the covers and snuggle by my side, she'd sit on my lap while I wrote at the computer, and she followed me everywhere. Tucker loved playing with Zoe, but when it was time to eat she knew who her meal ticket was. I was smitten with this dog and now she was gone. I trembled and tears rolled down my face while I tried desperately to steady the steering wheel.

By the time I arrived, a search party of five had already assembled and dispersed with handwritten signs announcing "Lost Dog." Tucker had a nametag and was micro-chipped. Surely we'd find her. For hours I walked with food in one hand and a squeaky toy in the other. As the sun sank my spirits followed. I'd have to return to my husband empty-handed and break the news. I told Dee I'd come back the next day. All we could do was pray and stay by the phone.

Despite the next day's even bigger search party, Tucker was nowhere to be found. We were going to have to tell Zoe. Alarmed that we picked her up early from a sleepover party, Zoe collapsed into a heap of wails when she heard.

"We'll keep looking for her," I said stroking Zoe's hair. "We won't give up."

That night I prayed, "Dear God, please keep Tucker safe and let her find her way home."

I allowed Zoe to miss school on Monday so we could print 500 flyers and post them. We visited every shelter and pet store in a twenty-mile radius. By the day's end we were exhausted. The house was eerily quiet and our hearts ached.

Months went by and every so often someone would call with a sighting, and our hearts would soar with expectation, but it was never Tucker. While our grieving deepened, I continued to pray. At the suggestion of a pet psychic, I left Tucker's crate outside on our front porch hoping one day I'd find her in it.

After six months, we adopted "Lucy," another Yorkie, and she kept us happy and busy with her own special puppy antics. While Lucy tempered the grief of our loss, my heart still ached for Tucker and I continued to pray that she'd find her way home.

"How will Tucker find us when we move out?" asked Zoe as we packed for a nearby apartment in anticipation of our eight-month home renovation.

"We'll leave the crate here," I said. "I'll check on it every day, and we'll keep our same phone number."

Another six months went by and still I looked and prayed for Tucker. I was cooking dinner when the phone rang.

"Is this Mrs. Tanzman?"

"Yes," I said a bit impatiently, expecting a phone solicitor.

"This is the Blue Shield vet clinic. We have your dog Tucker."

"What?" I gasped, nearly dropping the boiling pot of water. "Is she all right? She's been lost for over a year."

"Well she's got two bad cuts under her eyes and she's infested with fleas, but other than that she seems okay. Can you be here soon? We close at six."

"Zoe," I screamed, "they have Tucker!"

We both burst into tears as we fled the apartment, putting Lucy safely in her crate and barely remembering to turn off the stove. The vet was an hour away and it was five o'clock.

How did Tucker get there? Where had she been all this time?

Would she remember us? Here I was on another white-knuckle drive flooded with anticipation, fear, and excitement. Had Tucker searched for us as we had for her?

We were laughing and crying as we raced up the steps of the vet and they brought Tucker out. She leaped into my arms climbing all over me while licking away my tears.

"She definitely remembers you," smiled the vet.

As we drove home, I looked in the rear view mirror. Tucker was once again protectively nuzzled in Zoe's arms. It had been a year and twenty-three days since Tucker went missing from our lives. She wasn't that cute ball of fluff anymore. In fact she was fat, smelled horrible, had a bizarre haircut, oozing wounds, and a cone around her head, but we thought she was the most beautiful dog in the world.

"See Mom, I knew Tucker was a good name for her."

"Why's that?" I asked. "Because she's everlasting?"

"No, because she never got tuckered out looking for us."

~Tsgoyna Tanzman

Brave Susie

I think dogs are the most amazing creatures;
they give unconditional love. For me they are the role model for being alive.
~Gilda Radner

"**D**onna, did you see the news tonight?" asked Ramona. I hadn't. It was another late evening and I was packing up to leave the hair salon that I had owned for the last sixteen years.

"A puppy was dropped off at the shelter, and it had been beaten and set on fire," she said. Ramona was nearly in tears telling me the horrific details. My heart sank. I didn't understand how people could be so cruel. The wounded Pit Bull mix puppy had suffered second and third degree burns over sixty percent of its body, the dog's jaw was broken and the tips of its ears were singed. Everyone assumed the injured animal would be put to sleep, but at the shelter, in spite of its pain, the dog continued to wag its tail and lick anyone who came close.

In the weeks following, Ramona was chosen to foster the four-month-old puppy until a permanent home could be found. The courageous dog had been named Susie and had already endured a number of surgeries. Susie needed around-the-clock medical care. Ramona was scheduled to go out of town one weekend so I volunteered to bring Susie home and care for her. When I walked in the door, my husband Roy looked skeptical.

"It's a Pit Bull. Are you sure you want to do this?" he asked.

His concern was legitimate. A year earlier I had been attacked by a Pit Bull and Roy knew I still had nightmares from the incident. A family in our neighborhood had moved, leaving behind their dog chained up with no food or water. I was appalled and was trying to find the animal a home. Every evening I filled up its empty food and water bowls. But on this particular day I turned around and the dog clenched down on my calf. He shook his head back and forth, gnawing into my skin. His strength knocked me to the ground where he let go of my leg and began biting my neck. I could see the blood pouring onto the ground beside me. With all my might I pushed the animal off with both of my hands and began running. Doctors would later tell me I was lucky to be alive. I endured forty stitches and was unable to walk for six weeks.

But Susie was different. There was nothing intimidating about her big brown eyes or her always-running wet nose. We welcomed her into our home. And within a few weeks, Ramona helped us make it official. We adopted her.

The joy we experienced as Susie became a part of our family was short-lived when we heard that under North Carolina animal cruelty laws, Susie's attacker wouldn't receive jail time. I was disgusted. What type of message did this send to other abusers? Attorneys shook their heads and apologized, but their hands were tied and nothing could legally be done. The injustice fueled a passion in me that I had never felt before. I refused to let Susie's story be swept under the rug. With Susie by my side, I rallied friends, family and anyone who would listen and began a grassroots effort to tell others what had happened months earlier. Our team quickly grew from a handful of animal advocates to thousands. Within weeks, our humble Facebook page had 24,000 followers. We spoke at rallies, local events and inundated our communities with Susie's story.

Our hard work paid off. After long meetings with our local representatives, they agreed to speak on our behalf. Our state legislators decided that anyone who tortures, starves or kills an animal would face jail time. In North Carolina, the malicious abuse of animals would be deemed a Class H felony, punishable by up to ten years of prison, even for first-time offenders.

On June 23, 2010 I woke up with a spring in my step and whispered to Susie, "Today is the day."

We traveled to our state capital. Susie enjoyed the car ride with her nail polished paws on the door and head hanging out the window. I watched her from the corner of my eye as I steered. She was a far cry from the scared puppy who been beaten, burned and left for dead. When we arrived, I smiled at our governor as she approached, but before I could shake her hand, she wrapped her arms around my neck and whispered "Thank you." But it was I who was thankful that day. Thankful for a little burned puppy that had the will to survive and who change my life—not to mention other lives in the years to come.

~Amanda Dodson

A Little Thing Called Sisterhood

How do people make it through life without a sister?
~Sara Corpening

Nineteen ninety-six was a big year for my husband and me. We finished school, got our first real jobs, bought our own house, and yes, decided that we needed a dog. In fact, I had told my husband that as soon as we returned from our two-week post-graduation vacation, we were getting a puppy. I even wrote on the calendar in our kitchen "July 14, buy our new friend."

My husband tried as hard as he could to put off the puppy purchase date. After all, we would both be working full-time and our house wasn't that large. Who would take care of the puppy when we were gone all day? And, where would the puppy run around? Yet I completely ignored my husband's practical perspective in exchange for my emotional one. And, on July 14, I forced him into the car with me in search of our new family member.

As soon as I saw Snickers, I was instantly in love. A tan-and-white Sheltie, just twelve weeks old, she was frisky and energetic. I knew that she was destined to be mine. My husband was hard pressed to disagree, as the tiny ball of fur licked him furiously, with a look in her eyes that practically begged him to take her home.

As certain as I had been that we had found our dog, I began to have doubts on the half-hour car ride home. The entire way, as I held my new baby in my arms, she shook, shuddered, and looked simply terrified. My husband reassured me that her fear would subside once she got used to us and her new surroundings. Still, for the next twenty-four hours, Snickers shook, moped, whined, and cried. Something was wrong and we felt helpless. Despite treats, toys, and lots of petting, Snickers was unmistakably miserable.

Then, without warning a thought sprung into my head.

"Maybe she misses her sister," I announced.

"Are you suggesting…" my husband began.

"I'm simply saying that I think I know how to make Snickers happy," I informed my husband. "Now, get in the car."

I picked up the sad mass of fur that had been drooping around all day and put her in the car. Less than an hour later, we were back at Snickers' original home. I set my lonely puppy on the ground, and within seconds she was romping and barking and even chasing her tail. In an instant, my woebegone pup was vivacious and animated. Minutes later, the breeder came out with the other female from the litter. The two animals ran toward each other like a scene out of a movie. Once they began frantically chasing and licking one another, my husband and I looked at each other. That evening, we relaxed at home, curled up with our two happy Sheltie puppies.

Snickers and Skittles were completely inseparable from the beginning. They ate together, played together, and even got into trouble together. When one of them sucked down a pair of knee high stockings, leaving us wondering which dog had actually committed the unthinkable act, they were even forced to vomit together. The point was, though, that they were twin sisters with an invisible bond so strong that attempting to break it would also, as we'd seen in the beginning, break their spirit.

When our canine children were three years old, I gave birth to a beautiful baby girl named Hannah. I'm pretty certain that the dogs thought of her as their human sister, because they refused to leave her side. They licked her tiny toes as she sat in her bouncy seat and watched her closely as I'd feed her. They even slept beneath her crib at times. My dogs knew who was in their pack and were aware of their family responsibilities.

But pregnancy with Hannah had been difficult for me. I was nauseous and tired and even had to go on bed rest for almost a month. Thus, the thought of having another baby made me nervous. I wasn't sure I wanted to go through all of that ever again. One night, as I was telling my husband my reservations about getting pregnant again, he looked at me sternly and said, "So you want to deprive Hannah of the joy that Snickers has?" I had never thought of our situation in that way. However, my husband was right. Snickers loved having a sister to share her experiences and play. How could I possibly deny my daughter that same happiness and contentment?

Today, as my puppies approach their fourteenth birthday, I am heavyhearted as I watch them limp with arthritis and ignore my commands due to failed hearing. Still I get so much joy from watching them play with my two human daughters, Hannah and Jordyn. The dogs taught me how to love and laugh. They showed me how to play hard and how to relax. Yet most importantly, they taught me the importance of a little thing called sisterhood. And for that, I will always be grateful.

~Sharon Dunski Vermont

Delilah, Take a Bow

A dog is the only thing on earth that loves you more than you love yourself.
~Josh Billings

Have you ever felt totally unappreciated? Have you ever needed support and your loved ones were not there for you? Dog School graduation was one of those times when I felt very alone in the world. It seemed as if no one cared about all the hard work I had done. Aside from being disappointed, something else happened that night of a positive nature. I had an awakening that completely changed my perspective about reveling in my own personal glory.

We brought Delilah, our new Doberman, home at eight weeks old. She had a wonderful temperament. Over the first six months, she grew to a generous seventy-five pounds. She was basically good, but a bit unruly being her puppy self. Our two adolescents were behind many of her shenanigans. She was both high-spirited and headstrong. Our home was not spacious. She was a large "house dog" who definitely needed to be controlled. It soon became apparent she had to have some training. I was the only family member with tenacity enough to tackle the rigorous ten weeks of daily dog training sessions. Delilah's predecessor had been a huge, energetic, male Doberman. I had taken him though obedience training with good results. He became an enjoyable member of our household, a great pet, and we missed him terribly. We had gotten Delilah hoping to fill the large void left when he died. We immediately fell in love with her and anticipated she would be the same kind of wonderful pet he had been. She quickly worked her way into our hearts.

Classes began in late May. It was already hot and ten more weeks would take us into August, the hottest month of the year. Although I knew my artificial limb was going to be a problem for me with the intense heat, I was determined to get through it. It had to be done. I had expected Delilah to be stubborn and difficult, but as we worked together I saw a different side to her temperament. She had an innate desire to please me. The only problem was the long hours of training in the dreadful heat.

Although she learned quickly, it was necessary to repeat the exercises over and over until she could do them by rote. There were times I became frustrated and impatient, and I yelled at her. I felt bad about that because once she understood what I wanted her to do, she never forgot the command or what I expected of her. She was attentive and not easily distracted. Our male Doberman had been far more interested in anything and everything but the commands I was trying to teach him. She was a delight by comparison. Nine weeks of training had passed and it was the week before graduation. There was a final rehearsal before we actually faced the judge. Delilah did beautifully and I was proud of her. I was even prouder of myself for my major accomplishment. Graduation week arrived. I asked my husband if he wanted to go to the graduation. He said his allergies were bothering him and he felt he would be miserable sitting outdoors for that long.

"I am disappointed," I said. "But you might be right. I don't want you to be miserable for my sake." Truthfully, I thought it was just a lame excuse. I was certain that the children would be anxious to go, but I was mistaken. They had gone to a couple of sessions and sat sweating and swatting mosquitoes. They hesitated when I ask them if they wanted to go, and I could tell they really didn't want to.

"Mom, do we really have to?"

"Of course, you don't *have to*," I said.

Foolishly, I believed some of the family would simply "want to" for my sake. I had worked hard all summer and wanted their support during the trials. It became apparent that none of it mattered to anyone but me. Graduation night was long and hot. Even though I knew my family would have been uncomfortable, it still hurt that no one had wanted to come. Out of the twenty-seven dogs, Delilah was one of the last to face the judge. The auditorium was stifling and we were both hot and weary by the time we started the drill. Delilah responded to every command to perfection, but lagged slightly on the turns, losing a couple of half points. We formed a straight line across the floor in front of the judge awaiting her decisions. She announced first place, then, second place. I was looking down at Delilah when I heard, "The Doberman, Delilah, third place." I felt the blood rush to my face. Reaching down, I encircled her big head with a hug. The crowd applauded as we stepped forward to receive the trophy. I knew Delilah had done well but I never expected to be in the top four.

On the drive home, I chattered incessantly at Delilah who was curled up in the seat, trying to sleep. She was relieved to be back in the air-conditioned car, headed for home. I was bubbling over with the excitement of winning third place. I could hardly wait to tell the family. It was eleven o'clock when I arrived home. The family had all gone to bed. I felt yet another pang of disappointment that no one had waited up to see how I had done. I put the trophy in the middle of the breakfast bar and stepped back to admire it. I walked back to living room to sit down and unwind a little before turning in. Delilah was curled up at my feet, her shoulder leaning against my lower leg. I stroked her head and she sleepily wagged her stubby tail. My good girl. She had worked so hard for me, every night for ten weeks, and performed like a real champion when it mattered most. What a wonderful dog.

I began to think back over those weeks of training. Suddenly, I sat straight up. It hit me like a bolt of lightning. What was wrong with me? It was Delilah that had learned all those many commands and it was her score that won the trophy. I had won absolutely nothing. I was self-indulgent enough to believe that graduation was "all about me." The truth was, I was only a small part of it. The training sessions must have been just as stressful, frustrating, and tiring for her as they were for me. She did her best out of love for me and to please me. She never cared about trophies or winning. The only reward she wanted was to hear me say to her, "Good girl, Delilah!" and pat her on the head. I stood up and walked to the breakfast bar, took out a marker and a big piece of paper. Smiling, I wrote: "WAY-TO-GO, DELILAH!" in large, black letters. I stood the paper up in front of the trophy and went to bed, a little less full of myself.

~Joyce E. Sudbeck

A Puppy Named Runt

When the world says, "Give up," Hope whispers, "Try it one more time."
~Author Unknown

He was just a small bundle of dark fur, not even breathing. So small and helpless that I didn't think he would survive, but Pepper kept licking her puppy and my son, James, gently nudged the puppy's lifeless body.

"I'm sorry, honey," I said. "He's probably the last one and he's the runt of the litter. I don't think he'll make it."

James looked up at me for a moment, his jaw set in quiet determination as he refused to give up and continued to nudge the puppy's limp form, as if willing him to live. Suddenly, the little body jerked and you could see his small chest rise and fall with spastic breaths as he struggled to move his body around. He was so tiny that you could hold him in the palm of one hand. Gently, James laid him down with the rest of the puppies. Pepper was exhausted and lay down beside them. She had given birth to seven puppies and all of them were alive.

As the days passed, I noticed that something seemed different with Runt. James had already named most of the puppies: Bear, because he was so big, Romeo, because he was so handsome and loveable, Sad Girl, because, well, you get the picture. Yet we continued to call the last puppy, Runt. Somehow, it was the only name that fit. We decided to find homes for all but one of the puppies and I was letting James pick which one we would keep. He wanted to keep all of them, but of course that was impossible. I grew up always having a dog around, and if it was left to me, we probably would have kept two or three, but then I was always a sucker for dogs and especially puppies or any helpless animal. That's probably why I felt compelled to look after Runt.

Pepper would not feed Runt and didn't seem to want him around. All the other puppies were bigger and stronger and pushed him off during feeding time. I started taking Pepper and Runt into my home office, away from the other puppies so he could nurse. It was the only way he could get any food. I had to stay with them though, or Pepper would not lie down to feed him. As the puppies grew, they seemed to be twice Runt's size. When they were six weeks old, we gave five to a placement service and kept Romeo and Runt. One of the neighbors wanted Runt and James wanted to keep Romeo. My aunt was going to keep Pepper until we could find a good home for her.

I had delayed weaning Runt until the other puppies were gone. As soon as I started, the problems began. When Runt ate his puppy food, he threw it up, so I bought soft food and whipped it with the fork. For a while this worked, and then he started throwing up again. Watching his little body spasm as he threw up was like a knife through my chest. He didn't want to eat, only nurse, and I was getting very worried. He was almost eight weeks old and had hardly grown. I took Runt for his puppy shots and described his problem to the vet.

"Runt has a constriction in his esophagus. He may need surgery to correct it," he said, after he examined him. When he told me how much it would cost, I dropped my head. I did not have the kind of money he was talking about.

"What other options do I have?" I asked.

"You could try a liquid diet for a while," he said. "Or you could put the dog food in a blender and see if he can digest that. If that doesn't work, he may have to be put to sleep."

I felt my chest constrict. Runt looked up at me with brown trusting eyes that seemed to say, "Make it better, Mommy Person."

Mommy Person was a joke between James and me that started when Runt was very little. I would tell James to bring Runt to me, and he would say, "Come on Runt, Mommy Person wants you."

Standing in the vet's office, I blinked back the tears that filled my eyes. Runt deserved a chance to keep living. Even when the other puppies were walking and his little body was too weak for him to stand, he would drag himself around. He pushed under the other puppies if they didn't get out of his way and kept trying until he was able to limp around. Runt was a fighter, and since he wouldn't give up on himself, I wasn't giving up on him.

The puppy and dog food didn't blend well and he continued to throw up. The more helpless I felt, the more upset I became. One day at work, I told my friend Denise, "I'm so worried about Runt. I've mashed up the puppy food, whipped it, blended and pureed it. Nothing seems to work. He still throws it up. He's hardly grown at all and if he doesn't keep some food down soon, he'll die."

That's when she said two simple words, "baby food." I was silent for a moment, and then I repeated her words.

"Baby food?" So simple, yet I had never thought of it.

"That's what we feed our dog," she continued. "She's old and can't digest anything solid, not even the very soft dog food."

That evening I picked up some baby food on the way home. When I fed it to Runt, he licked the bowl clean. I waited, dreading the usual convulsions that shook his tiny body after he ate, but nothing happened. I continued feeding him baby food and he started getting stronger and even gained a little weight.

When he turned three months old, he was a little ball of energy. He continued to grow, although slowly. When he reached six months, I decided to try small amounts of soft dog food again. I whipped it until it was smooth as pudding.

"Mom," James protested, "he's not a baby. Why are you doing that?"

"Honey, he's only had baby food for the last four months and this is a lot thicker," I answered. "I'm trying to make sure he doesn't choke."

I gave it to him in small quantities, even coming home on my lunch hour to feed him. As he was able to eat more of it, I decreased his baby food and finally stopped it altogether.

When Runt turned nine months old, I bought him puppy biscuits and fed him one with each meal. He was able to eat it with no problem, and I gradually gave him a few more. I had to be careful not to let him eat when he was excited since he would choke. One time I had to do the Heimlich maneuver on him. When he turned a year old, we had a birthday party for him. I got his favorite treats and even made him a little puppy cake, which he gulped down in a few seconds.

Runt will never be as big as his brothers and sisters and his legs may not be as strong as they could have been, but he never gave up, no matter how hopeless things seemed and for now, I'm content to have him hopping around the yard barking and chasing James.

~Brendalyn Crudup Martin

Treat, Pray, Love

You may have a dog that won't sit up, roll over or even cook breakfast, not
because she's too stupid to learn how but because she's too smart to bother.
~Rick Horowitz, Chicago Tribune

I opened the cupboard door under the sink and reached for a sponge. Ginger, our six-month-old Boykin Spaniel, darted in, grabbed something and disappeared, her nails scratching along the tile as she scooted away from the scene of the crime and crouched under the coffee table.

"She's got a Brillo Pad!" I yelled, in hot pursuit. "Drop it, Ginger! Right now!"

Richard blocked one end of the table while I blocked the other. Ginger darted out between Richard's legs, over the sofa and into the bedroom.

"Richard!" I screamed. "I can't take it anymore! This dog has got to go!"

Ginger was the devil in disguise. As she grew, I waited for horns to sprout behind her soft silky ears. The amazingly cute, chocolate-brown puppy with a gleaming smile and sparkling eyes had captured my heart the minute I saw her. I soon tired, however, of chasing her around the kitchen table to retrieve socks, towels, eyeglasses and everything else she snatched when I wasn't looking. Only a biscuit would make her relinquish her prize. I kept the treat jar filled at all times in order to retain my sanity.

I stomped my feet in frustration. "Take her to the pound! I'm done with her!"

Richard calmly snapped the leash on her while I picked pieces of steel wool out of the carpet. Ginger trotted behind him as he headed out the door. My heart began to pound. I leaped up and ran after them.

"She can stay," I sobbed. Richard laughed. He knew full well Ginger wasn't going anywhere. Ginger, oblivious to her close call, sniffed the garbage can.

"She's going to obedience school," I decided. Obviously I couldn't train her myself and I certainly couldn't let her get the best of me.

"Whatever you say, honey," Richard answered with a grin.

I immediately signed her up for school at the local pet store. The instructor billed himself as a world-renowned dog trainer who could cure any behavioral issues. I laid down my credit card without hesitation.

On that first night, we were six women gathered in the pet store parking lot. The drill sergeant, Gordon, barked orders at us.

"Wear flat shoes to class. No spike heels. No stopping at happy hour. If I smell alcohol, I'll tell you to leave. And absolutely no smoking," he said, emphasizing every word with his hands on hips. "Does everyone understand?"

We nodded in agreement.

"I've trained dogs for years and it's the owner that needs the training," Gordon bellowed. "No treats! Dogs can't be trained with treats."

On week two, owners and dogs lined up in the parking lot. Big scraggly-haired mutts of various shapes and colors towered over tiny Ginger. Not the least bit intimidated, she immediately stuck her nose in the pile of bags and purses lining the sidewalk. I jerked her away before she had a chance to steal a set of car keys.

"Sit!" yelled Gordon.

On command five dogs landed on their rumps. Ginger darted off to chase a squirrel dragging me along with her.

"Obviously you didn't do your research on this breed before you bought her, did you?" said Gordon.

"Why do you think I'm paying you?" I snapped back. "When are we going to learn 'drop it'?"

"That's in the advanced class," replied Gordon. "She has to learn how to sit first."

I took Ginger to school the next week full of hope. We had worked on sit and stay every spare minute I had. She didn't seem to get it but I had a feeling it would sink in soon. If she could learn one simple command, I hoped that "drop it" wouldn't be far behind. The biscuit jar verged on empty.

On cue the class lined up as Gordon called out commands.

"Sit!"

All six wagging tails hit the pavement. Ginger's face lit up as I dealt out praise—along with a treat I'd hidden in my pocket.

"Stay," Gordon called. Ginger was off like a dirty shirt, as my father used to say. But one out of two was progress.

"Stay," I repeated. Ginger yanked her leash and I pulled her back. We played tug of war. I glanced at my watch. Ten minutes left. I prayed the time would go quickly. My arm hurt. A classmate's screaming startled me.

"She's got a cigarette! She's got a cigarette!" someone said.

Gordon spun around. "Who's got a cigarette?" he screamed.

"Ginger! Ginger's got a cigarette."

I looked down at the little imp to see a cigarette butt dangling between pursed lips as if she'd been smoking for years.

"Drop it, you little juvenile delinquent. You're going to get us expelled," I scolded her.

Ginger looked up at me as if I were speaking Chinese. I retrieved the butt from her clenched jaw and walked toward the trashcan, bouncing dog in tow, as she desperately tried to grab her smoke from my hand. She wanted that cigarette back. I wanted a dog that obeyed me. If I had had a match on me that moment, I'd have lit it so we could both take a drag, and I've never smoked a day in my life.

With my stomach in knots, I drove Ginger to the last class. We'd have to pass a final exam to get our obedience school certificate. I worked sit and stay into every interaction with her. My pockets bulged with treats just in case she responded to a command.

"Good luck, Ginger," I said as she leaped from the front seat of the car into the now familiar parking lot. Excitement lurked in every corner of her asphalt playground. She couldn't wait to find it. Each dog took its turn performing four different tasks: sit, stay, come, and down. Ginger got an "A" on sitting, and an "F" on everything else.

"I'm sorry, Ginger, you flunked obedience school," Gordon said, breaking the news in his usual matter-of-fact manner. "Call me," he whispered in my direction. "I'll give you a discount to repeat the course."

I led Ginger to the car, leaving the graduation party in full swing. I slid onto the seat and rested my forehead on the steering wheel, tears flowing down my cheeks. Lifting my head, I read her the riot act.

"You're so bad. How can I keep you if you'll never listen to me?" Ginger calmly climbed up on the center console and stared at me. "I'm mad at you. Go away."

Before I could push her down, her soft pink tongue touched my cheek and licked my tears away. A little brown bouncing ball hopped into my lap and I could no longer resist. With her tail wagging, she kissed me on the lips.

"I can't live with you. I can't live without you," I said as I hugged her.

Ginger kissed me again. Then she stuck her nose into my pocket of treats. I fished one out and she gobbled it down before curling up in my lap. She rested her head on my chest, and her warm, sweet puppy breath soothed me as we drove home together.

~Linda C. Wright

"Thank you for teaching me to fetch and roll over, but these are not skills that will help me in the long run."

My Man Harry

*No animal I know of can consistently be more of a friend
and companion than a dog.*
~Stanley Leinwoll

Just as I was beginning to feel confident about parenting two children, my husband David announced, "You know Kim, the kids really need a dog. You don't want to deprive them of that experience, do you?" Unlike me, my spouse grew up with black Labradors and was already a dog lover. My closest similar childhood pet experiences involved barn cats and basement-dwelling hamsters. Both species had numerous, impersonal cycles of arrivals and departures, but the looming guilt trip immediately pushed me over to the ranks of a reluctant dog owner. As a family we researched a suitable breed. No slobbering, minimum shedding, not too large, not too small, good with young children, and no loud nocturnal barking or high pitched daytime yelping. "Could there be such an animal?" I wondered. Then my husband brought home a book about Cairn Terriers.

An eight-week-old, this reddish-brown puffball captured our hearts the moment we saw him. On the ride home the children tenderly protected their puppy with a warm blanket in the back seat of the car and talked to him in hushed voices. We quickly agreed upon his formal name. The first part, Harry, came from a favorite storybook, *Harry the Dirty Dog*, and the second, Tanqueray, paid tribute to my husband's select gin. David explained to the children that a purebred needed to have two names. Harry slept in a metal cage in the laundry room since I insisted that he be crate-trained. For company we put a small ticking clock in his bed, a plastic squeaky hamburger dog toy for entertainment, and several blankets to keep him warm in the drafty room.

Soon Harry was running the show. Paper training did not go well for this independent canine and I stocked up each week at the grocery store on carpet cleaner. The living room was often decorated with upside down paper plates signaling still damp accident zones. All of the rubber tips of our downstairs doorstops were immediately chewed off and two lamp cords and the vacuum cord had to be replaced due to excessive gnawing in order to prevent potential fire hazards. The backyard looked like the gopher exhibit at the zoo, with small divots and even deeper holes everywhere. We learned that terriers were "ratters" and were bred to flush out vermin in the underbrush of the Scottish countryside. Since neither was our scenario, Harry simply made indiscriminate holes to satisfy his urges and we were left with the fallout. That summer each of the rear mud flaps of David's new car were missing large bite-size chunks. During the challenging puppy stage I just could not handle too many indoor doggie days, and I often banished Harry to the garage. David was always very patient and reminded me, "He will outgrow it."

In the following months our pet started to grow on me and I officially became a devoted puppy mother. I forgave his many indiscretions and his territory grew. Our dog sat in the recliner for hours with the children when they were sick and guarded our home when we were away. He warned new visitors of his presence with a confident series of selected barks, which were followed up by excessive sniffing. He became a great after dinner cleanup assistant, even eating vegetables. Eventually he graduated from sleeping in his crate to a soft dog bed in the mudroom.

For his bathroom needs Harry figured out how to ring a small brass bell on the front door with his nose and then wait for a reaction. David and I usually took turns walking Harry in the evening. One night my tired husband neglected to securely attach the leash to Harry's collar. Out the window I observed the duo plodding in tandem up and down the street, the metal clip of the leash dragging solo along the macadam. Unconnected and unaware, Harry loyally followed his owner on their prescribed route, stopping to relieve himself at the usual mailboxes until they were back home.

Five years after we got Harry my husband died from injuries he suffered in a car accident. Harry immediately sensed that something was wrong. He became particularly protective of the three remaining members of the family and started to follow me upstairs at bedtime. At first he slept at the foot of my bed, but he soon inched his way up to the vacant pillow next to my head. His deep breaths and gentle snoring were comforting and Harry's warm body filled the cold, empty side of the bed. Occasionally his pointed ears perked up in the middle of the night and he jumped out to stand guard at the top of the stairs. Because I did not hear or see anything myself, I was unnerved by his agitated behavior. I wondered secretly if perhaps he sensed David's spiritual presence in the house. With his head cocked to the side and a reassuring wag of his tail, Harry seemed to signal a secret, positive message to his master and then would leap back in bed and fall fast asleep.

Ten years later it was time to let go of Harry. At almost sixteen years old, his lively pace had been reduced to a slow crawl. For the past ten years we had relied on Harry for our peace of mind. We felt safe at night knowing that he was guarding the house. As I took my now-graying animal friend on his final ride to the vet I could not stop the flood of tears down my face. My grief was complicated and intense. I was crying for my own loss. I was crying for the children's sadness for their beloved pet and for the end of an era. And I was still grieving the loss of my husband. The vet encouraged me to stay with our dog as he drifted off but my persistent mourning prevented me from staying. I whispered goodbye, and clutching his red nylon collar, I exited the office. Although it was only four o'clock in the afternoon, I had to fulfill a pledge that David and I made when we first got our dog. We agreed when it was time to say goodbye to Harry that we would toast him with a Tanqueray martini. Now, as the surviving partner, I ordered two martinis at a nearby bar, one was for David, his master, and one was for Harry.

"Goodbye Harry!" I toasted out loud. "Thanks for taking care of us."

Now whenever I order a martini, it is with Tanqueray Gin and double olives, one for each of my departed men.

~Kim Kluxen Meredith

A Little Sister for Hudson

Having a sister is like having a best friend you can't get rid of.
You know whatever you do, they'll still be there.
~Amy Li

There comes a time in most couples' lives to decide about children: When? How many? How far apart? In the same way, the time had come for us to make a decision about pets. Should we welcome another dog into our family?

"Wouldn't Hudson like a sibling?" I asked my husband one day, looking down at our older, and I was sure, lonely yellow Lab.

"I think Hudson believes one dog is enough," Mike answered diplomatically.

"But he must get lonesome. He needs a friend." I tried to make my best pleading puppy-dog-eyes at Mike. Mike shot me a doubtful look.

Eventually, Mike warmed to the idea. We brought home a silky little mixed breed from the rescue shelter. Her name was Kelly. Part Cocker Spaniel and part longhaired Dachshund, we guessed she was about eight months old.

"Here you go Hudson," I said, setting the wiggly pup gently on the rug. "A little sister."

Hudson studied her for a moment. He put his big yellow nose

down to her face. Kelly looked up with big innocent eyes. Then, quick as a viper, she curled her lips, growled and snapped.

Mike lifted Kelly away. "No! No growling!"

"And no biting," I added.

Later, I knelt next to Kelly and gently stroked her soft fur. She'd been in a shelter and was probably frightened by all the changes. I hoped she'd soon feel a part of the family. And she did. In the following weeks she jumped and played in the backyard, bounded after a ball, and claimed the best spot at the foot of our bed. She followed Mike around the house. She even jumped on the back of the couch and draped herself around my neck like a scarf. But with Hudson? Although she never growled or snapped at him again, she didn't play with him the way we'd hoped. She never chased him or frolicked like most dogs. In fact, when she did pay attention to him, she bossed him around and took his toys. If she was a sister to Hudson at all, it seemed she was a bratty little sister.

One day I opened the back door to let the dogs out. Kelly pushed past Hudson to be the first one out. Later, I offered them doggie treats. First Kelly. But as soon as I gave a treat to Hudson, she dropped hers and grabbed Hudson's biscuit right out of his mouth. I sighed. If there were two chew toys, she'd end up with both. Two bowls of food. She ate both. She even tried to drink all Hudson's water. Worse, whenever we went to pat Hudson, Kelly sprinted from across the room and nipped at our hands.

"No, Kelly," I said. "Hudson deserves some loving too." Not to be ignored, Kelly plunked down close by. Poor Hudson. What could I do? Kelly's behavior stumped me. Perhaps it had to do with the fundamental differences between the two dogs. Hudson was big on brawn and a little short on brain. He loped happily around the house, his main goal to please us for the mere reward of a pat on the head. Kelly, however, was cute and little with delicate paws and flowing long hair that looked like a fancy gown. Somehow she got the idea that she was queen. Poor Hudson seemed only to be a serf in her fiefdom. We did all we could to discourage her bossy behavior. We separated their food and water bowls. We took Hudson on walks and gave him extra attention. We slipped him treats in secret. Still, as much as we loved both dogs, I felt guilty. Hudson was there first. Did he really deserve this interloper?

"I'm afraid my idea backfired," I finally admitted. "Kelly hasn't been much fun for Hudson at all."

One day Hudson was more lethargic than usual. I could tell he didn't feel well. He just sniffed at his food and plunked down in the corner. When we took him to the vet, they wanted to keep him overnight for observation and a few tests. That evening, Kelly wasn't herself. She curled up on the floor with her head between her paws. She didn't eat her dinner, but just looked at her bowl, then Hudson's, and walked away.

"Maybe she's sick too," I worried.

Early the next morning, the veterinarian called. All the tests were negative. Hudson was going to be fine and we could bring him home. When we got home and let Hudson in the door, Kelly pushed her way between us and made little circles around our legs. Typical. But then she bounded over to Hudson and rubbed her face against his neck. She wagged so hard her whole body wiggled and she even licked his face. Our mouths hung open as we watched.

"What do you make of that?" Mike asked. I laughed. But then it all made sense.

"It's like when I was a kid, and my brother went off to camp. I thought I couldn't wait for him to go. But when he was gone, I discovered I missed him after all," I said.

It seemed that Kelly had room in her heart for Hudson after all. Over the next few weeks I occasionally noticed Kelly following Hudson or lying down beside him. One night I even saw her licking his face. Hudson responded with gentle acceptance. The more I watched them, the more I noticed moments of interaction. Sometimes Kelly was jealous and bossy and other times she was affectionate and loving, but they were bonded together as part of a family. In that way, just as I'd hoped, Hudson did get a true little sister.

~Peggy Frezon

Spider-Dog

*In all affairs it's a healthy thing now and then to hang a question mark
on the things you have long taken for granted.*
~Bertrand Russell

A round the time the Olympics came to Atlanta, my friend Sara called to tell me about a new litter of puppies born at her house, a mix of Poodle/Pekingese and Lhasa Apso. There were seven little black fur balls and one of them, she said, was mine. I reminded her that I was not in the market for a dog.

"You don't understand, there are only two females and one is mine and one is yours," she said. "She is your birthday present and you can't refuse a birthday present. Just come down and see them," she said. "You will want all seven." I agreed to a 300-mile, round-trip drive to visit since I was long overdue, and, I had to admit, I wanted to see the puppies that she was so smitten with. She was right. I could have brought home all seven. When it was time for me to leave we loaded up my suitcases, said "goodbye," and I put Prissy in my car. She had the cutest face that I had ever seen. She had the subtle features of a Pekingese, long black silky fur with a soft feathery blaze of white on her chest, a little pug nose, and an underbite with one tooth that stuck out on the bottom. She was a romping ball of fire, always making us laugh, and always into something. Since no one could figure out exactly what kind of dog she was, my daughter called her a "La Pookinese." It fit.

A few months after we got her, my mother came to live with us.

Shortly after she moved in I got a frantic call at work. She was upset because she couldn't find Prissy. We live out in the country and Prissy had twenty-six unfenced acres to roam. She was always running after Canada geese, treeing a squirrel, or chasing an occasional rabbit, so I tried to calm down Mama by promising we would look for her when I got home. Mama was waiting in the driveway as I pulled in and met me.

"Well I found the baby dog but I can't get her to come down," she said.

"Come down?" I said.

"Yes, she's climbed up a tree and I can't get her to come down," she said.

I laughed. Mama had never really spent time around dogs.

"Mama, dogs cannot climb trees," I patiently explained. "It must be a cat you are seeing in the tree. But let's go take a look."

"Maybe so but I'm pretty sure it is the puppy," she said, leading me around the house to where a small pine tree had been blown over and had caught in the fork of another taller tree. Apparently, Prissy had been chasing a squirrel and had followed it up a pine tree that was leaning. There about fifty feet up, in the fork of the old oak tree, sat Prissy, happily wagging her tail. How on earth was I going to get her down? She had been up there for at least four hours and there was only one hour of daylight left. We didn't have a ladder that would reach her, and I couldn't climb that tree.

I quickly ran to our closest neighbor to see if I could borrow his ladder. His jaw dropped when I said I needed it to get my dog out of a tree. Although he looked at me like I was crazy and shook his head, he didn't hesitate to help. Fifteen minutes later he descended the ladder with Prissy in his arms, still shaking his head in disbelief. Without a word he sat my wayward dog on solid ground. Now he says that whenever he hears a dog bark, he finds himself glancing upward.

~Andrea Peebles

My Dog's Life

Chew on This

All in a Day's Work

Gratitude is the best attitude.
~Author Unknown

The daily adventures of a school administrator are rarely predictable. Many of my early adventures as a leader took place at a large elementary school situated upon several acres of land that included a city park. I am sure that over the years I logged many miles walking from one end of campus to the other.

One morning, I was called from the main walkway to the primary playground to remove a mangy mutt that had been loping around the equipment, lapping up rainwater and wagging his tail at the first graders. As I hurried to the east side of campus, the aide described, on her cell phone, an evil, almost rabid creature. When I approached the sandpit, the demon dog scurried up to me and dutifully followed me to a fenced-in storage area. (Okay, the breakfast ham helped.)

As I relished my new hero status, a swarm of fifth and sixth graders came running from the park on the other side of campus screaming, "Save the puppies, Mr. Ramsey! You've got to save them! Hurry! They're trapped under the bridge."

I had been at this school for nearly four years, had covered every inch of the campus and could not recall ever seeing a "bridge" at the park. I hurried nonetheless to the west side of campus accompanied by my junior humane society representatives. A superhero, after all, must answer when danger calls.

I arrived at yet another sand pit and stood near the jungle gym listening to the sounds of unhappy puppies and to the voices of approximately three hundred pre-adolescents. Nearby was a tiny wooden overpass that barely covered a small patch of grass and a puddle of rainwater. Beneath this "bridge" were three scared puppies. Stocky and squirming, they kept slipping from my grasp as I tried to extricate them from their safe haven.

After much effort and continued cheering, weeping and fretting from the crowd, I managed to remove all three dogs. I took two of them and an eighth grader picked up the third. I carried my two—one under each arm—back to the east side of campus. They wriggled and struggled to climb up to my shoulders and, throughout the journey, attempted to lick my face with their little slobbery pink tongues.

With my shirt covered with fur, fleas and filth, I entered the front office with an entourage of kids all simultaneously screaming, "Can I keep one, Mr. Ramsey? Can I, please?" I announced that the pups would go to the first three kids whose parents agreed. Immediately the children dashed for the office phones or simply pulled from their pockets their forbidden cell phones.

The grandmother of a new student was at the front counter when all of this took place. I was sure she was thinking, "What kind of school is this? Never mind the registration packet!" Instead, she asked if she could have one of the puppies. Even though the school day had yet to officially begin, I stood there—exhausted—and willingly consented.

About a month (and 800 adventures) later, I received a thank you card from the puppy (I'm pretty sure Grandma did the writing). Next to the photo of the now much larger pup were these words: "Thank you for saving my life. Love, Lucy."

~Tim Ramsey

Memo to Oreo

If you get to thinking you're a person of some influence,
try ordering somebody else's dog around.
~Will Rogers

TO: Oreo
FROM: Dave (Nominal Head of Household)
CC: Cheryl (Spouse), Sarah (Daughter)

A belated welcome to the Martin-Brooks household. I know there was some initial reluctance on the part of some to your joining the family. But I am happy to say that, for the most part, we have ironed out our differences.

The fact that you are a Portuguese Water Dog is apparently a big plus. Since both Cheryl and Sarah are allergic to dogs, it was mandatory that any new member of the house be a non-shedder. As far as I know, despite my advancing years and increasingly hairy back, I, too, still qualify on that count.

As you may be aware, the family vote on your proposed membership was not unanimous. However, your candidacy did garner a clear two-thirds majority. Given the secret ballot nature of our quasi-democracy, I am not at liberty to divulge the specific breakdown of the vote. Suffice it to say, we are now all on board to varying degrees.

Initially, I would like to stress to you that your acquisition was not a frivolous decision on our part. I'm not sure if you are aware that Cheryl purchased you at two months old for the not insignificant sum of $1,700. We are not asking you to contribute to that amount in any way. But I thought you should know that we are financially committed to your wellbeing. Just to reassure you, please note that we paid nothing for Sarah and yet she is still with us ten years later.

You may have noticed other expenditures for your benefit. The high-end crate and the stainless steel dog food bowls are not inexpensive items. And, by the way, in case you're wondering, the three baby gates blocking off the kitchen doorways did not come with the house.

I hope you are enjoying the $800 Afghan carpet on the stairs. Apparently that was purchased to help you avoid developing hip dysplasia. I only wish that it had been there ten years earlier to help with my arthritic hips. But, never mind; better late than never.

The $300 gate in the backyard was also a recent acquisition for your benefit. As were the various bricks and boards used to block off any exits under the fence. I get the sense that you are not fully appreciative of these improvements. Rest assured; they are necessary. Much as you think you can take on the neighbor's cat, trust me, you can't.

As for health care, I am told that you do not have any medical insurance coverage. That's unfortunate. However, until you do, we are prepared to cover your vet bills including the upcoming neutering operation (don't ask). I would only ask that you take appropriate precautions to minimize further expenditures on medical treatments. From now on, that means no more eating feces or rolling around in dead animal matter.

We expect all of our family members to be housebroken. If I am required to always put the toilet seat down, I trust that you can at least refrain from urinating or defecating indoors. I know the living room rug looks vaguely like a lawn, but please restrict yourself to the real lawn. After all, it's not as if we're asking you to pick up after yourself.

Our expectations for you are fairly modest and I believe entirely reasonable. In return for three meals a day, assorted treats and at least two walks, all that we ask is that you feign excitement when we come home and occasionally sit and/or lie down on command.

As for schooling, we were pleased with your recent satisfactory performance at obedience school. However, we do not foresee any postgraduate studies for you in the near future. In fact, if the slipper chewing and failure to come when called continue, it is possible that you will be repeating obedience school, possibly with a private tutor.

I believe you have already recognized and accepted Cheryl as the alpha female. I understand that I am supposed to be the alpha male. Let me just say that I am a tad disappointed since your behavior to date suggests otherwise (e.g. biting, barking and general disobedience). I'm not going to press the matter right now but this will have to change.

Which brings me to the subject of walks. In keeping with the original terms of ownership, walking you is not my primary or even my secondary duty. You are to look to Cheryl and Sarah for the performance of this particular function.

That is not to say that I am averse to the occasional walk with you. I am concerned, however, that the gradual increase in the frequency of such walks over time may result in my *de facto* membership in the ranks of other aging males on our street who seem to be the only ones walking the family canine before sunrise, after sunset and during any outbreak of significant precipitation. This matter should be revisited periodically to prevent any further drop in my already tenuous standing in the family hierarchy.

Notwithstanding the concerns expressed in this memo, I anticipate a cordial, dare I say friendly, relationship developing between us over time. Once you have learned to stop chewing anything within reach and to cease eating non-edible items, I fully expect that we can spend many pleasant years together on or near the rec room sofa watching sports, drinking beer and/or eating dog biscuits.

~David Martin

"What do you mean even in dog years I'll NEVER
be old enough to get my driver's license?"

Dirty Dancing

What soap is to the body, laughter is to the soul.
~Yiddish Proverb

Once in a great while, something so crazy happens that all you can do is cry. Or, if it is bad enough, laugh. Our crazy moment happened on a relaxing and beautiful day. The windows were open and the patio door was flung wide, letting the warm spring air flow through the family room and kitchen. On this glorious day, Bosun, our Newfoundland, was a four-month-old puppy. Black, fuzzy, and sweet, Bo was destined to weigh 150 pounds. But then he was little—sort of—and funny. He was forever falling over his fat puppy paws onto his nose, picking himself up, and rumbling on as if nothing had happened. We laughed more during his first year of life than we had in ages.

It was a busy day. I had errands to run, shopping to do. I left my husband, Marc, deep in a book. His beloved pup was next to him, flopped flat on his fat tummy, snoozing in adorable Newfie puppyness. An hour later, I returned to a scene that still is impossible to forget. As I entered the family room, no bouncing fur ball had come to greet me. The house seemed too still. Yet there were some slapping water sounds coming from the kitchen. Odd. My eyes adjusted slowly from the brilliance of sunlight to the cool darkness of the house, but as I reached the kitchen I could see clearly. A scene of disaster was before me. The place was covered in mud—splattered, smeared, squished.

Marc was on his hands and knees, surrounded by mud, wielding an old dish towel. He balled up the gray cloth and rinsed it in a bucket of muddy water.

"Great Scott!" I gasped. "What are you doing?"

Realizing that was a stupid question, I tried again. "What on earth happened?"

With a trace of false humor in his voice, he pronounced slowly, "I think I'm actually spreading mud all over the floor."

"I see you are, and you're doing very well, but where did this mess come from? I can't believe this."

Marc sat back and flipped the towel into the bucket. "I can't either. And it's not just this floor," he said nodding his head toward the adjoining hall.

Dreading what I was to see, I tiptoed through the least muddy spots and peered down the hall.

"Oh, no! It looks like the grandkids rode a muddy Slip 'n Slide down the hall."

"Yep, all the way down and back again," Marc added, not smiling. "But look closely at the stove. Have you ever seen a more artful job of splattering? Look at that beautiful smear on the dishwasher, and the impressive polka dots on the fridge. While you're at it, check out the table and chairs."

My eyes followed his words. Aghast, I mumbled, "... and the walls... and the glasses in the glass cupboard... and the..."

"How did you fail to notice the furniture in the family room — and the rug?"

I returned to the family room. A trail of paw prints led from the patio door to a puddle in the middle of the room where Bo obviously had stopped to shake himself, covering the brown leather furniture with a mottled mess of drying mud. The only clear space was where Marc had been sitting.

I turned around. "Oh my gosh, even the lampshade. This is so bad. So unbelievably BAD. How could one little dog..." At last, I couldn't help it. I started to chuckle, then couldn't hold back the laughter at this absurd mess. Marc looked at me as though I had tipped over the edge into madness. Then, he relaxed and settled back on his heels. Slowly, a smile washed over his glum expression, and he, too, began to chuckle.

Dropping my packages in the clean chair, I said, "I'll get the mop and help you."

While we mopped, Marc recounted the tale.

"I was sitting peacefully in my chair, absorbed in the attack on Hornblower's frigate. The French were swarming over the side, the mast was in splinters, the sails in shreds, blood everywhere, when I felt a weird sort of spray—like I was in the story—sea spray or maybe the splatter of blood. When it happened again, I noticed I wasn't covered in salty spray or blood at all—but mud. I snapped out of my reverie. But by then it was too late. There was that dog-gone puppy, dripping in muck. All you could see were his two round eyes, rimmed with those innocent little white half-moons, and his pink tongue flapping as he bounded joyously around, careening off furniture and walls...."

He shook his head, recollecting the scene, and then his shoulders began to shake with more laughter. "I wish you could have seen that little devil!"

His laughter set me off again. We both chuckled off and on until the floors were, at last, semi-clean. Now that we were able to move around, we decided to take a break for a cup of tea. Before the tea-kettle could whistle, we saw movement from outside the patio door. In roared the muddy dynamo, newly coated in fresh slime, his eyes sparkling, ready for a reprise of his idyllic puppy joy. He bounced through the family room, hit the kitchen and began his tumbling, smearing romp of happiness. Down the hall he tore. But this time, there was no return trip. Marc regained his senses first and corralled that really dirty doggie in the hallway. Clutching him with utter disregard for getting a mud bath of his own, Marc hauled a wriggling Bo outside, trying to avoid a barrage of sloppy kisses that seemed to say, "Are you coming out to play with me?"

It didn't take long to find the source of his fun. I had set the water on the rose garden for a deep soak, and then forgotten about it in my push to get the errands done. There on the edge of the rose bed was a churned up lake of mud—paradise for a water-loving Newfie pup. Another cleaning project followed, getting silt and grit out of the puppy's thick wooly coat. Finally, after the bubbles were gone and the rinse water ran clear, we wrapped him in towels and brought him inside. Here, on his big soft bed, an exhausted Bo fell sweetly asleep. And we finally shut the door. From time to time we still find a stray mud stain on a lampshade or the ceiling, and we recall that moment of Bo's puppyhood with nostalgia and a quiet chuckle. No, we never scolded him. He didn't then, nor has he now, any sense of guilt, so it would have done no good. He is five now and tries hard to please, and thankfully, he has never done his dirty dancing in the house again.

~Meg Stragier

Hanger

Dogs are not our whole life, but they make our lives whole.
~Roger Caras

My dog burrows into his pillow beside my bed like he has for the last twelve years. He doesn't ask for much. Occasionally, he'll plunk the tennis ball at my feet. The game we play is less "fetch" and more "keep away." I know I did us both a disservice by not teaching him the difference. But we enjoy it all the same.

On the day we met, persistent spring rain kept me interred in my tiny apartment that, after eight months, still looked like I hadn't unpacked. There were no curtains, no family photographs, no decorations, just a desk, table, TV and a daybed against builder-beige walls. Even the refrigerator was bare except for a gathering of vegetables in the crisper drawer. When the rain subsided to a drizzle, I slogged the mile to White Rock Lake. There would be people at the lake: jogging, skating, biking, walking dogs. Granted, we wouldn't speak as we passed, but passing was affirmation enough. When they stepped a little to the right to let me pass, I knew I existed, and for a split second, I was not alone. The city sidewalk ended at the park gate. Rain puddled on the pedestrian trail, so I walked on the steamy asphalt. Car traffic would be light.

Up ahead a small dog loped in my direction. It was black and amber like a German Shepherd, but its bent ears were more Tramp than Rin Tin Tin. Bicycles whined passed me, spitting mist up through the thick Texas humidity. The dog bolted up an embankment, across the road, into a ditch, and back. A stray, I reasoned, no park-required leash, collar, or human companionship. Behind me, a car engine revved, its radio drowning out the chirp of summer cicadas. Intent on catching the skittish dog, I held my breath. If I moved, it could dart away from me and into the path of the car. That's how it happened. The rear tire of a powder blue convertible rolled over him. The car stopped a few yards away.

"I am so sorry," the driver said as he sauntered over to see what he had hit.

Pulling my eyes from the convulsing puppy, I looked at him. He swayed slightly. He appeared to have been drinking, and he shouldn't have been driving.

"I'm so sorry," he said again. "So sorry." He waited anxiously for me to absolve him of responsibility. The dog's nose bled a thin red line, nothing else moved.

The man and I dragged the limp body across the pavement to the gravel shoulder before he left, speeding away. As I stood wondering what to do, the puppy revived, jerking his legs and neck, trying to stand. I struggled to pick him up. He didn't fight, just hung his head over the crook of my left elbow, legs dangling. "Hang on," I said. "Just hang on and I'll get you to the veterinarian." Before I'd gone one hundred yards, I had named him Hanger. My arms were already tired when I noticed a cyclist stopped at the concrete pedestal water fountain next to the lake's spillway. He lingered curiously over the ancient spigot that no one ever used. He was tanned and toned, and had razor cut hair under his aerodynamic helmet.

"Most people let their dogs walk," he joked as I came within earshot.

"Yeah, it's not my dog. He just got run over by a car," I said.

"Wow. Wait here," he replied. "I'll get my car and drive you home."

"That's okay. I can walk," I said, deferring to admonitions about stranger danger.

"Really, wait here. It's no problem."

He returned ten minutes later in a black Mustang with a bed of towels in the trunk. If we talked, it was about what happened, the puppy under the tires of the car, the driver's behavior. It was a short, quiet mile to the gate to my apartment complex. He lifted the dog out of the trunk. "Can I call you sometime? Would you like to have lunch?"

"I'm moving to California in a month, so. Thanks for the ride."

"I'm Todd Cohen," he offered as I took Hanger from his arms.

"Thanks Todd. I'm Rhonda Richards. I've got to go call some vets."

At the Emergency Veterinary Clinic a woman in a white coat explained that strays are treated and turned over to the SPCA. "If you decide to keep him," she said, "you pay for the treatment, which averages about $300." I was pretty sure this dog would not survive until morning, much less be going home with anyone.

The clinic called the next day, "That puppy you brought in is fine."

"Fine, how can he be fine?" I said. "He got run over by a car."

"He's young. His bones are still rubbery. He's too sore to walk or eat. His vital signs are good, though. Do you want to adopt him or send him to the SPCA?"

I heard the question, but my mind was somewhere else. I wanted a dog. I had already planned to find a rental house in California with a fenced yard so that I could get a dog and wouldn't be alone.

"What do you want to do?" she repeated.

"Um, I guess that's my dog. I'll keep him," I said.

That day at the lake changed my life. I don't spend as much time away from home as I used to. Hanger has to be fed, even if I'm not hungry. And home isn't as lonely as it used to be. He warms my cold feet, leaves hair on the bathroom floor, and requires a little bit of affection every day. He is tolerant to a fault. Children have toddled through our lives, clobbering him with happy fists. He doesn't seem to mind. He's just like my husband, that way. The cyclist who gave us a ride back to my apartment that fateful day—I married him.

~Rhonda Richards-Cohen

15

Surprise Me

Dachshunds are ideal dogs for small children, as they are already stretched and pulled to such a length that the child cannot do much harm one way or the other.
~Robert Benchley

I t was two o'clock in the morning, and our dog, Mocha, hadn't adhered to the timeline I had set for her. She was supposed to deliver her puppies in the evening so that my ten- and twelve-year-old children could observe the wonder of birth. I thought it was ironic that, as a pediatrician, I was being called on to help our dog. I was on my third cup of coffee while Mocha labored.

Since we acquired her, Mocha had always done things her way. She couldn't be broken of the habit of eating tissues out of the garbage cans or the cat's droppings. Now, Mocha was again doing things her way, delivering at this ungodly hour.

I sat at the kitchen table feeling sorry for Mocha because of the pain she was enduring, and sorry for myself for having to pull an all-nighter. I smiled when I thought of the idea to send my wife, Dotty, a bill for my obstetrical and pediatric services. It was her idea to breed the dog. But then again, I was the one responsible for bringing Mocha into our house.

• • •

Kristy Calabro was the mother of three of my patients. Her initial insecurity during motherhood gradually abated with each of her ensuing pregnancies. When her first child was born, Kristy would ask me the most basic and inane medical questions, not because she didn't know the answers, but because she needed confirmation. This took a lot of my time, but I didn't mind much because of her affability and gratefulness.

One day, after her third child was six months old, we had a non-medical conversation. "Do you like dogs?" she asked.

"They're okay, but my wife's the real animal lover."

"Are you thinking of getting one?" she asked.

"We've been talking about it, but haven't made a decision yet," I replied.

"What kind of dog have you been discussing?" she pressed.

"One that's small, but not too small," I answered. "Maybe a Beagle."

"What about a Dachshund?" she asked. "As you know, I raise Dachshunds. If you're interested, let me know. I'll find a nice one for you."

On each of her next four or five visits, Kristy would ask me the same question when she left. "You've been so nice. I'd like to get you a gift. What would you like?"

My response was consistent. "I appreciate the thought, but please don't get me anything."

After repeating this scenario on a few more visits, I shrugged in defeat.

"Just surprise me," I said.

About six weeks later, as I was finishing up with my last morning patient, my receptionist buzzed me on the intercom. "Mrs. Calabro is here. I think we should send her right back to your office." Before disconnecting, I could hear her giggle.

When I walked into my office, Kristy was sitting there with a cute, mocha-colored Dachshund puppy in her lap. She reached out and handed the puppy to me.

"Here's your surprise," she said.

"But we don't have any stuff—no bed, no food, no leash, no toys," I protested.

"That's why I came in this morning. Maybe your wife could pick up everything at the pet store this afternoon."

I was speechless. What had I wrought? I hoped Dotty wouldn't kill me. One thing for sure, I vowed never again to say "surprise me" if a patient said that she wanted to give me a gift.

"I'm sure you'll enjoy the dog," Kristy said. "She's a sweet little puppy. If you have any questions give me a call."

I think she sensed I was mulling over rejecting her gift. Before I could say anything, she waved.

"I've got to run," she said.

Like an apparition, she was out the door. I walked into the front office cradling the pup in my arms. She opened her eyes and fixated on my face. It was as if she was beseeching me to keep her, not to do anything rash. "Do me a favor," I said to my receptionist. "Call my wife and tell her to come right over—that there's an emergency in the office. Tell her I'm okay, but I really need her to come now. Don't mention the dog, and don't giggle."

I sat in my office with the puppy on my lap, stroking her head. When Dotty arrived, her frown turned into a smile when she saw the dog.

"How cute," she said. "Whose is it?"

"Ours," I replied.

"You're kidding."

I shook my head and told her the story. Dotty's frown, which had returned after I told her the dog was ours, was supplanted by a wide grin.

"I guess we have a dog," she said.

I nodded and returned her smile. "I guess we do."

●●●

Sitting at the kitchen table, watching Mocha in her birthing box, I chuckled at the memory. When she delivered her first puppy and licked its face until it was clean, I knew she would be a good mother. Despite her fetishes for tissue paper in the garbage and the cat's bowel movements, she had been a wonderful dog. The miracle of birth repeated itself three more times. The last puppy was small and having trouble, gasping to breathe. I jumped out of my chair, grabbed the puppy, cleared her throat, and gave mouth-to-mouth to her until she was breathing on her own. Mocha licked my hand as I put the puppy down next to her. It was her way of saying thanks.

I smiled at my dog, bent down and whispered into her floppy ear, "I'm glad I said 'surprise me.'"

~Paul Winick

16

I'm Not Crazy, I Just Have a Dog

No one appreciates the very special genius of your conversation as the dog does.

~Christopher Morley

I talk to myself, but that doesn't make me crazy. It just means I have a dog in the house. At least that's what I keep telling myself. I realized I did it when I first picked up my dog Eddie. He was a quivering, tiny ball of black fur. At around seven weeks old, I couldn't tell how this Poodle-Pomeranian mix would look. He just wiggled and looked cute with a red ribbon around his neck. He had been content with the dog and human parents who had raised him. Then I came knocking.

Eddie was originally named Jimmy, which happened to be the name of my late husband. I didn't name him. Kathy, who was great friends with Jimmy before his death, named the dog after her good friend. She wanted me to have him as I began rebuilding my life more than a month after Jimmy's death. I could take the puppy's cries, but I couldn't bear trying to soothe him by his name.

"I'm going to call you Eddie," I said, determined to stop crying on my way out of town. Jimmy's middle name was Edward. He had never used that, so I thought it would be a good compromise—it would stay true to the intent to honor Jimmy and it would allow me to not tear up every time I called the dog's name.

"It's going to be okay," I told Eddie as he lay in his crate. He had his zebra toy, but it comforted him very little. We stopped at a gas station about a third of the way through the six-hour drive to our new home. With the gas tank topped off, I pulled over to a grassy area.

"You need to go," I told Eddie, attaching a small leash to his collar. I stood around watching him stumble on his short legs. He was so low to the ground, I couldn't tell whether the fuzz ball had relieved himself or not.

"Sorry, we've got to get on the road," I told him putting him back into the borrowed crate on the front seat. I pulled the seat belt through the handle so he was secured. The front seat was the only empty space in my Honda Civic. It was bursting at the seams with stuff I deemed not eligible for the movers, who had arrived early at my rental to pick up my stuff. It was my first experience with movers and their estimate ranged between a couple of days to a week before they would arrive with my belongings. I had probably over-packed my car, but I knew I would need some stuff before they arrived. Eddie cried as we pulled back onto the interstate.

"Please don't," I told him. "I promise I've had dogs before. You'll be fine with me."

I don't know who I was trying to convince. I had not had a dog for more than two years. After Jimmy's catastrophic stroke, his care took over our lives. I found new homes for each of our seven dogs. When Jimmy died, I knew I would begin rebuilding my life—I just really didn't expect Eddie to be part of it. There were a lot of new beginnings waiting for me at the end of this ride with Eddie—a new job, a new state and a new house. As Eddie cried and seemed miserable, I began second guessing my effort to introduce a dog into my new life. It took hours of zooming down the darkened road before he was calmed, or more likely worn down, and his crying stopped.

At our new home, Eddie seemed content to follow me around as I made lists and worked on small projects before the movers arrived. I moved his new bed from room to room. The box-shaped bed was about four times bigger than he was. He curled up in one corner and slept while I worked. Sometimes, he would listen to my plans. I was talking to him whether he wanted to listen or not. I set an alarm for every two hours in an effort to train him to do his business outside. He didn't seem to agree with me on this plan as I found small puddles on the hardwood floor.

When the movers arrived, they noted my new addition. "Ma'am you need to watch out for those birds," one guy said, pointing to the circling black birds over one part of the subdivision. "They may snatch your dog."

I kept Eddie in my arms throughout the move. He didn't like being held. He liked to explore, but the only way to keep him calm and unharmed was for me to hold him.

When my job began, Eddie and I established a new routine. I worked later in the day, so he spent a large portion of his afternoon crated. I came home during my break to let him run around and do his business. Eddie and I spent our mornings watching cable news channels.

"You're a Republican!" I yelled at him as he sat still watching President George W. Bush at a news conference. I was moving around, but Eddie didn't miss a single move by the President. My talking out loud to Eddie continued. He learned a few essentials such as "You need to go potty" and "I'm going to work," and also a few nonessentials such as "What's for breakfast today?" and "Laundry time." The truth is I talked to the dog about everything that popped into my head while I was by myself. Before Eddie arrived in my life, I did not talk to myself, even before when I had dogs.

Eddie somehow gave me permission to talk to him—he knows I'm not crazy, even if he is a Republican.

~Stacy S. Jensen

Puppy Therapy

There is no psychiatrist in the world like a puppy licking your face.
~Ben Williams

It had been a tough year for my father. He had already buried a brother, a sister, and a best friend. Then, in the late fall, my brother, his only son, was a suicide. It was almost more than he could endure. I watched his health deteriorate with an ulcer, a hiatal hernia, high blood pressure, heart trouble, and the list went on. The thought of losing Dad was more than I could bear. I remembered reading somewhere that older people respond positively, both physically and emotionally, to pets. I immediately began the search. My family and I found a litter of Poodle puppies—four cute, cuddly, auburn balls of fur. We each held one. Mine snuggled up to my neck, licked my cheek, and rested his head on my shoulder. This was the dog for Dad. We left him with his breeder until we could pick him up on Christmas Eve.

My parents were staying with us. So after I picked up the puppy on Christmas Eve, I hid him in my bathroom and kept Dad and Mom away from there. I wrapped up a box, big enough for our surprise puppy, in beautiful, festive paper. I spent most of the night holding him to keep him from crying and giving away our surprise. Christmas morning, I put him in the beautifully wrapped box, placed the lid on carefully and slipped the box under the tree. I made sure that the box was the first gift handed out.

I handed the box to Mom and she put it back down immediately.

She pushed it to Dad and said, "Here, it's all yours... it's moving!" Dad took off the lid. As if on cue, the puppy rested his chin on the edge of the box and looked up. His big, brown, puppy dog eyes met Dad's. It was all over for Dad. He loved him already. But Mom was not exactly smitten. "What are we going to do with a dog? We can't keep him. I'm not training a puppy again. He'll ruin our house. How will we get him home?" I showed her his carrying case and his airline ticket back to their home. What could she say?

Dad named him Rusty. And the rest of the story amazed all of us who were looking on. In two months, Dad's ulcer problems had subsided, as well as the indigestion problems and the hiatal hernia. Even more surprising, his blood pressure went back to normal and his heart condition was under control. The doctors were surprised. I wasn't. I knew exactly what had happened.

Rusty, a cute, little, red Poodle had jumped into Dad's life, filled it with unconditional love and helped heal the pain of loss. Many times I saw Dad holding Rusty in his lap with Rusty's head nestled on Dad's shoulder. I was amazed at Rusty's sensitivity. Unlike some Poodles, nervousness was not in his character, and he never barked. He was calm, loving, and intuitive.

Seven years later, Dad had a heart attack and was placed in intensive care in the hospital. We knew his days were numbered. My son, Jeff, arrived at the hospital one evening sporting an overstuffed parka. He walked directly into the ICU to visit Grandpa. He closed the doors to the room and slowly unzipped his parka. We watched Rusty climb carefully onto the bed and lay his head on Dad's shoulder, lick his cheek, and stay there while they said last goodbyes.

~Suzanne Vaughan

What's Your Poison?

A piece of grass a day keeps the vet away.
~Author Unknown

Our nine-month-old German Shepherd puppy, Sheba, was intelligent, obedient, and most of the time, quick to learn. However, she loved to play, especially in the middle of the night. One night I threw open the door to the kitchen.

"Sheba!" I screamed as the dog pranced forward to meet me. Her dark brown eyes gleamed with joy and anticipation. Her tongue, hanging to one side, gave her mouth a lopsided grin.

"No Sheba. I'm not going to play with you. It's one in the morning," I scolded. "Get back in your basket...." My voice faded as I gaped at the war zone that had been a clean kitchen floor just two hours ago. The dog's tail slowed from an enthusiastic wag to an occasional twitch, as it sank between her legs. She gazed at me through confused eyes that seemed to say, "What? You don't like this game?"

The kitchen floor in front of me was littered with tins, packets and chewed-up wads of mushy paper. I spotted some minute fragments of torn foil, some scraps of yellow cardboard and a few dregs of red powder. It was the yellow cardboard that caught my attention, or rather the black drawing of a skull-and-crossbones.

"Oh no. How did that get into the food cupboard?" I attempted to smooth out a piece of soggy cardboard. "Rob!" I yelled. "You'd better come quickly."

Sheba slunk into her basket and lowered her chin onto her front paws and watched, her face a portrait of dejection. Only her dark eyes moved, studying me as I rummaged through the debris on the floor. Obviously her mistress wasn't in the mood for a game. Rob joined me and together we searched through the soggy mess for information about the product. Sheba hadn't left anything legible. There were only enough fragments to identify a previously unopened packet of Fly Death, a highly toxic powder for use in a garden flytrap. I dashed to the phone and rang our vet.

"Our puppy's eaten a whole pack of fly bait," I blurted out. I could hear him struggling to understand, his brain doubtless fogged with sleep.

"Fly bait? What's in it?" he said.

"I don't know. She's eaten the instructions," I said.

"Can you read any of the packet? Anything at all?"

"Yes—a skull and crossbones," I said. "And the words, 'Highly Toxic.'" He swore.

"We must get her to vomit—at once. Have you a syringe?" he asked. I did. "Make a concentrated solution of dishwashing soap and water and squirt it down her throat. Keep going until she vomits. Then piece together any paper you find and phone me back. I need as much information as possible so that I can give her the right medication to counteract the poison. Work quickly or you could lose her."

I slowly returned the phone to its cradle and stared at it for a moment. Piece together the regurgitated paper? He had to be joking. "We" must get her to vomit? It sounded pretty one-sided to me. I briefly considered changing vets, but it didn't seem to be the best time to do this.

"Come, girl," I coaxed. "Come into the garden." Sheba's ears perked up and she sprang from her basket. We had obviously changed our mind. We were going to play.

She wagged her tail cautiously as Rob gripped her firmly, then somersaulted in panic as I forced her jaw open. I squirted the green, soapy mixture into her mouth. At least, I tried. Most of it hit Rob's face as the terrified dog broke loose and hurtled to the bottom of the yard. For half an hour we battled with the young animal. The more stressed we felt, the more frantic she became. She rolled her eyes in terror and thrashed around, constantly breaking loose. Foam frothed from her mouth, either from saliva or soapsuds, as we chased her round the garden in the dark in our nightclothes.

"Sheba, here sweetheart! We don't want to hurt you. We're not cross. Come on girl," I called. She cowered in the darkness. "If you don't want to hurt me, then what are you doing?" she seemed to ask. Her huge eyes glinted orange in the neon glow from the street-lights. We grew desperate—the dog petrified. Still she didn't vomit. I phoned the vet again.

"This is taking too long," he admonished. "You'd better bring her in at once and I'll contact the poison center."

I wondered why he hadn't suggested that in the first place. We pulled on outdoor clothes, and attempted to get the dog into the car. Normally, Sheba loved the car. Not tonight. She had no intention of getting into a car with two deranged humans. Always a fool for bribes, she eventually succumbed, and we lifted her into the vehicle. I tried to comfort the terrified animal, as Rob raced the car towards the vet's surgery, hazard-warnings flashing.

"What did I do wrong?" her wide eyes seemed to ask. "Where are you taking me?"

When we arrived at the surgery all the lights were on. The vet met us at the door with a drawn-up syringe.

"This is a morphine mixture. It'll make her horribly sick. As soon as I've given her the jab, take her outside onto the lawn."

Sure enough, within minutes, she heaved out the entire contents of her stomach. She examined the soapy, bubbly mess, then looked at us with hurting eyes. "How could you do this to me?" The vet insisted on keeping her in hospital overnight. As he led her away, she went berserk, seeking to break loose from this man who was taking her away from her crazy owners.

"Go, Sheba. It's all right girl," I assured her. "We'll see you in the morning." Tears of relief and guilt ran down my cheeks. She gazed back at me for a long moment, then lowered her head and trudged after the vet. She didn't know what she'd done wrong, but it must have seemed we wanted to give her away.

The next day she was home, apparently willing to forgive, if not forget. Her playful spirit returned, but not at night. If we ever came into the kitchen when it was dark, if she wasn't in her basket, she would scoot to her bed with an expression of panic that said, "Sorry, sorry! I'm in bed! I'm good. Really I am." I think she believed all the drama of that dreadful evening happened because we caught her playing when the lights were out. We also learned a lesson. The next morning, my husband attached childproof clips to all the lower cupboards. Sheba may have had four legs, but she was still underage, and needed to be treated accordingly. She never burgled a cupboard again.

~Shirley M. Corder

Almost Twins

The reason a dog has so many friends is that
he wags his tail instead of his tongue.
~Author Unknown

On a warm Fourth of July morning, I absentmindedly walked with Bunny, my three-year-old Cockapoo-Terrier mix, when suddenly we were joined by what could easily have passed for his twin. The other black-and-white dog had the same fluffy hair and started prancing along Bunny's side. It must have been love at first sight because the two of them rubbed sides and noses all the way back to my house. Bunny's new friend had no tags or collar and I'd seen no signs posted for her return along my walk route. Revelers anxious to set off their fireworks had already begun terrorizing the neighborhood pooches with their loud, sharp whistles. For her protection, I decided to keep the newcomer inside with Bunny. Bunny couldn't get over having a playmate, and the two of them would never retreat more than a few feet from each other before a joyous yip would signal another round of rolling and chasing. Eventually, they'd collapse into a tired pile of fur.

After the Fourth, I put a free ad in the paper describing the dog who had found Bunny and me. The ad ran for ten days with no response. After that, a woman called from a local animal rescue agency.

"Do you still have the dog?" she asked after identifying herself.

My affirmation seemed to brighten her tone to a congratulatory pitch.

"She's legally yours now! You've attempted to find the owner, but being unsuccessful, she becomes yours," she said.

Hanging up the phone, I was both stunned and relieved. Glancing out the window to see Bunny and Fluffy, the name I'd begun calling my little guest, wrestling on the grass together, I realized Bunny needed to keep his new friend.

A visit to the vet to check out my new pet led to a startling discovery. Fluffy was just a puppy without an ounce of Cockapoo or Terrier blood in her. What was apparent to my vet was that she was primarily an Old English Sheepdog. Translation: she had a lot of growing to do. I sighed, realizing that Bunny wasn't the only one to fall victim to her charms. Regardless of her potential size, she was now part of the family.

Fluffy was friendly to everyone who met her and she managed to work her way into their hearts almost immediately. On several occasions, she managed to get out of the backyard. One time, a message was on my answering machine that Fluffy had been found by a lady at the apartment complex next door to my house. I called immediately—it was after 9 p.m.—and the woman said, "Fluffy's sleeping on my sofa with me. Come by in the morning."

The next morning I was greeted by the lady in her bathrobe and bunny slippers alongside her tail-wagging sidekick. If I didn't know Fluffy had been living with me, I would have sworn the pair had enjoyed a long happy history together. Another time, Fluffy was missing for several days. She had managed to lose her collar during the escape. My newspaper ad was answered by a wealthy family whose home was a mansion. When I arrived to pick Fluffy up, the tiny lord and lady of the estate were brushing Fluffy as she sat on their porch between them. Their mother said it broke their hearts when she told them Fluffy would have to be returned to me. Like the Shmoo character from the *Lil' Abner* comics, Fluffy instantly transformed into my closest friend once I got her beside me in the front seat of my car.

The last time Fluffy went on an adventure was on Halloween. Her tags had been replaced and I responded to a kind woman's call. When I arrived, she told me Fluffy was out back with her three dogs. I didn't know if I should laugh or cry as I saw my huge Fluffy running gleefully around with three miniature, white Poodles. She was blissfully unaware of any difference between her size and theirs. Since Fluffy's Halloween bash, I've reinforced the wood fence with cyclone fencing. Now, if she manages to shove out another plank or two, the metal crisscross will put a halt to her next adventure. Oddly, Bunny, who is inseparable from Fluffy at home, never chose to join her on any of her excursions. He always remained in the yard barking at her latest point of egress.

~Marsha Porter

Playing Hard to Get

Scratch a dog and you'll find a permanent job.
~Franklin P. Jones

"**C**an we have a dog?" my siblings and I begged as we crowded around Dad after he walked in the door from work. Dad did not even pause to consider our request. "No," he replied. "Absolutely not."

Dad was not much of a dog lover but he eventually gave in. Maybe it was the irony of his six children declaring undying devotion for a creature they had never seen that unnerved him, because one day he picked up a stray from the dog pound and brought him home.

We named him Fifi and lavished him with love for three weeks. Although the novelty of feeding, walking, and grooming him lost its charm, Dad made us stick to our promise to care for the dog. Dad continued to ignore Fifi completely, but Fifi's response was astonishing to us. When Dad reclined in his easy chair, Fifi lay at his feet and dozed.

"Somebody take Flea Flea for a walk," Dad would announce after sneaking a few scratches between the dog's ears. A few pats here and there from our disinterested father delighted Fifi more than all the games we played with him. Just when I thought that Fifi had won my dad's heart, the dog's belly began to swell. It soon became apparent that Fifi was not a pup after all. Fifi was not even a "He." Fifi was pregnant.

"Pups for everyone!" declared the kids. Dad and Mom were not so optimistic. Dad had lost his job and had decided to move the family to another state to find employment. Fifi went into labor just days before we had to vacate our present home.

"One's coming out!" declared my little sister while we huddled around a large cardboard box. Fifi lay inside on a blanket, her large dark eyes focused on the task at hand.

"There's another one!" yelled my brother.

Just when we thought she was done, several more wet bundles slid out. By the time the night was over Fifi had delivered eight pups. My siblings and I stared at them as they wiggled and squirmed and nursed at their mother's breast.

"Mom," someone cried while observing the pups the next day. "Fifi's snapping at her babies when they try to drink her milk."

One look at Fifi's swollen breasts and mom called the vet. She purchased a large bottle of ointment and several rolls of first aid tape. Mom applied the ointment to the swollen breasts and wrapped the paws of each puppy so that they could not scratch their mom while nursing. Then, she shooed us kids away from the box to give Fifi privacy.

Before Fifi had a chance to recover, it was time to move. Dad crammed all our worldly goods into a small trailer hooked behind the family station wagon. Then, he gently picked up the large cardboard box housing Fifi and her family. After a little maneuvering he secured it in the back of the station wagon.

"On to Oklahoma!" we yelled as we drove from Michigan toward middle America. With six kids, a convalescent dog, and a full litter of pups the trip seemed to take forever. Dad stopped frequently so that we could go to the bathroom and Mom could check the bandages on the pups' paws. The last task before pulling out of the rest stop was to apply Fifi's ointment.

After we reached our destination Fifi quickly recovered. The pups found homes with other dog lovers, and Fifi spent even more time following around my dad and sitting by his chair in the evening.

"How come she likes *you*?" I cried one afternoon when FiFi refused to leave Dad's side to play with me. "You don't even like dogs."

Dad just shook his head and kept on reading the paper. After one last bid for Fifi to follow me I stomped outside in disgust. It just didn't seem fair. But, Fifi's instincts were better than a degree in psychology. The name Fifi rang from our lips with the affection we would give a favorite toy. Dad's distracted murmuring of Flea Flea expressed a dedication to her wellbeing and survival. He may not have professed to be a dog lover, but he loved our dog. No wonder she honored him by lying at his feet.

~Renee Willa Hixson

Destiny

My little dog—a heartbeat at my feet.
~Edith Wharton

For years, my daughter Stephanie craved a miniature Dachshund to call her own. She loved our family dogs and appreciated their status as rescues, but the Dachshund breed captured her heart and she always knew one day she would be a Dachshund's "mom." Stephanie's yearning for a miniature Dachshund puppy remained steadfast throughout middle school and high school, though she stopped asking us to gift her with one. The closer she came to her college years the more she realized getting a puppy was unrealistic. She attended college in New York, and toward the end of her senior year talked about staying in New York to live and work after graduation.

"If you come home to Georgia," I bribed, "I'll get you that puppy."

"I'll hold you to that," she said.

After graduation Stephanie did indeed move home and reminded me of my promise.

"Happy college graduation to me!" she teased, though she knew we were less than eager to add a third dog to our household.

The September following Stephanie's college graduation we took a day trip to Helen, Georgia. Helen is a beautiful re-creation of a German Alpine village nestled in the North Georgia Mountains. There are myriad shops to entice tourists and the restaurants are unique, many of them serving German fare and imported beer. The Chattahoochee River flows through Helen and the sight of people lazing in tubes as they float down the river is a common sight. Helen is a leisurely place to spend an afternoon, and we meandered about, shopping and enjoying the warm sun and mountain breezes.

My husband noted some commotion around a truck parked in a lot near where we stopped for ice cream. We wandered over to discover the cause of the hullabaloo. There were puppies for adoption. Stephanie honed in on one floppy-eared pup and turned to me with big eyes.

"He's so cute, Mama," she said. "And you did promise me a puppy."

"So I did," I agreed, unhappy with this turn of events. How to convince her that she did not want this pup? We already had two dogs and two cats at home and that was enough for me.

"You know," I said, rubbing Stephanie's back. "I think adopting this pup would be a mistake. You have always wanted a miniature Dachshund. This pooch isn't the 'right' dog, sweetie, he's the 'right now' dog, and that is the wrong reason to adopt. Getting a dog is a long-term commitment and you shouldn't compromise. You want a miniature Dachshund, and you should wait for a miniature Dachshund. Besides, you'll be moving into your own apartment soon and this puppy is already twenty pounds. He's going to be big."

Stephanie's disappointment showed on her face, but she agreed with my logic. As we walked away from the truck and the puppy, I told her, "Somewhere out there is the perfect little miniature Dachshund, destined to be yours. You'll find him when the time is right."

We walked in the direction of another set of shops and followed some steps leading down to a store we had yet to visit. As we came into the center of the shop, Stephanie gasped. So did I. There on the counter sat a small kennel and inside lay a sleeping puppy, an eight-week-old miniature Dachshund.

My jaw dropped. How could this be? Less than five minutes before I had talked her out of a puppy and now, here lay the dog of her dreams. The shop proprietor explained that the puppy was the last of his litter and the owner was anxious to adopt him out. She opened the kennel and lifted the tiny ball of fur. Curled up, he fit in the palm of Stephanie's hand and weighed less than two pounds. He opened his button eyes and they locked onto Stephanie's face. He wriggled up to snuggle against her chest, licked her face and sighed, as if to say, "Mama! What took you so long?"

"You were right." Stephanie snuggled the pup. "If I had adopted that other puppy I would have missed out on McGee, and he's perfect. He was here just waiting for me to find him!"

"Did you just call him McGee?" I asked.

"Yep." She chuckled and rubbed her nose in the puppy's soft fur. "Special Agent McGee after my favorite TV character. It suits him."

The pup was in her arms less than five minutes and he had a scored both a name and a home. And Stephanie was right. McGee was perfect in every way.

~Lisa Ricard Claro

My Dog's Life

Who's the Boss?

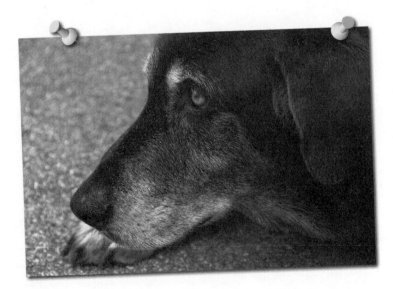

My Fan

My dog is usually pleased with what I do,
because she is not infected with the concept of what I "should" be doing.
~Lonzo Idolswine

We have a new addition at our house. Not a baby (thank goodness), but a puppy. If you think that I got the dog for my three kids, you're wrong. I got the dog for me. With two teenagers in my house, I need to balance their criticism of my clothes, my jokes and my driving ability with someone who will give me unconditional approval and wet kisses. I want someone who will roll over, not roll their eyes. My friends without teenagers don't understand. "A puppy is just like a baby," they say. "Your kids are barely out of diapers. Why would you want to start the whole housebreaking process all over again?"

I have to admit, during the first few weeks of new puppy parenthood I've been sleep deprived and slightly frazzled, but in lots of ways having a puppy is better than having a baby. My nipples aren't sore from nursing, and I know that in fourteen years the dog won't be a surly adolescent. He'll probably be dead. Having a dog is easier than having kids, too. I can leave the puppy locked up when I go out and the ASPCA thinks it's just fine. If I tried to crate my teenagers (and sometimes it seems like a pretty good idea) the child welfare authorities might not be real sympathetic. When I come home (even if I've locked him in a crate), the dog is happy to see me. In fact, he's ecstatic, and he covers me with those wet kisses. My teens don't even bother to look up from the computer screen. They just ask, "When's supper?"

When it's dinnertime, the dog thinks that I'm Julia Child. He is happy to lick up any crumb that falls on the kitchen floor. He never complains when I serve him dry puppy chow in the same bowl for two weeks in a row. In fact, he likes it. My teenagers aren't impressed with my culinary skills. "Eww... meatloaf," they complain. "Why can't we get pizza?" Maybe I should serve them puppy chow, too.

The dog always comes when I call. My teens can't hear me call them unless I jump in front of the television screen and yell. Even then, they don't move. They simply roll their eyes and say, "Hold on, I'm about to kill these trolls." The dog never rolls his eyes. When I talk to him, his ears perk up and he looks at me intently and listens. He thinks I'm fascinating. My teenagers think that I am a hopeless geek.

The dog doesn't run up the phone bill with text messages about his love life or put perfectly clean clothes into the laundry hamper. He doesn't need braces or a ride to the mall. The dog doesn't want clothes from Abercrombie & Fitch. In fact, Abercrombie doesn't even carry his size. The dog never asks me for money or borrows my good leather boots to walk to school when it's raining. Unlike my kids, the dog actually plays with his toys and seems grateful for the one or two that I have brought home from Petco. The dog doesn't mind if I sing along with the car radio. I can walk the dog around the block and he's not embarrassed to be seen with me. He doesn't sigh or even roll his eyes when people comment on how much we look alike. In fact, he looks flattered.

I'm pretty sure that the dog will never deplete my life savings by spending four years at an expensive, private college drinking beer. He is, however, enrolled in Canine Kindergarten. Tuition is only seventy dollars and they promise that in eight weeks he'll learn to walk on a leash, sit, and stay. I just hope he never learns to roll his eyes.

~Carol Band

Schooner's Big Test

Perseverance is not a long race; it is many short races one after another.
~Walter Elliott

We were on our way to a class in downtown Stuart so Schooner, my two-and-a-half-year-old Labrador Retriever, could try out to become a therapy dog. He was standing on the back seat, his head next to mine, his furry cheek brushing my cheek, and he started to hyperventilate. Maybe it was the cars whizzing by or the trees, but something outside made him very excited. He breathed in loudly and then held it. I feared he might pass out.

A neighbor had told me that the local pet therapy program was looking to add more big dogs. She didn't have a phone number and suggested I drop by the class. Schooner was a long shot. We parked next to the meeting area, and I saw Rottweilers, Bull Mastiffs, Greyhounds, Pugs, German Shepherds, Chihuahuas, Corgis, Papillons, and Dachshunds. He saw them too. He flailed against his heavy-duty seat belt wanting to play and wanting to do it now. He bellowed and pulled. How would I control him? All I had was a four-foot leash and flat collar. Maybe my dog trainer was right. I should go home and work with him for another year. Maybe my brother-in-law was right, and Schooner could never become a therapy dog. Maybe my neighbors were right when they said they'd never seen such a wild puppy. But we had gotten to the parking lot, and I refused to give up so soon. I would keep the seat belt on him and use it like a harness.

Out of the car, Schooner rushed to a Golden Retriever and began to sniff. The handler said, "No sniffing or touching during class." My face flushed as I pulled my dog away. I'd already broken one rule. The woman in charge strode over and said, "Hi, and who are you?" She gave Schooner an appraising look.

"Donna said we should try out," I said. "I'm Janice and this is Schooner."

Schooner gave her one of his wagging all over greetings that started with his frenetic tail and eventually engulfed his entire body in wild undulation. His body wiggled in glee for a full minute. He ended his greeting with a long look and a broad smile.

"Nice looking Lab," she said. I beamed. He's the most beautiful yellow Lab I had ever laid eyes on. A little skinny in the chest, with curly hair on his shoulders, but a handsome face, with a dark nose and eyes outlined in black.

Then she turned and took off, a string of dogs and handlers following her down a street, like a canine conga line. We would walk down the city street to see how the dogs behaved. I found a place in the middle of the line where I hoped no one would notice us. It took sheer force to keep Schooner from pushing his nose into every dog's rear end. I remembered—no sniffing or touching—and worked hard to follow that rule, but Schooner was in a swoon from the sights and sounds of so many dogs. He couldn't keep his nose away from them. The dogs and handlers snaked past downtown storefronts and pedestrians stood out of the way to watch the parade. When we reached a street corner, the other dogs stopped and waited before crossing. Schooner bounded across the street like an out-of-control sled dog. At the next corner I sat on him so that he would wait. As my dog leaped ahead, I kept a death grip on the seat belt. It had already blistered my hand, but it gave me more control than a flat collar and leash would have. It must have looked odd, the black webbing flopping against Schooner's yellow body. We stopped to greet friendly shoppers and Schooner wiggled and wagged. When something else grabbed his attention, he prepared to bolt. I pulled and struggled to keep him somewhere near the line of dogs. When the walk was over, I knew Schooner had failed. By the time we got home my arms ached. I swallowed a pain reliever, took a hot bath, and jumped into bed. The next day, I called.

"He's not ready," she said. My heart sank. She continued, "To go into a facility, that is. But I think he would make a wonderful therapy dog with more training. He likes people and is happy and friendly." I took a breath. She added, "And he really wants to please you." I couldn't believe it. This was something I hadn't realized. I had always felt that I was invisible to Schooner, that he followed only his own desires. If he wanted to please me, I could have some control over him. There was hope.

It took us more than six months of additional training to pass the requirements to become a certified therapy team. We attended classes every month and eventually got permission to visit a nursing home. The first evaluator flat out refused to approve us, saying that a wild Lab like Schooner could never be a good therapy dog. The second evaluator noticed his winning personality and explained how to keep him under control in close quarters, and to tell him to sit when I worried that he was getting away from me.

To date, he and I have volunteered with the Humane Society of the Treasure Coast in Florida for almost seven years. He still spends a lot of time sitting. He participates in reading and humane education programs in the schools, assists with shelter tours, visits nursing homes, models in fashion shows, and poses for photographers. At ten years old the kids still think he's a puppy because of the wriggle in his greeting and the bounce in his step. Each new class of wanna-be therapy dogs and handlers hears about the wild Labrador Retriever in the seat belt who eventually made it into the program. We've inspired dozens of therapy teams to stick with the training in order to qualify. The other day, one kid summed it up. "Lady," he said, "you have a very cool dog."

~J.J. Kay

"You dropped something."

Barkley, Blow Your Horn

Dogs feel very strongly that they should always go with you in the car, in case the need should arise for them to bark violently at nothing right in your ear.
~Dave Barry

Barkley was a pitiful soul the first time that I laid eyes on him. He was a one-year-old AKC-registered Lhasa Apso, but he had never been groomed and had never been let out of a small wire-bottomed crate. He never stopped barking. Not surprisingly, his family was at wit's end, and I was a lonely female looking for a dog to ride shotgun in my Kenworth 18-wheeler truck when I read the ad his family put in the paper: "Free to good home." That's how I got Barkley, a sentry dog bred and "trained" for enclosed places. He jumped into my truck and we both knew he had found his forever home.

Over the years Barkley managed to mark his territory in every single state except Hawaii. He was so much more than my co-pilot. He was my confidant, my protector, and my "fella." He loved to bark, and did so a lot—anytime anyone would walk near my truck. He wasn't mean, just vocal. He loved to sit in the driver's seat when I got out at a shipper or receiver, and it didn't take long for him to learn how to blow the city horn on the steering wheel. I finally had to disconnect it since he would stand on the horn to look out. Barkley was determined to be heard.

One evening we had been trucking a long time. It was 2 a.m. when we finally pulled into a large truck stop just off the interstate. I told Barkley to "get your leash" and he did, then hopped up front. I hooked him up and we jumped out. Barkley was never known for doing his business in a timely manner. This particular night it was very cold, and a cold snow was blanketing the ground. It was Barkley's favorite weather. He was, after all, from Tibet, where the weather is brutally cold. After a long time waiting for him to sniff the snow and make a couple of yellow spots, I was freezing. I put Barkley back into the truck to snuggle up in the sleeper while I went inside for some food.

The place was empty, which was strange even at 2 a.m. at a truck stop. The snow was closing the interstate for the night so I figured that all the drivers were in their trucks sleeping. As I was eating I suddenly heard a trucker pull his air horn in the parking lot. Now, that is a major no-no in the trucking world. You don't make unnecessary noise when drivers are sleeping in their trucks. Then, there it was again, and this time it went on forever. Drivers started appearing, complaining about "some jerk out in the lot." I decided to go and investigate, and the closer I got to my truck, the louder the air horn got. As I rounded the row of parked semis, and approached my own, there was Barkley sitting up on the dash with his chin hooked around the air horn chain blowing away. Apparently he had not finished his business. I got some really nasty looks as Barkley finished what he needed to do, and later that night driving on the road I heard what a few drivers thought about Barkley over the CB radio.

Barkley loved that trick that he taught himself. Shortly after that episode I had to remember to disconnect one end of the chain on the air horn, so that he couldn't blow it anymore. I thought that would do it, but soon Barkley learned how to pull the chain with his mouth.

~Maria Mills Greenfield

Wonder Dog

The dog was created specially for children. He is the god of frolic.
~Henry Ward Beecher

His name suggested a dog much larger, but Brutus weighed in at thirteen pounds and stood one foot high, full-grown. A curly, black, cocka-pomma-peeka-poo, he puffed out his little barrel chest and swaggered around the house like a big dog. He loved hanging out with us kids and we loved including him in everything we did.

We lived just north of Seattle and snow was a rarity. A foot of snow was cause for a celebration. School was cancelled, and the road to our house became a giant hill for slipping and sliding. Brutus knew something was up when all four of us started pulling on our coats, boots, mittens and stocking caps. Naturally, he wanted to go with us. He immediately started his "we're going for a walk" prance by the front door.

"No, Brutus," said my sister, shaking her head. "You're too little."

"Yeah," said brother number one, "the snow's taller than you are!"

Brother number two frowned. "I'm little, too," he said with trembling lips. "Brutus can go. He can follow the trail like I do."

"But you've got snow gear," said my practical sister. "Brutus would get all wet."

I looked from Brutus, eagerly standing by the door wiggling all over, to my little brother, struggling to fight back tears. "What if we made Brutus a snowsuit?"

I went to the kitchen and got a Wonder Bread bag. "This should fit him."

Brother number one got the scissors and we fashioned a covering for the dog by cutting out leg and tail holes in the bread sack. We pulled it on his trembling body. He looked ridiculous but I don't think he cared.

"He's a Wonder Dog!" said brother number two excitedly. "Now he can go with us!"

Mother took pictures of us tramping out in the snow, Brutus in his Wonder Bread bag scurrying along behind. But it wasn't long before we realized we'd forgotten something important. Brutus had been inside all day, and after only fifty yards or so, he hunched over to poop. We suddenly realized we had forgotten to leave the business end open.

We all screamed, "NO! NO! NO!" and chased after him to remove the sack. Of course he ran, staying just out of our grasp, thinking we were playing. We floundered in the snow until total exhaustion set in, when we literally collapsed upon the front porch steps. Brutus then took care of his business, while we all moaned from our seats on the stoop, still trying to catch our breath. Mother came out the front door, laughing so hard she was crying.

"Here," she said, holding out the scissors. "You cut the bag off him, and I'll run him a bath."

"Why me?" I asked incredulously.

"Because you're the oldest, and you should have known better."

"Why didn't you stop me?"

Mom laughed. "I honestly didn't think of it either, but you're the brilliant one who came up with this great idea."

Brutus was running in circles in the snow, trying to figure out what the bulge was trailing along behind him weighing him down. Seeing him dragging his poop behind him put us into fits of laughter. Mother called him, and he came to her for help. Together, we held him still and cut the bag off him. Brutus loved his bath time, and ran around the house dragging his towel along with him until he was dry. We'd had almost as much fun as if we'd been out sledding… almost.

~Jan Bono

The Good Dog

A good dog never dies. He always stays. He walks besides you on crisp
autumn days when frost is on the fields and winter's drawing near.
His head is within our hand in his old way.
~Mary Carolyn Davies

We were in the Berkshires visiting my mother-in-law, and my brother-in-law was calling my name from the kitchen where he was doing dishes. I got up from the dinner table and found him looking down at my dog, Scout, a two-year-old, eighteen-pound Bichon Frise. Scout was standing, all four legs splayed, with his head hung low, mouth open, and his girth fully expanded. His breathing was loud and labored.

"I think he just ate a corncob," my brother-in-law explained.

Suddenly Scout heaved and up came a four-inch-long piece of a corncob. Recently tossed into the kitchen garbage after our Labor Day dinner, Scout had rummaged, eaten the cob, and tossed it back up again. What kind of crazy dog would try to eat a corncob almost as big as he was? Scout, of course, who, above all and anybody else, loved food. Although cute like a stuffed animal, my small non-shedding dog was stubborn, hard to train, curious, prone to relieve himself indoors if I made him unhappy, and would eat anything.

After the long weekend, my husband Ted, Scout, and I drove back to our home in New York City. Everything returned to normal for a few days until Scout started throwing up. I took him to the vet, whose office was only three blocks away, and explained about the corncob incident. The vet thought that the vomiting was probably caused by the other half of the corncob. Although it wouldn't show up on an X-ray, he said that to rule out that he swallowed something else, we should take an X-ray. As he suspected, after the X-ray, nothing showed up. However, he said, if the corncob was still in his digestive system somewhere, it had to come out, since otherwise it would eventually get lodged in his system and kill him. He explained that what Scout did was common — and dangerous. If we saw no change in the next few days, and Scout couldn't get it out himself, we would have to go in and get it.

Besides the occasional vomiting Scout was acting like he normally did. He begged, gobbled down his food, wouldn't sit when you asked him to, came to me only if he felt like it, and searched for disgusting things on the New York City sidewalks to rub in during our walks. However, after a few days the vomiting hadn't improved. The vet said that it was clear that his body was trying to rid itself of something that wasn't coming up. He suggested surgery.

Surgery was scheduled for that Friday. I could pick him up Saturday. As I left Scout at the vet, I gave him a kiss on his fuzzy little head and wondered just how much that piece of corncob was going to cost me.

At just after midnight on Friday night, as Ted and I were turning off the TV to go to bed, the phone rang. It was Natasha, the vet's assistant.

"I am really sorry to call this late, but we have done all we can do. Scout is bleeding. We have gone through five pints of donated blood, but he is not keeping it in," she said.

"What?" I said, trying to understand what she was saying. "Is he dying?"

"Um, yeah, can you come?"

I grabbed the apartment keys, and Ted and I ran the three blocks to the vet's office. Tears from fear and shock ran down my cheeks. They buzzed us in and brought us directly into the operating room. It was only the vet and his assistant.

"He's lost so much blood," the vet said. "I am so sorry."

Scout lay on the silver operating table, his eyes closed. A towel covered his midsection and back end. Only his shoulders, head, and front paws could be seen. The vet flipped back his ear, and showed us the skin. It was white, not pink like it usually was. The vet pulled back Scout's lip and his gums were pale, too. He was losing blood.

"We even held a kitten to his nose to see if we could keep him with us a little longer," Natasha said.

Trying to stifle sobs and be strong for my dog, I held Scout's front paw and put my head near his head. I took a long sniff of his fur. It didn't smell like Scout anymore. It smelled like the vet's office. I put my lips to his ear and whispered how much I loved him.

"Scout, you are a good, good dog," I said, crying into his fur. Suddenly, I felt a lick on my cheek. I picked up my head to look at him. His eyes were half open, and he was trying to raise his head. He tried to lick again. The movement of his mouth looked like a smile. Scout had never smiled before.

Relief flooded over me and I laughed. I put my nose to his nose, and my eyes level with his eyes. "Yes, you are a good dog, Scout. A very good dog. A good, good dog," I repeated. "Now please don't die on me."

Ted and I stayed there for three more hours watching the pink slowly return to his ears and gums. Fortunately the corncob had been found and removed. Today, Scout is fourteen and ever since we have been very careful with corncobs. However, looking back on it, I'm not sure that Scout was really that close to the pearly gates of doggy heaven. I think he just wanted me to tell him that he was a good dog.

~Jennifer Quasha

Warning!
Beware of Dogs!

Dogs teach us a very important lesson in life:
The mail man is not to be trusted.
~Sian Ford

I was just dabbing on the last of my hair dye when I heard a familiar metallic bang. "Oh, no," I muttered. "Not again!" Panda had escaped. She had spied the mail carrier and was now accompanying him on his route. My adolescent Golden/Lab mix had recently learned how to finesse the storm door handle to free herself and roam at whim. We'd been meaning to get a new storm door.

I looked in the mirror to see if I was presentable enough to make a public appearance. In my pink, reserved-for-hair-dying-only robe, I wasn't. I looked like the Pink Panther with "medium-blond" polka dots dribbled all over her, a plastic bag atop her head.

Forty minutes later, the gray in my hair tinted medium-blond, I caught up with them. Panda was standing guard at the edge of a neighbor's yard as the mail carrier approached a porch mailbox. The rusty fur at the nape of Panda's neck and above her rump rose to the tune of her best "chase-away-the-intruder" bark. The USPS worker, a bulging mailbag slung over his shoulder, shot me a glance that burned a hole in my conscience. I apologized profusely (sparing him the details of the hair dye).

"I've been bitten by dogs while delivering mail," he said.

I felt the heat of shame tint my face.

"We're going to be hanging a new storm door very soon," I said contritely, as I clicked the leash in place on Panda's collar. "She's afraid of people in uniforms, but she'd never hurt you."

Several months after the new storm door was installed, I discovered a neon orange card stuck in my mail stating, "Warning: Beware of dogs!" Evidently postal carriers use such a card to flag substitute carriers to dangers en route. Somehow a substitute accidentally left the card in our mailbox.

"My sweet Panda, labeled a danger, and our innocent, senior mutt, Trixie, implicated as well," I lamented to my hair stylist not long after. She smiled, consolingly, as she mixed my medium-blond tint.

"I sacrificed the trust and respect of a dedicated civil servant and besmirched the good names of my canine companions on the altar of pride," I admitted.

"Tsk, tsk!" she said.

~Linda Elmore Teeple

28

Hope and Kindness

The world is hugged by the faithful arms of volunteers.
~Everett Mámor

The room was awash in crumpled gift wrap as my brother, sisters and I tore through our presents before the sun was even over the horizon. I was ten, the oldest of five children, and we were busy playing with our gifts when my father poked his head through a doorway into the room and announced, "You kids forgot something! There's one more present!" He opened the door wider, and a bundle of sable-and-white fur bounced into the room, pouncing on piles of wrapping paper and greeting each of us with puppy barks and kisses. The room erupted with squeals and shouts as we met the newest addition to our family, a Collie puppy.

In all the excitement, the puppy's registration papers, along with his regal, registered name, were lost in the mounds of wrapping paper and thrown away. We settled on Andrew, a fitting Scottish name for a Collie puppy, and he stole our hearts from the first minute we met him. I loved the outdoors, and because Andrew did, too, he chose me as his special buddy. My best friend also had a puppy, and we took our dogs on walks through the woods and on all our after-school adventures. Andrew staked out the end of my bed as his own, and I loved to snuggle my feet against his warm body at night. He grew into a strapping, handsome Collie with a dignified presence that belied a sweet, mischievous nature.

My father owned an advertising agency, and when a client, the

Deerskin Trading Post, needed a dog for the cover of their national catalog that year, Andrew was chosen. I was allowed to attend the photo shoot as the dog handler and I was very proud of Andrew as he sat patiently through hours of location photography. When the catalog was printed, we kept a framed copy of the cover in our living room. Despite his local fame, Andrew was a modest homebody, spending his days following my mom around the house, bounding down the driveway to meet me when he heard the school bus rolling up our street every afternoon.

Two days before our second Christmas with Andrew, he disappeared. We called the police, the animal control officer, and all our neighbors hoping that someone had seen him. We rallied our friends to search the woods and streets around town. As the hours, then days, went by, I was inconsolable, fearing that Andrew was lost or injured. I couldn't sleep or eat, and our Christmas that year was a somber one. My father wrote a press release about the disappearance of the dog that had graced the catalog cover, hoping to help get the word out, and we placed "missing" posters at veterinary offices around the area.

My parents speculated that Andrew had been stolen, as there had been a rash of thefts of pedigreed dogs in our area prior to Andrew's disappearance. All I knew was that my best friend was gone, and I was heartbroken. It was a particularly cold winter, and with every blizzard that rampaged through New England, with subzero wind chills and a fresh blanket of snow, our hopes diminished to the point where we had just about given up on finding Andrew. My schoolwork suffered and at night I cried myself to sleep, missing the warmth and security of his warm body at the end of my bed. I couldn't imagine how Andrew could have strayed away from our loving home, and I couldn't imagine how anyone could steal a family pet from five children. Andrew was so handsome and friendly though, he would have been an easy target. I wondered if Andrew missed us as much as we missed him and every night I prayed for his return.

On a late March day, three months after Andrew disappeared, a woman made a quick stop at a department store in downtown Salem,

Massachusetts, eight miles from my home. Salem is a waterfront city whose harbor is open to brutal Northeast winds in the winter, and it was a particularly blustery, cold day. She was hurrying to a luncheon and her mind was on her afternoon plans when she stepped out of the store and almost stumbled over a dog lying on the sidewalk. Hot tears welled up in her eyes as she looked down at a filthy, emaciated creature trying to pull himself to a standing position, wobbling and stumbling on legs that were too weak to hold him up. His sable and white fur was tangled and matted in fist-sized knots, and when she reached out a gloved hand to touch him, she could feel his bones in sharp relief beneath his skin.

Despite being late for the luncheon and dressed in a fine outfit, she bent down and gently picked up the dog. Placing him carefully in the back seat of her car, she rushed him to a local veterinarian before heading off to meet her friends. During the luncheon, she recounted the story of finding the pathetic dog, expressing dismay that so many people had walked past a starving Collie without bringing it to the attention of the store manager or local police. One of the women at the table remembered reading a newspaper story about the missing Collie that had appeared on the cover of the Deerskin Trading Post catalog. The two women called the company to tell them that their cover dog might have been found.

The owner of Deerskin Trading Post called my father, and by that night we were on our way to Salem, hope rising with every mile. Before we arrived at the vet's office, my father cautioned us about what we were going to see, telling us that the vet had made it clear that the dog was in very bad shape. He told us not to get our hopes up because the chance of this dog turning out to be Andrew was low. But even though he was telling us not to get excited, I could hear the hope in his voice, too.

Sitting in the waiting room at the veterinarian's office, the minutes stretched on, dragging like hours. I could barely contain my nerves and energy, knowing that behind the office door, joy or desolation was waiting. When the door opened, a thin, mangy-looking dog stepped gingerly into the room. His noble head looked impossibly big for his ragged body, and he sniffed the air cautiously. This wasn't the same bundle of joy that bounded into our living room that wonderful Christmas morning, but a frightened, confused shadow of a dog. What fur he had was dull and thin, and there were huge bare patches where the veterinarian had shaved off mats and treated his ulcerated, flea-bitten skin. He faltered as he stepped into the room, but his tail struck a happy beat as our eyes met and I said, "Andrew?" He looked right at me and in that instant, I knew it was him.

Andrew came home and made a full recovery. The story of his return made the front page of our local newspaper, and once again Andrew became a minor celebrity. We never found out how he wound up in Salem, but Andrew lived for many years after his return. He followed me everywhere and again took up residence at the foot of my bed, waking me every morning with a doggy smile and wagging tail, ready for adventure. The only change in Andrew was a new, fearful reaction to the sound of a certain truck engine that stayed with him for the rest of his life.

The compassionate woman who found Andrew refused any reward from my parents. I am grateful for her selfless act of kindness and I wonder how many other people passed by the sight of the starving dog on the sidewalk. She set a strong example for the children in my family about the importance of doing the right thing, and how important and far-reaching the effects of that can be.

~Susan Graham Winslow

29

Crawl Before You Hike

You need special shoes for hiking—and a bit of a special soul as well.
~Terri Guillemets

I hate exercising. It's not that I'm lazy. I just don't see the point. Sure, it's great for the body, but running in place on a treadmill, lifting heavy things over and over and over... I just don't get it. However, adopting Lily, a one-year-old pup, has changed my perspective on a lot of things. I like taking her on walks, wrestling with her, chasing her all around the condo, and it's good for us both, but when my wife suggested hiking, I was skeptical. This sounded dangerously like exercise. Walking up and down dusty trails, getting passed by power walkers, mountain bikes, being overtaken by the occasional new mommy with baby in sling, weights on ankles, all while curling five-pound rocks... that's not for me. But for Lily I decided to give it a try.

"Let's start out easy," my wife, Karen, said. "We don't know how far Lily can hike."

This was a great plan and certainly in the best interest of our new dog. We went to Fryman Canyon, which I learned is challenging. I have no words for the kind of all-consuming fire that ravaged my muscles and lungs after the first one hundred yards of steep incline. But Lily pressed on, so I pressed on, powered by pride in the little dog at the end of my leash. She was so shy and so timid, but on that dusty climb from hell, she was all heart, bounding, pulling with excitement to see what was around the next bend. While I could only hope it was our car, she was excited every single time, her little stump tail wagging so fast, I was afraid she'd re-injure her newly healed pelvis. She was still on the mend from being hit by a car before we adopted her. Lily loved hiking. Until she didn't.

It was hot, I'll give her that. She was the only reason I hadn't sat down and sent up a flare, calling in the forest service to airlift me back to my couch. Her joy was enough, simple as it was, to keep me going. Not trained to walk on a leash, Lily was constantly running in circles, sometimes behind me, sometimes ahead, but I didn't care. She was like a child exploring, and it warmed my heart. But suddenly, I felt a tug behind me. I turned around to see Lily spread-eagled in the dirt under the shade of a leaning eucalyptus tree.

Fryman Canyon is about a 2.5-mile hike, and after we'd reached the top, Lily decided that she had had enough. Somehow we had to get back down. Seventeen pounds doesn't seem like much, but it is when you have to carry it. Sometimes I wonder if she did it on purpose. I looked down at my dog lying on her back, cradled in my arms and looking up at me with her big sad eyes.

And as it turns out, I loved her—enough to exercise. Five hundred dollars later, for tech shirts, vented sunglasses, lined shorts, patellar straps, breathable socks and of course, a water bottle for Lily, Fryman Canyon has become a bi-weekly trip. The steep grade at the beginning has gotten easier, my muscles burn with less intensity and, to my surprise, I have yet to call in the forest service. Lily can tackle the trail like a wild jungle cat, but she takes it easy on me—always looking back, her big brown eyes ever encouraging. And sometimes, whether she needs it or not, I pick her up and carry her.

~Josh Gloer

"I have a lot of experience
in leadership positions."

30

A Loving Heart

One man's trash is another man's treasure.
~Kevin Smith

I remember the day my heart fully opened to love. It was a sunny fall morning and as I walked home along the country road after finishing my morning run, I saw his silhouette framed by the red, glowing beauty of the rising sun. His tail was wagging, his head was high, and he had waited for me. My heart opened to receive the love of Max, a Border Collie.

Our journey together had started a month earlier. I had just moved from the urban sprawl to the country, and while visiting my new neighbor I noticed Max at his farm. Max was emaciated, matted, and paced endlessly. His exhaustion was evident. His eyes were bleak and unfocused, his tongue hung out, his breathing was labored—and yet he kept pacing. My query about Max provided me with his sad tale. He'd been purchased as a puppy, but quickly, his disobedience and high energy caused the farmer and his wife to give up on him. The farmer couldn't destroy him so he fed him and ignored him. For almost two and a half years Max was a nonentity. He wasn't touched, wasn't acknowledged in any way but negatively, wasn't spoken to, but simply fed. When I asked the farmer if I could work with Max he said, "Do whatever you want. You can take him. I don't want him."

The next day I began working with Max. Not in any forceful manner—I wasn't trying to modify his behavior by training him. I simply wanted to give him attention and love. As an animal intuitive and communicator I knew that Max would die that winter unless something was changed in his life. I walked and ran every day along the country road. That day I took raw chicken necks with me and at the end of my property, adjoining the road, raised my voice and called for Max.

He came. His head almost touched the ground, his knees were bent, his tail wagged cautiously, but he came. I offered him a chicken neck. He almost took my hand with it as he gulped. His eyes lit up and he grinned. I talked to him and told him what a magnificent fellow he was. He moved closer for pats and a hug. I then moved out a few feet, called him to me and when he timidly came forward, rewarded him yet again with another chicken neck. Thus we moved, ever so slowly down the country road, until he stopped. No amount of coaching or bribing would move him further. We had come to his boundary and there he stayed. Although he wagged his tail at me and looked cooperative, he did not move another step forward. Reluctantly, I turned away to continue my run and he left for his home.

This became our routine. Every day he traveled a little further on the road and then stopped, refusing to move forward. Although my calls in the morning soon turned to a whistle and an immediate response from Max, we could not seem to move past his invisible barrier. I would eventually and inevitably continue on alone and return to my home by myself. I began to talk to him constantly. I asked him to wait for me if he didn't want to go further. I told him that I would have a treat for him if he waited for me. His response became more and more open. He held his tail and head higher, his grin was broader, and his response to my whistle was instant. We both looked forward to our daily interactions.

As the fall deepened, it was clear to me that our daily encounters and half dozen chicken necks were not going to keep him alive. Further, it seemed that Max didn't care if he lived or died. His self-esteem was minimal. I began creating a raw food diet for him and incorporated cooked oats to help put weight on him. I began intuitively treating him with herbs in his food and fed him each evening. I did not want to infringe on his bond with his home and the farmer—yes he'd bonded with the farmer, a testament to the love he had to give—so I took the food there.

I took a dish of food to Max every night. This was not without incident. The first time, the other dog at the farm attacked Max and tried to run him off the food. It was then that I heard from the farmer that the other dog, the Alpha dog, wasn't letting Max eat anything. I upped my food delivery to twice a day, and I even brought the other dog chicken necks so that Max could eat in peace. Meanwhile Max and I continued our daily walk with the invisible barrier remaining as a border.

Then the day came when I returned from my run to see that Max had waited for me. I rewarded him with a chicken neck. We grinned at each other, both inordinately pleased. My heart felt so full of love I couldn't contain it. I knelt down beside him, placed my left hand on my heart, my right hand on his heart, and sent him the love. It was in the color pink and it was ever so warm, my hands vibrating with the heat. Max stood there and accepted my love, leaning into my body. We stayed like that for several minutes and then parted. That was the first time as an adult that I fully experienced an open, loving heart, a heart without defensive barriers.

This became our new routine. Max would stop at his boundary, which was getting further and further along the road, and would wait patiently for my return. Then he would bound along beside me until we reached my driveway, where we would hug, share our love, and move on to whatever daily activities we had.

~Camille Hill

Free Dog to Good Home

For me a house or an apartment becomes a home when you add one set of four legs, a happy tail, and that indescribable measure of love that we call a dog.

~Roger Caras

With shaking hands, blurred vision, and tear-streaked cheeks I read over the notice I had just typed. It began with the words: "Free Dog to Good Home." I couldn't believe that I was actually going to give away Wolfie. Wolfie, the dog I had nursed back to health after a blood transfusion as a six-week-old, five-pound pup. Wolfie who, as a puppy, would sleep with and carry around his beloved stuffed Cow until Cow became nothing more than a mere rag. Wolfie, who with his one blue eye, one brown eye, beautiful black coat, and muscular ninety-pound body, was the most striking dog I had ever seen, especially when he was listening for something, or running at a full-sprint on the football field at the school near our house. The same Wolfie who we "baby-proofed" and who merely cocked his head when our eight-month-old son took his bone out of his mouth.

And, yes, it was the same Wolfie who an hour before had dug up and chewed through, in a matter of minutes, the lawn sprinkler lines that my husband had, by staying up half the night before leaving for his two-week trip, reburied only hours before.

Yes, Wolfie had spent two weeks at dog obedience school. And yes, we continued to go to the follow-up classes. And yes, we knew that at nearly two years old he was still an "active adolescent." But he was also bringing unneeded stress into our stressed-out home, and I had to preserve what sanity we had left before everything fell apart.

I held that paper in my hand and continued to reflect upon my dog's life. I wondered what I would remember the most about Wolfie. How quickly he was potty trained? Yes, I was diligent about never letting him out of my sight, but he quickly learned to paw at the back door if he needed to go out. Or maybe it was the first time Wolfie spent the night in my parents' downtown triplex apartment. My mother knew that it would take a while to walk him down to the lobby and then across the street for him to go to the bathroom, so she built him a little grass square and kept it on her terrace. We took him out to use the grass square and he took care of business right away. Or maybe I'd remember how, full of pregnancy hormones, I was so worried that I asked Wolfie's trainer if Wolfie might react aggressively and hurt the new baby.

"Wolfie doesn't have an aggressive bone in his body," he replied.

Or maybe I'd remember how nice it was to have him at home while my husband traveled. It didn't take long to realize that the best way to get rid of door-to-door salesmen was to, upon hearing their first knock, put Wolfie's leash on him and jump up and down. Wolfie would notice my excitement, get excited himself, and then, once I opened the front door, it looked like I had an uncontrollable ninety-pound dog.

As these memories came to mind, I was overcome with such sadness that Wolfie could no longer be a part of our lives. Even with all of the extra attention we gave him, he continued to destroy our yard, and inside, he was a bundle of unspent energy, constantly pacing, never just sitting and being still. There was no other choice.

Unless... maybe... possibly... The next day, I went and bought a huge crate for Wolfie even though my husband didn't want me to get another one. "They take up too much space," he said.

But he was out of town and I was desperate to try something, anything. We had crate-trained Wolfie as a puppy but had given it up a few months earlier since he was potty trained and he had outgrown his second crate. I thought that perhaps Wolfie needed a place for a time out. Somewhere where he couldn't ruin anything and where he could rest calmly. Sure enough, the crate was exactly what he needed: secure, free from temptations, and a place of his very own.

Over time, the grass grew back, the digging stopped, and the constant pacing diminished. It's been four years since I wrote that notice. Since then new Wolfie memories have been made. I am so grateful that we made it through those rough patches with Wolfie, my beautiful, smart, loyal, energetic, and gentle Wolfie.

~Michelle Sedas

My Dog's Life

It's a Ruff Life

The Rock Lover

We cannot live only for ourselves.
A thousand fibers connect us with our fellow men.
~Herman Melville

Jake was a wanderer, and no one in the neighborhood was exactly sure where the large black Lab had come from. It's lake property here. There are year-round residents, summer residents, vacationers, and a steady stream of people who come to fish for the day. Seeing a wandering dog that summer was not an unusual sight. Seeing him on and off for weeks was. Upon first glance, Jake was a pretty indistinguishable black Lab. I'd like to say he had special markings or a particular gait, but he didn't. What he did have was an innate ability to expect only the best from everyone he saw and the tenacious temperament to make sure his expectations were met.

His demands were simple: throw a rock or a stick for him to fetch and return. He would drop a rock or a stick at your feet, and prance around and bark a time or two to make his intentions known. If that didn't work, Jake could make himself look pathetic or lonesome, thereby appealing to our kinder nature. Either way, Jake got to play, and the rock/stick thrower usually finished with a smile, greater self-esteem, and the momentary gift of distraction from worrisome thoughts. In time, we all came to think of Jake as our friend, but it was my neighbor, Ben, who bonded most with Jake, and I was to understand just why in the days to follow.

Because property owners on a lake often build walls of rock to stop erosion, no one was surprised when a truck filled to capacity with rocks pulled up to Ben's home. There was a powerful wind that day. What we saw as an opportunity to stay indoors and catch up on household chores, Jake saw as an opportunity to play. The sight of a truck carrying twenty tons of rock and a man who just might throw them to him must have seemed like a dream come true for Jake. The noise of the wind coupled with a loud truck engine and a cargo of rattling rocks echoed through our closed windows as we continued with our daily work.

The truck driver, intent on completing his delivery, never saw Jake playing with a rock that had fallen behind the truck. That wind kept up for three days blowing small branches and yard debris, and on the third day, the man building the wall came to do the work. Minutes later, he stood at Ben's door. Pale, shaken, and almost unable to speak, he said he had heard the whimper of a dog beneath the twenty-ton pile of rocks. A shout went out, and all within hearing distance came running. The situation was assessed, a plan was calculated, and rocks were gently lifted so as not to make them tumble and cause further injury.

Maybe it was God. Maybe it was some universal force that made the rocks fall in just the perfect way to save him. Maybe it was the right people at the right time. Maybe that wind kept the air circulating through the small spaces in the rocks so Jake could breathe, or maybe it was just Jake's unwillingness to leave his new friends.

But, out of that pile he came, fragile, feeble, and hovering near death. After an immediate trip to the vet, Jake was placed on a mattress in a space in Ben's garage that had been hastily prepared just for him. The unmistakable smell of death soon permeated the area. With rotting flesh in shades of pink and red, and the word "raw" in my mind, I stood back, witnessing what was taking place. Ben tenderly put his face down on that ailing dog and repeatedly uttered a loud hum. Jake responded to the sound and the comfort offered by the hum. The connection from human to animal was complete.

I was humbled by Ben's quiet strength and his ability to teach simple courage to the rest of us who just wanted to help. In the days that followed, the garage became a hub of activity. Ben moved a cot out there to be close to Jake. A card table was set up in the corner, and the chairs around it were always occupied by a changing array of friends and neighbors who came to check on Jake's progress and to keep Ben company. The dual role of supporting both Ben and Jake soon grew to include taking on the task of slowly waving a flyswatter over Jake to keep investigating or intrusive summer bugs from landing on the salve protecting his open wounds.

Although our neighborhood had always been one of friendly "hello" and "isn't it a nice day" courtesies, Jake had brought out the best in each of us and helped our neighborhood grow closer. He became the topic of discussion, and in so doing, gently melted away any boundaries that kept us disconnected. Cordial words and routine politeness gave way to sincere emotion, caring, and friendship. We became comfortable with each other, able to share our joys and sorrows, and, in the process, learned more about each other as individuals.

In the weeks that followed, Ben's wife and daughter continued with the constant care and cleaning and frequent trips to the vet. After months of recuperation, Jake was Jake again and the first thing he wanted was to fetch a rock. Jake had reached celebrity status in the neighborhood and he had also become distinguishable. His mouth was crooked, a toe had been amputated, and some of the body damage was permanent. He now kept his wandering to just our street, but he spent most of his time at his new home with Ben's family. Five years later, Jake died. He simply crawled on his mattress, since moved to the living room of Ben's house, and fell asleep. We carried him to a lovely place, brought a few flowers, put some rocks and sticks on top of his grave and shared our stories. It was a peaceful death for a dog who had gone through so much, and in the process, united a neighborhood in a common spirit of kindness and love.

~Pamela Underhill Altendorf

Rottweiler Rescue

Wherever a man turns he can find someone who needs him.
~Albert Schweitzer

I had made it a minor mission in my life to help lost dogs... even when they didn't want my help. I was the owner of two Beagles: Daisy and Bessie. Bessie was a very "sexy" little dog. Even though she was properly spayed at six months, she had that extra pheromone attractant about her, and a special swivel of the hips as she wagged her tail in friendly greeting—no dog would fail to approach with a glad sniff. Whenever I spotted a lost dog, if I could not get the dog to come to me, I would get Bessie and parade her casually on leash. Inevitably, the lost dog would approach her and get pleasantly distracted in the midst of her scent, giving me the opportunity to grab the dog's collar, read the tags, and take the dog back to its owner.

A few weeks earlier, one of my neighbors down the street had acquired a puppy. My neighbor was a UPS deliveryman, and the puppy was a Rottweiler. Both were handsome guys, my neighbor in his cute little brown shorts, and the Rottweiler in his birthday suit. So I had been glad to stop by a couple times for some chatting and petting time while walking the Beagles.

Sometimes I would see the "UPS Man" in his front yard, doing work on his bushes or his lawn, shirt off, nice muscles glowing in the Florida sun, and the Rottweiler puppy, watching his owner, tied with a heavy rope to a front yard tree, nice muscles shining in the Florida sun, and I would slow down the car and smile and wave.

On this particular day, I was walking the Beagles with my husband, and as we passed our neighbor's house, I noticed the Rottweiler standing loose at the edge of the road, and the rope tied to the tree, with the knot undone. I quickly verified that our neighbor was not home, and decided to take matters in my own hands; this dog needed saving! I called him to me, but he ignored me. I cooed and smiled and spoke to him in a friendly voice, but he continued to ignore me, even though I thought we were buddies.

So I did what always worked—I took Bessie's leash and paraded her in front of the Rottweiler. He couldn't resist my irresistible Bessie, and when he came closer, I grabbed his collar. At that point he turned his head and growled deeply at me, all his muscles bunching up in protest in the most unfriendly manner. Having schooled myself with numerous dog-training books, I knew better than to show any fear. (Even though he did look quite imposing on that day—goodness, these Rottweilers grew fast!) So, I sternly took him by the scruff of the neck, and in a gruff voice told him to knock it off. (I mean, really, I wasn't going to get pushed around by a pup, and one I knew, even if he was a Rottweiler.) His body language changed to a more peaceful demeanor, and not knowing what else to do with him in his owner's absence, I retied him to the front yard tree, and left him there to continue my walk with my husband and Beagles.

A few days later, I saw the neighbor doing work in his yard, and the Rottweiler pup tied to the tree. I stopped the car to let the neighbor know I had been his dog's savior, and told him what I had done for him. The UPS Man looked at me and chuckled, "Oh, I was wondering how I ended up with a strange full-grown Rottweiler tied to my tree. My puppy was home inside."

~Mimi Pollack

Sam's Sulks

A cat, after being scolded, goes about its business. A dog slinks off into a corner and pretends to be doing a serious self-reappraisal.
~Robert Brault, www.robertbrault.com

Sam wasn't just a big black Labrador, he was absolutely huge. As I am only five feet tall, my husband, Eric, used to joke that Sam's legs were longer than mine. It was Sam that taught me a very important lesson about myself, even if he was probably concentrating more on his treats and his pride.

Eric and I had only been married for a couple of years when we got Sam as a puppy. I suppose like most people in the first few years of marriage, there are always adjustments to be made. Sam was huge, but gentle and such a character that it would be easy to think we learned our lessons from all his good points. It wasn't quite that way, but he certainly did show me that I had a bit of growing up to do. Until we got Sam, I never knew that dogs could have a sense of humor, but he actually used to play tricks on me.

We live on the coast and since our neighbors had to work weekends, we used to take their little boy, Gavin, down to the beach for the day. Sam had watched me dig holes for Gavin, and decided it was time to join in. I was so busy building a sandcastle for Gavin that I never saw, and Eric never enlightened me, that Sam was busy digging behind me. He dug a deep hole behind me so that when I sat back and put a hand out to steady myself, I tipped back into the hole. Everyone nearby on the beach had been watching, and the sight of my short legs waving in the air brought the beach to a standstill. Sam took off and ran huge rings round me to make sure he wasn't in trouble. Laughing at his tricks on me was never a problem. I thought it was funny too.

Sam, however, could not stand to be laughed at and would go into very serious "sulks" when that happened. One very cold winter, we were taking him out for a walk and didn't realize our front door path was completely iced over. Sam bounded outside as usual, but the next minute his long legs were flying all over the place as he tried to stay upright. Almost in "Bambi" style he slid down the path on his side and bumped into our hedge. None of this happened with any great impact, it was almost done in slow motion, so we knew he wasn't hurt, and it was so comical, we both burst out laughing. Sam's pride was hurt and when we got back home he went into his "sulk" corner and only came out to eat and for walks for two days.

Even worse was the incident with a pop group called Boney M who were popular in the United Kingdom at that time. Sam was already beginning to recognize certain words and "bone" was one of them. He was lying in the living room, stretched out under a small coffee table, while we were watching a pop programme on television. When the DJ said something about the next record being "A big hit for BONEY M," Sam's shot upright, banging his head underneath the little coffee table. It wasn't a serious "bang" and so we both laughed. That sulk lasted three days.

In bed that night, I said to Eric, "It surprises me that a dog as intelligent and as good-natured as Sam takes our laughing at him so seriously. You would think he would know how much we love him."

There was a slight pause before Eric said quietly, "People can be like that too. Some people can't take criticism, even though it's given out of love too."

I laughed and pretended not to know that he was subtly trying to tell me, since that was my failing. When we were first married, it was always okay for me to criticise Eric and he would just shrug. The first time he said that something I cooked had no taste, I did a "Sam" for two days. And once when I tried to open a wine bottle with his fancy bottle opener, only to find it was a screw top, he thought it was hilarious. Eric laughed for ages and I sulked for days.

I lay in bed making the comparison and realized that although I took exception to criticism from Eric less than before, that was because he didn't give it so much. I realized too that he probably secretly laughed at my big mistakes, rather than annoy me. Eric liked to keep the peace but I knew he really shouldn't have to do that.

I thought about Sam and all the ways he was so brilliant. His sulking was his only fault. Sam, however, was a dog, whereas I was supposed to know better. I vowed that night to not only accept criticism, but openly invite Eric to make it every now and again. At first he was wary of that, coming from me, and offered it warily and ready for fireworks. As he saw his subtle comment had worked, we talked about it openly and I explained that I had learned my lesson not only from his comment, but really from Sam.

"I'm not sure that Sam's sulks are entirely about hurt pride. He is a very crafty dog," Eric said.

"What do you mean?" I asked him.

"Well, I think they might have started out that way, but whenever he sulks, both you and I fuss over him. He gets lots of attention and you give him something special to eat to bring him out of his mood."

I smiled at Sam as he lay on the rug and asked him, "Are you really that smart?"

His huge innocent brown eyes looked up at me. He raised one ear and I could almost hear him say, "Who me? I'm just a dog!"

~Joyce Stark

"First it was 'The dog can't roll over,' then 'The dog can't fetch.' No wonder my self-esteem's in the gutter."

Sunny Delight

Everything has beauty, but not everyone sees it.
~Confucius

I heard a shotgun blast echoing through the valley between my house and my neighbor's. I looked up at the clock and noticed the time, 2:10 in the afternoon. Rising from my desk, I looked out the window facing the valley. That was when I saw her for the first time, running for her life. With her tail tucked between her legs, the small yellow dog ran as fast as her short legs could carry her, stopping only after she made her way to the top of the hill a good 300 feet in front of me. I watched as she settled down into a small heap, panting, her head resting on her front paws as her eyes scanned the horizon.

Not another stray! But it was really no surprise. The road behind my office had no houses for miles, the perfect spot for dropping off unwanted animals in a county with no animal shelter. My neighbor and I were often the recipients of these strays who foraged for food, water and kindness in an unkind world. My neighbor, however, wasn't as understanding as I was. He'd taken in his share of strays, nursed them back to health if the expense wasn't too great, and then found loving homes for them, but only if it didn't require much effort on his part. I wondered why he'd fired the shot to scare this one off. I found out soon enough.

I opened the door and made eye contact with the frightened creature. From where I stood I couldn't see the severity of her problems.

I gently called to her and I watched as her tail started wagging. I coaxed her in my direction, anxious to see if she was friendly. She picked herself up and looked at me, tail wagging, probably wondering if it was safe. I went out onto the porch and opened the plastic bin where I kept food for such emergencies. I poured out a generous helping and proceeded toward her. We met halfway. It was then I understood my neighbor's reluctance to let her stay.

Her face was swollen from infection, her eyes nearly closed. Her neck was puffy and raw and the fur was almost completely gone from her legs, face, and neck. Mange. I'd never had any dealings with it and was reluctant to touch her because I had other dogs to think about. She, however, didn't know she had mange and her tongue drooled at the smell of the food. She consumed it in five bites and then licked the bowl, her small face looking up at me for more.

I knew at that moment I would not let her suffer. I went back inside and made a frantic call to my vet.

"I have a stray dog here and she's eaten up with mange I think. What should I do?"

"Any signs of rabies?" he asked.

"No. She appears normal in every other way."

"Will she let you touch her?" he continued.

"I haven't tried."

"Can you get her in your van?" he asked.

"I don't know, but I'll try."

"Bring her in if you can. It's not the end of the world. Mange can be treated," he said.

"What about my other dogs? Is she contagious?"

"It depends on what kind of mange it is," he said. "Let me have a look at her before you let the other dogs around her."

"I'll be there shortly."

That's all I needed to hear. I went back outside and gave her water, which she lapped appreciatively.

How would I get her in the van? I started across the field to my house to get a clean towel to wrap around her. She followed me, close on my heels, probably hoping I wouldn't leave her behind. Towel in hand, she and I walked back across the field to my utility van. I opened the back door, placed the towel around her, and picked her up. She offered no resistance as I placed her in the back and closed the door.

The vet met me outside. One look at her confirmed his suspicions. Red mange.

"Can it be treated?" I asked.

"Yes, it can be treated, but red mange is the hardest form to cure. We can get rid of the infection quickly by treating her with a high dose of antibiotics, but it'll take about a year for her hair to come back."

"Is she contagious?"

"She's not contagious to your other dogs because red mange is hereditary. It's in her blood. We can keep it under control, but she should never be allowed to have pups. We'll need to spay her as soon as we get the infection cleared up."

"Okay, let's get started," I said.

"Do you have a name picked out for her?"

A name? I had no idea because I wasn't expecting such a bundle of neediness to come knocking on my door. As I looked at her, her blond tail wagged in tune to my thoughts and I could see her smiling with her puffy eyes. Suddenly it came to me.

"Sunny Delight."

"Okay, let's get Sunny Delight inside," he replied as he picked her up and carried her gingerly through the door to his examination room. Her thin, bony body trembled as I reached out and touched her head for the first time. I thought, God, why does this happen to your beautiful creatures? How can people be so mean?

The next few months brought great changes in Sunny D's appearance. With daily treatments of antibiotics, the infection went away. Her eyes began to look normal and bright and her fur started growing over the once-raw skin. She developed a healthy appetite, but she no longer wolfed down her food as if it would be her last meal. The scar from her spaying healed over nicely. Happiness exuded from her as she made friends with the other animals that call my rescue farm their home.

A year later Sunny D shows almost no signs of red mange. She's a fat, healthy bundle of joy who lives up to her name daily. She greets me enthusiastically whenever she sees me and rides beside me in the golf cart as we check fences every day. Nothing goes unnoticed by her now-clear eyes. She chases butterflies and barks at blue jays when they fly down at her. She loves the farm pond and stands knee-deep in the water barking at the fish as they nibble at her.

My neighbor, the one who'd shot up in the air to scare her away, saw her the other day as we rode through the pasture on the golf cart. "Where'd you get the cute dog?" he asked, unaware of his shortcomings. "My kids would love her."

"Oh, she was a stray who adopted me," I told him.

~Carol Huff

Living in the State of Joy

The average dog has one request to all humankind. Love me.
~Helen Exley

Tara was the family dog during my childhood. We lived in Huntington, Long Island in New York. It was the suburbs and a time when kids and dogs ran freely in the neighborhood. There was no fear of abduction or leash laws. Tara was my brother Ricky's dog. She would walk Ricky to the bus stop every school morning and be there when the bus dropped him back off. During school hours, she would rally her dog friends to her yard where they would play with twigs, logs, rocks and occasionally my mother's freshly cleaned laundry hanging on the line. My mother used to lament that she did not know why Tara's friends always had to play in our yard. It was an idyllic time and place for Tara but that was all about to change.

We were moving to Italy so my parents could launch a business. Taking a dog overseas required a lot of paperwork, and in addition, we would be living in a small apartment where she would not have the same freedom she was used to. My mother decided that it was best for her to find a new home. We kids were devastated.

Tara must have sensed the change in the household for she began haunting my mother day and night. Literally, she sat beside my mother's bedside at night with her head on the mattress just staring at her while she slept. My mother found that sleeping with Tara staring at her made her feel so guilty that she went to talk to the veterinarian about the situation. He explained that Tara was part black Lab and part German Shepherd and as such considered herself very much a part of the family. He stated that he felt Tara would find it very difficult to adjust to a new family and would have a better chance of adjusting to a new environment. Mom came home that night and announced that Tara would be getting the much-dreaded shots just like we were in order to travel overseas. There was a unanimous "Hurrah!" I think Tara knew she was going to Italy too, because after that night she resumed her sleeping spot at the beginning of the hallway instead of beside my mother's bed.

Tara was remarkable. During the first two months in Italy, my parents, who grew up in Italy, took us three kids touring the country. Tara, of course, came along. She went on a gondola ride through the waterways of Venice, spent New Year's Eve on the Isle of Capri and rode through the mountains of Northern Italy. She adjusted to apart-ment living and being walked on a leash instead of freely exploring her new neighborhood. She became my confidante and my ever-present friend during the summer months when we lived in an area where there weren't many children my own age. I would read Nancy Drew books to her and she always appeared to be listening. I would dress her up in whatever I happened to think was the rage, and tell her all of my adolescent problems. She often went to work with my parents and was the guard dog for the business.

After my father passed away, we returned to America where my brother was to attend Fordham University. He insisted on taking Tara with him, and against my mother's better judgment, she let him. Tara became a regular at his classes. One day during a particularly long and boring lecture, Tara stood up from beside my brother's chair, loudly yawned and stretched. The professor stopped in mid sentence, looked at Tara, and looked at my brother. My brother thought that he would surely be expelled. The professor promptly dismissed the class because Tara said it was enough.

When my brother got a job selling cars, Tara learned to stay on the car lot, in his office, or sleep in his car. When it was hot, she taught herself to use her paw to roll down the windows. Tara even had a say in my brother's love life. Since Tara was always with him, it seemed only appropriate that she would go on his dates. Tara did not always like the girls he dated and had no problem letting him know her opinion. My brother was so used to having Tara with him, that he did not always remember to introduce Tara to his dates when they got in the car. Imagine their surprise as my brother held the passenger door open for them to get in, then closed it and walked around to the driver's side, only to have this large black Lab rise up and poke her head over the front seat to inspect them. To Tara, it was not important where she lived. It only mattered who she lived with. Tara adapted and adjusted to her surroundings, loving each day wherever it may have been as long as it was with the people she loved the most—her family.

~Loretta Schoen

A Small Detour

If you think dogs can't count, try putting three dog biscuits in your pocket and then giving Fido only two of them.
~Phil Pastoret

Patton was a sleek German Shepherd who was responsible for being Debbie's eyes. He was a godsend to the teenage girl, the blind daughter of my friends, Becki and Kent. When Debbie and Patton became a team, I was excited about meeting him. For years, dog training had been my hobby and along with just about everyone else in the world, guide dogs intrigued me. They are on the top of my Wow-List when it comes to service dogs. When I was a teen, I read a book about the first guide dog in the United States, Buddy. Until I met Patton, I had been relegated to admiring service guide dogs from afar. I finally got my chance to become personally acquainted with one of these fine working beasts.

On our introduction day, Becki, Debbie, Patton and I went on a minor outing. Patton pretty much functioned simply as part of our group. We humans just chatted and walked, so there was really not much to see on the part of the dog's training. As a dog trainer, I wondered how well these dogs transitioned from training school into the real world. Sometimes human students do quite well in college but just cannot make it when thrust into the responsibilities of the real world. In a sense, Patton was a recent college graduate embarking on his working career. I felt blessed by being able to observe his transition. On the way back to Becki's home we stopped at a grocery store for coffee and bread and I got my opportunity to see the dog truly work—and also be a bit of a sneak.

Loving her newfound independence and being a typical teen, Debbie requested, maybe demanded, that her mom stay in the car while she, Patton and I went grocery shopping. I must admit that being a dog lover, there was a bit of rebellious satisfaction at being able to enter a grocery store with a dog. It was fun to watch the admiring glances of people who tried to avoid staring at the Blind Team. Staring would have been okay. There was a blessed beauty watching the dog guide Debbie up and down the aisles. It was inspiring to see the Debbie-Patton team head to the coffee section as well as anyone with sight. The coffee aisle is perhaps the one grocery store aisle I could find without using my sight, the odors being so incredibly strong. I wondered how the dog could tolerate the smells in that store without being distracted from his work. I was awed when we passed the meat section and Patton did not even take a whiff of the delectables that might send an ordinary dog into conniptions. Patton focused seriously on his work. We made our coffee selection and moved along.

"Forward," Debbie commanded, and off we went to the bread section. On the way to the bread, Debbie and I chatted about specific commands the dog was trained to flawlessly obey.

"Does he know to go to the check-out first?" I asked.

"If I want him to follow Mom, I just say 'Follow,' and Patton will follow Mom wherever she goes. I don't shop alone."

"How does he know to go to the store exit?" I asked.

"I say, 'Outside' and he goes to the door we came in."

"That is amazing," I said. I wondered if service dogs were generally a lot smarter than most dogs or if pet owners just lowered the bar of expectations.

We completed our shopping and Debbie gave Patton the command to go to the front of the store. I was shocked when the dog headed to the rear of the store. It appeared to be a mistake but then I realized that perhaps he was just retracing our steps.

He was not. The next aisle over, he turned back toward the front of the store down an aisle where we had not previously walked. I assumed he was readjusting his bearings. After all, he was a young working dog and maybe he did not have his skills perfected. It was then his true intentions were exposed. He was leading us down the dog food aisle and for the first time I saw his nose wander. Those big bags of dog food stacked on the lower shelves drew his attention from his duties. I laughed because it made perfect sense. The dog knew everything else in the store was verboten. Dog food was the one thing in the store that he was allowed, and the attraction was too great. To his credit, he only sniffed.

~Jane Marie Allen Farmer

38

A Special Delivery

A person who has never owned a dog has missed a wonderful part of life.
~Bob Barker

I t wasn't fair. We had spent a year planning our wedding and honeymoon—a beautiful ceremony and reception followed by eight exquisite days on a Bermuda beach. An unwelcome telephone call from Russ's office changed our plans. Our eight-day escape was shortened to seven days and we caught an early flight back. To make matters worse, we returned home to learn that the reason for our change in plans had changed yet again. We could have stayed the extra day after all. Like I said, it wasn't fair.

One more thing about our new life together wasn't fair. The man I had fallen in love with had a prior love. I had to share my husband with Lord Cardigan, a sixty-pound, full-grown, five-year-old English Bulldog. Cardigan slobbered. He drooled. He snored. Calling him ugly was an understatement. As the saying goes, he had a face only a mother could love. I might have thought better of Lord Cardigan if I had spent time around dogs when I was younger, but I grew up in a dog-free home. Mom and Dad didn't like dogs. Or cats. Or any other four-legged animals. I learned to fear dogs, rather than love them. The closest thing to a pet in our house was a couple of goldfish that lasted a few weeks before being disposed of with a flush.

I loved my future husband. I did not love Cardigan. However, I could not have one without the other. And I knew better than to ask Russ to choose between us. The early return from our honeymoon only hastened the beginning of a precarious co-existence with the one who came before me. Somehow, I would have to learn to love—or at least tolerate—Cardigan, too. The day after we returned was overcast, but matched my mood. The gray, New York sky mocked the clear Bermuda-blue heavens I had left a day earlier. We ate an early dinner while listening to the sounds of a violent storm as it quickly moved in. Booming thunder accompanied flashes of lightning and pelting rain. I was thankful we were indoors—and not in a plane. That's when we received a special delivery.

I glanced out the window to check on the storm's status when something caught my eye. It appeared as if a white plastic grocery bag had blown up against our fence. When I checked again a few minutes later, it was still there, but it wasn't a bag. We ran outside to find a cowering Lhasa Apso sitting in front of our gate. She cringed at each clap of thunder, but did not run away. It seemed like she was waiting for us. Russ scooped her up with one hand and brought her into the house. She sat calmly as we patted her dry with a towel. It was clear she had been on the streets a long time. Her hair was tangled, matted, and dirty. She had no identification and her collar was so tight a tumor had grown over it. No matter how much Russ tried to comfort her, she trembled all night and flinched at any sudden movement. My first thought was that the last thing we needed was another dog. I wasn't crazy about the first one, but with Cardigan I had no choice. This one was different. I was determined that we would not keep this stray.

The next day I put up signs in the neighborhood, but no one claimed her. No one recognized her, either. As the days passed, she and I began to bond. Soon I was privately hoping no one would come for her. By the end of the week I was glad no one stepped forward. I named her Pumpkin—a term of endearment Russ used for me, and now I used for her. Pumpkin was thirteen pounds and fit perfectly on my lap. She was an ideal first dog for me. She delicately kissed me with soft, tiny licks—a far cry from the slobbering deluge Cardigan presented whenever he was near me. When Pumpkin jumped on me, it felt more like a brush against my legs, nothing like the force of sixty pounds knocking me off my feet. And when Pumpkin ate, she did it with the manners of a lady, without leaving puddles of drool on the floor around her dish.

Pumpkin quickly became my dog, while Cardigan remained Russ's. She tortured Cardigan, stealing his food and his toys, much to my secret delight. She ran for the softest pillow and was always first in line when we opened the box of treats. I allowed her to sleep on the bed with us, even though I did not permit Cardigan the same privilege. To his credit—and my shame—Cardigan tolerated my double standard. He also let Pumpkin get away with her antics. His continued patience with her caused me to see him in a different light. Perhaps he wasn't so bad after all. I soon realized that Cardigan's unattractive exterior concealed a heart of gold.

Pumpkin's presence helped me in other ways. For the first time in my life, I had a dog of my own. She taught me what it meant to be responsible for another life. She also taught me to relinquish my fear of animals, something that came much easier with a lapdog than a Bulldog. God had sent me exactly what I needed. Life is not always fair, but if we had not returned from our honeymoon a day early, I would have missed the special delivery left at our home that stormy night. Following Pumpkin and Cardigan, six other dogs have blessed us by being part of our family during the past thirty years. Some were purebreds, some were mutts. But every one of them had Pumpkin to thank for softening my heart and teaching me the joy that comes from opening my life to the unconditional love of a dog.

~Ava Pennington

Paws Off

The belly rules the mind.
~Spanish Proverb

We often heard people say that Poodles are exceptionally smart, so when we decided to get a new dog, we opted for a large, white, Standard Poodle puppy. In addition to wanting an intelligent breed, I also wanted a tall, shaggy-haired dog I could "see eye-to-eye with," so this big, Royal Standard Poodle puppy fit the bill. We named our Poodle "Dudley" after Dudley Do-Right of the Royal Canadian Mounted Police, a character in the old *Bullwinkle* cartoons, and our Dudley surely was a keen thinker.

Growing up in our family of two adults, with no children and no other pets, Dudley took it upon himself to believe that he, too, was human. Dudley operated under the assumption that whatever people do, he could do, too. When the light bulb in the front hall ceiling fixture blew and my husband had to replace the bulb, Dudley was alongside him, standing with his two, front paws on the chair upon which my husband was standing, peering up at the ceiling, as if to assist.

When we sat on the living room sofa to watch TV, relaxing with our feet atop the coffee table, Dudley would sidle up to the couch, backing into it, so he could place his rear end on the cushions adjacent to us, and then extend his long, fuzzy, front legs straight out onto the coffee table, so he would be sitting as we were.

Dudley also had a strong commitment to maintaining "his"

possessions, and whatever we people did, he did too. When my husband or I would carry a bowl of pretzels to the living room to snack on while we watched TV, Dudley would pick up his bowl of kibble from the dining room floor and carry it to where we were sitting, so he could enjoy a TV snack, too. This worked fine until one day when Dudley lost his grip of his glass food bowl and it fell from his mouth and shattered on the floor. Then there were also a few times when Dudley attempted to carry his glass water bowl with him from room to room when we carried our beverages with us. We soon learned that Dudley required non-breakable plastic bowls for his food, and we stationed additional water bowls throughout the house, so he wouldn't need to carry around his big one.

Everyone loved Dudley and thought he was a big sweetheart, and Polo, a large, white Samoyed who lived around the corner thought so too. Dudley and Polo were always so happy to see each other and to frolic on our lawn when Polo's owner took him around the corner for a walk. One afternoon, there were scratching noises coming from outside our front windows. Dudley pushed open the curtains with his nose to take a look, and there was Polo, wagging his tail and looking in. Polo had broken loose from his outdoor run and had come over to visit. I opened the front door and Polo came running in. He gave Dudley a quick sniff "hello," and then, when he saw Dudley's kibble bowl sitting nearby, he took it upon himself to enjoy a snack. While Polo was sampling Dudley's food, I found an extra leash so Dudley and I could walk Polo home.

Although Polo seemed hesitant about returning home, the stroll back to his house was uneventful, and Dudley and Polo enjoyed walking together. After Polo's owner profusely thanked us for returning her dog, Dudley and I returned home, but I could sense from his demeanor that something was on his mind.

As soon as we walked into the house, before I could even remove his leash, Dudley ran over to his food bowl—the bowl Polo had been nibbling from a few minutes earlier. Dudley picked up his bowl, but instead of carrying it to the living room sofa/TV area or to our bedroom as he frequently did, Dudley carried his bowl of food into our home office. This was unusual since the office was not a room into which Dudley generally would bring his food. Dudley crawled underneath my husband's desk into the farthest, back corner of the room, and gently placed his food bowl where it would not be visible to anyone. Dudley decided to send a message to Polo: "You may come into my home to visit, but you are not going to eat my food!"

~Ronni Pollack Geist

A Healing Friendship

A friend is one of the nicest things you can have,
and one of the best things you can be.
~Douglas Pagels

Our Boxer, Biscuit, was a Christmas present to me, but she has proven to be a true gift to my middle child, willful, loving Jackson. He was three years old when Biscuit came to us, and they took an immediate liking to each another. Each night, Jackson would call to her in his little voice, "Biiis… cut!" And that puppy would bound into his room, throwing her front paws on his big boy bed, wag her little stump of a tail, and wait for Jackson to lift her hind legs up onto his mattress, where she would curl up and wait for her best friend to lie beside her.

Fast forward three years. We are in a tiny exam room at the vet and Jackson has flown into a tantrum so wild, even the animals are shocked into silence. The veterinarian, Dr. V., had just asked to keep Biscuit overnight for observation. At six, Jackson had already been through the loss of two beloved dogs, and he wasn't about to let anyone take another. So the minute the assistant reached for her, Jackson unhooked Biscuit's leash, and unleashed his temper, kicking, biting and demanding they let her go, tears streaming down his bright red cheeks.

The day after that visit, Dr. V. told us that Biscuit's left hind leg was badly infected. If we didn't remove the leg, the infection could spread, he warned us, possibly risking her life. We sat the kids down and told them what we needed to do. Admittedly, we were a little unsure of having a three-legged dog.

"It may take her a long time to heal," I warned the boys. "I'll need your help."

"I'll do it!" said Jackson.

"How will she get around?" asked Connor, our oldest.

"I'll help her," said Jackson. He had enough confidence for all of us. One thing we all agreed on was that we could do without her having four legs, but we just couldn't do without her.

So Biscuit underwent surgery. She was in the animal hospital for a week, and we'd visit every day. Jackson would bring the shirt he'd slept in the night before to each visit, and when I would open her crate door, Jackson would climb in. He'd curl up next to her, and reassure her with gentle pats and soft words. At the end of each visit, Jackson would place that shirt under Biscuit's head, saying simply, "So she feels like I'm here."

The day we brought her home, Jackson took all the pillows and blankets from his room and made a bed for himself on the floor next to her crate. My mothering instinct was to send him back to his bed—it was, after all, a school night. But the look in his eyes, and in Biscuit's, stopped me. And so, Jackson slept on that floor until the crate was no longer necessary.

Spring turned to summer, and we slowly began taking Biscuit for her beloved walks, first just around our cul-de-sac, then a little further, until she was pulling against the leash, her inborn desire to chase those tricky squirrels getting the best of her.

Now, several years later, when Biscuit runs, you'd never know it was on three legs. We take her to the park, and unlike the other dogs, parents encourage their kids to come up to Biscuit and ask if they can pet her. We get stopped at the pet store, on walking trails, and in our own subdivision. When we moved into a new house, a mile away from our old one, a whole new set of neighbors came to know Biscuit. And the first time I ordered pizza at our new house, the delivery guy greeted her at the door—by name! Who could forget Biscuit, the three-legged Boxer?

Wherever we go, we inevitably get asked the same questions, "What happened to your dog?" Younger children are a little more uninhibited, yelling, "Hey! That dog only has three legs!"

"Shhh," Jackson tells them, leaning in conspiratorially. "Don't let her hear you, she doesn't know!"

Like Biscuit, Jackson, too, faces challenges. He has been diagnosed with ADD and has a temper that is not easily controlled. But just as Jackson nursed Biscuit back to health with loving pats and calm words, Biscuit takes care of Jackson. She gives him a focus when he's feeling out of control, and has a calming effect during even the most violent outbursts.

When Jackson's dad and I separated, and later divorced, Jackson's sadness manifested itself in anger. He lashed out at his dad and me, and even his older brother, frequently scaring his baby sister. But not Biscuit. She was his saving grace. A stroke of her fur, or a sloppy, wet kiss on his neck from her is more effective than any patch or pill has ever been.

What our dear forty-five-pound friend with only three strong legs has taught me and my kids is the value of love, regardless of handicap. Biscuit can run, catch tennis balls, and play tug-of-war. She can cuddle in our laps, greet us with big, sloppy wet kisses, and make us feel loved. But she also brings something special to Jackson. She offers calm, comfort, and strength.

As Biscuit gets older, she has had more trouble with arthritis and stiff joints, but Jackson is there. Each night at bedtime, he calls to her, "Biiis… cut!" And in she runs, stopping right in front of his bed. He whispers "okay, girl," and she lifts her front legs up onto his mattress. Jackson reaches down and gently lifts her back leg up onto the bed, where she curls up in the same spot every night, with just enough room for her best friend to lie down beside her.

~Beth Fredericksen

Throw-Away Dog

*The gift which I am sending you is called a dog, and is in fact
the most precious and valuable possession of mankind.*
~Theodorus Gaza

Five years ago I had to do what every dog lover dreads the most, bring peace to a suffering friend and companion who had been at my side for eighteen years. My Lady Bear, a white Husky, could no longer walk, and at my age and with my arthritis I could no longer lift the large girl to carry her outside. I decided that after fifty years of dogs in my life, their lives were too short and mine was too long. Even though I figure I have about twenty years left, maybe more, and that would be about two dog lives, I was not going to get another and go through the pain of losing one again. But as the weeks turned into months, and even though I love my cats, I missed a dog around the house. My heart ached for Lady Bear. I missed the walks, the playing outside, the look of love in a dog's eyes when she looks up at you.

I started looking online and in the papers to see what a new pup would cost. I wanted either a Husky like Lady or maybe a Collie like my first two dogs. I'd always had big dogs. When I saw that breeders were asking three times my mortgage payment for a pup, it ended my search. I definitely could not afford it and even though my heart goes out to rescuing pets, I was loathe to try the animal shelter because any dog at my house had to get along with cats. I didn't want to bring one home, have a drama ensue, and then have to return the poor thing. So I simply stopped looking.

One morning, two years after Lady died, I heard a neighbor calling for help. There was a dog bothering her cat. I came out to help and found a Terrier-size dog sitting in her bushes with her cat. But the cat was not the one having the problem, the dog was. The dog was dancing around the cat and trying to lick the old Tom, who was not interested in being kissed by a dog. I grabbed the little dog to prevent him from losing an eye to the claws of the Tom, and took him to my yard until she could get the cat inside.

The neighbor suggested I turn the dog loose so he would find his way home. I hesitated but gave in. The dog seemed to be confused by his surroundings and started wandering in the street, obviously not used to traffic. He went from door to door in the neighborhood, scratching to be let in. People chased him away, and after I saw him almost hit by a UPS truck, I couldn't stand it and ran out and scooped him up. I brought him to the safety of my house and fenced-in yard.

The little dog was friendly and had obviously been raised with cats because he liked the neighbor's cat and wanted to snuggle up with mine when he came inside. I assumed he was a pet that had escaped from a local house because he was neutered and looked well fed, but he had no collar or ID. He found the cache of Lady's old toys immediately, pulled out several and started playing with them. It was as if he knew they were there waiting for him. I dismissed the thought that a greater force was at work.

I made signs and put them on the front fence and then proceeded to post them all around the neighborhood. I found an old puppy collar from one of my past dogs that fit him, hooked him up to a leash and started walking him for miles in different directions, asking everyone I saw if they knew the dog or his owners. No luck. This was no small task because the dog had no training and walking him was work. It was second nature for me to start training him as we walked, and I was surprised at how quickly he learned. At the park two blocks from my house a bunch of kids told me that they had seen a car pull up and toss the dog into the parking lot, and then drive away. Still I figured there was a chance that it was a mistake. The kids could be wrong. It might not be the same dog. It was summer and perhaps someone was on vacation and the dog got away. Maybe someone was dog sitting and the dog had accidentally slipped out through an open gate.

I took the dog to the vet and learned that he was a Puggle — half Pug and half Beagle — and about two years old. He had the coloring and was the size of a Beagle, but had the stocky build and the big round eyes of a Pug. He was a handsome little guy. I ran ads in both local and county newspapers in the "found" section, and posted online just in case he was lost by someone from another area. I had a few inquiries, but none was the right dog.

One day when I was talking about the dog with my neighbor from across the street, he said that I had done all that was humanly possible to find the dog's owners. He knew that I missed my Lady, and he said that God sent this little dog to me. The dog needed someone to love and I needed to mend a broken heart. By then, I had come to love the little guy. I named him Sparky because he came to me the week of the Fourth of July. That was three years ago. Today, he is my constant companion. He sleeps on my bed at night and only leaves my side to go out in the backyard. I have had great dogs in my life, dogs that I loved deeply and still miss, but my little "throw-away" dog has been the greatest gift I could ever receive at this stage of my life. I think we both found a way to heal our broken hearts when we came together.

~Joyce Laird

Chapter
5

My Dog's Life

For the Love of Dog

Room for One More

*"Hi," I said. She came over, licked my hand discreetly, allowed herself to be
scratched for a time, chased her tail in a dignified circle, lay down again.
I remember thinking: "There are times God puts a choice in front of you."
We took the dog.*

~Stanley Bing

"Lisa, if there is any way you could come and look at this yellow female while you're here Saturday, I would sure appreciate it. I've just been calling her Mama Dog," said George. I sighed. I really liked George. He was good to me and the animals stranded at the shelter where he worked. I had saved numerous Labs from this facility and George and I had worked out a pretty good relationship.

"I'll try," I said. "I can't make any promises because my kennels are full. But I'm excited about the big yellow male. I have a family ready to come look at him."

"Good," said George. I knew he was disappointed at my reaction to Mama Dog.

But, I had learned, you just never know. I am the founder of a Labrador Retriever rescue in Georgia. It is a true calling. I literally woke up one morning and knew this was what I was meant to do. Before I decided to do this job I had only owned one Lab, Mollie, and I had never visited an animal shelter before. I know it sounds crazy, but I didn't know that Labs were being euthanized at a rapid rate. The popularity of backyard breeding and the fact Labs were the number-one American Kennel Club registered dog for ten years in a row had created an excess of this precious breed. Almost a year after starting the venture, I had saved over five hundred Labs, had twenty kennels, and had twenty Labs on my farm that I was fostering. I was at full capacity. So when George asked me to take in one more, the likelihood was slim. But it is tough telling people "no" because that often means the dog will die.

The next morning, I loaded my 4Runner with two crates, just in case, and leashes. I was looking forward to my trip. By the time I had arrived at the shelter I was ready to save a life! As I pulled into the parking lot, George was there to greet me. He is a retired military man and has that air of respect. He has a passion for animals, and yet every day he comes to work and needs to decide who will live and who will die.

"Hey girl!" George shouted. "You are right on time as usual."

We went to the back of my truck to get the leashes and collars. When George saw the two crates, he gave me a quick look of approval.

"Softy," he whispered with a twinkle in his eye.

"Now hang on, you know that I am busting at the seams with foster babies and this is going to have to be a highly adoptable Lab in order for me to take her," I said. I was about to say more when George slowly lifted his hand.

"Mama Dog isn't much to look at. She just had pups and she appears to have a skin disorder... probably scabies or even mange, and her heartworm screening came back positive."

My heart raced as I did the math: Scabies or mange would cost about $50, the heartworm treatments $200, the basic checkup with spaying $150 and any unknown ailments. We were looking at $400 minimum to save this poor girl.

I broke the silence, "Well, we know one Lab is going home, so let's concentrate on that one first."

He led me to his front office and there in the middle of the floor was one hundred pounds of pure Lab love. The big boy I had come for was a beauty. His double coat was almost a peanut butter color with hues of blond and gold. He jumped up when he saw me and lumbered over.

"What is a dog like this doing in a kill shelter? He is great!" I cried. "I named him Sam on the way up here and it suits him."

"Well, Sam it is then," George beamed. Knowing this guy was safe and homeward bound made his day. I looked up at George and smiled.

"Well, let's go see Mama Dog," I said.

"I thought you would never ask," he replied.

As we walked into the kennel section of the shelter, I kept my eyes straight ahead. I had learned that to look into the eyes of all of these animals, and see their hopelessness and hopefulness would destroy me. And I had many more Labs to help. So, I made sure my gaze never faltered.

"Where is she?" I asked.

"All the way in the back," he said. I shuddered. If an animal is placed toward the back, they were considered unlikely to be adopted, and put on the kill list.

As we rounded a corner, I looked at George, and had to ask, "Why her? With so many good dogs here, why try so hard for her?"

George stopped a moment and reflected on this. "Well, she is special. It started when I got a call about six weeks ago that a stray dog was hanging around the dumpsters behind a local restaurant. When I got there I saw this mangy looking yellowish hound dog, sure enough, crawling out of the dumpster."

I nodded, "She was hungry… poor girl."

"Nah, she was saving," he said.

"Saving what?" I leaned forward.

"Her babies. It seems that someone had thrown them in the dumpster and she was pulling them out one by one. When I got there, she'd already saved four, and had two more to go."

George looked down at the cold concrete floor of the building, his army boot shifting from side to side. "I pulled out the other two. They appeared pretty healthy, amazingly enough."

My heart was racing, "Where are the puppies now?"

"All ten were adopted before Christmas, all except Mama Dog," said George. "Her Christmas was spent here."

"Wait a second, ten puppies? You said she had six," I said.

"She did, and we had four here at the shelter whose mother had died. Mama Dog nursed those babies like her own," he replied.

When people talk about love at first sight, I never really believed it. That was about to change. The moment I looked at Mama Dog, my heart swelled. There she was in a horrible situation after being treated unkindly by man, and yet her tail began the thumping that only a Lab's tail can make. I swear she sat up a little straighter, as if saying to herself, "This may be my last chance… throw in lots of charm." And charm she had, in a quiet reserved way. I gingerly opened her kennel. I laughed as she gave me sweet kisses on my cheek. I carefully ran my hands across her back. She was thin. It appeared she had been bred repeatedly because of the hanging skin under her belly. I could also see the skin irritations George had mentioned, but it wasn't bad. She was, to me, a highly adoptable Lab.

"Well, I'm glad I brought the second crate because she's coming home with me. I'll get her all fixed up and feeling like a champ," I said. "I know she'll find her forever home."

With tears in his eyes, George gave me a big bear hug, and I knew that words weren't going to come for him, and words weren't needed. Mama Dog was getting a chance, a second chance at life. I would be diligent in my efforts to find the perfect place for this great girl. Lord knows she deserved it. As we walked back through the kennel area, I looked up, and noticed the bright neon EXIT sign above the door. The symbolism did not go unnoticed by me. Mama Dog was exiting her once horrific life full of pain and suffering and entering one full of hope and promise.

"Olivia," I said to George. "Her name is Olivia."

"You and your names," he laughed.

Olivia recovered nicely from all her treatments and she gained twenty pounds. She also found her forever home. As I write this, she is curled up at my feet on my daughter's pink Tinkerbelle blanket.

~Lisa Morris

Saving Duno, Saving Dad

With the exception of women, there is nothing on earth so agreeable
or necessary to the comfort of man as the dog.
~Edward Jesse, Anecdote of Dogs

My father was just finishing up radiation for cancer when his dog, Duno, disappeared. To Dad, it was the final strike in a series of crises that threatened to put him out of the game. Duno, a Queensland Heeler in his golden years, had never left the farm that he had been raised on. My dad had trained Duno from a tiny, furry pup. On command, he would sit, heel, fetch a ball, and jump up into my dad's truck. The dog never left the man's side. I think my father loved that canine almost as much as us kids, maybe even my mother. Once when my son Christian was four, he stayed at my parents' house. When he came home, Christian told me, "I can't wait until I'm Grandpa's age... it looks like so much fun, just sitting around eating and watching TV with my lifetime companion."

"You mean Grandma?" I asked.

"No," he replied quickly. "With Duno!"

I laughed then, but now that the dog was lost, I knew how serious it was for my father. He already seemed depressed after his surgery. This new loss jeopardized his recovery. I decided to find that dog—whatever it took.

I searched and searched with no success. I put an ad in the local paper. No one called. For weeks, I watched the full-page ads from the animal shelter for our county, hoping to see a photo of my dad's lost dog. I called the shelter so many times asking if they'd found a Queensland Heeler that they started sounding irritated when they heard my voice.

Finally, one morning I studied that week's ad and called again.

"Do you have any Queenies in there today?" I asked for the umpteenth time.

"Actually we do," the receptionist said. My heart jumped in hope, then sank when she added, "But it's a female. You said your dad's is a male, right?"

"Yes," I replied, discouraged.

"And you said your dad's dog had a brown leather collar. This dog has a new red cloth collar," the receptionist continued. "Someone brought her in because she kept barking and they couldn't get her to stop."

My dad's dog never barked. Duno was the calmest, quietest dog a human could ever own.

I hated to call my father with the news, but I knew I had to.

"Dad, the shelter says they don't have your dog," I told him over the phone. "But maybe we should go in there and see for ourselves."

Why did I say that? I had lots of chores to do that day.

"Please help me find that dog," I prayed, wondering if God paid attention to petitions for pets when He had so many other major crises to control.

My father came by and picked me up in his truck and we headed over to the shelter. When we arrived, I explained to the workers that we just wanted to take a look at all the dogs they had in there. The worker led us up and down the rows of cages. There were so many dogs waiting for their masters to find them—Border Collies, Pit Bulls, Dalmatians, Lab mixes, Terriers and mutts. But no Queensland Heelers.

With all the barking, it was hard to converse. I shouted at the worker, "Are these all the dogs you have?"

He nodded.

"You don't have any other dogs anywhere on the property?" I persisted.

"Well, we have the dogs waiting to be euthanized," he said sheepishly.

"Where are they? I want to see them," I shouted again.

He led us to the other end of the property where a building housed the most unfortunate dogs. I hurried ahead of my dad, who was still trying to build up his strength after cancer treatment. I charged down the row of animals on Doggie Death Row, my head bobbing right and left as I quickly glanced into each cage for my dad's dog. At the end of the row, my hopes were dashed. I turned, stretched out my arms, and exclaimed in a discouraged voice, "Dad, he's not here!"

Just then, my dad rounded the corner of the building, coming into full view, for me—and the animals. Suddenly, a dog that had been lying in the back of a cage leaped forward from the dark shadows, barking and jumping. He stretched up to full height on his hind legs, putting his front paws on the cage, barking and howling at my dad. His bobbed tail wagged joyfully and a normally quiet dog was making lots of noise as he recognized his master. It was as if he was saying, "Man, am I glad to see you! Get me out of this awful place. I want to go home!"

Dad understood, in that unspoken language between owners and the pets that they love. He opened the gate, and wrapped his big arms around Duno's neck.

"Let's go home, Boy," he said quietly, patting his dog. "Things are going to be alright." Dad sounded more confident than he had in months.

Once home, Duno was treated to a bath and a new fluffy bed. My dad left the red collar on him. The people who had stolen Duno had thrown away his brown leather collar, replacing it with the new red one. They tied my dad's dog to their house for safekeeping. But the dog barked incessantly, so they took him to the pound to get rid of him. Weeks had gone by, and we had found Duno just in time.

I call this event our family's Mini Miracle. Many people might not want to bother God with something as minor as a man's lost best friend. But when that canine companion gives a man a new lease on life, I call that the major leagues, don't you?

~Cynthia Culp Allen

Scooby Knows

One of the most enduring friendships in history —
dogs and their people, people and their dogs.
~Terry Kay

When we adopted our Puggle Scooby, he was one year old, seven in dog years. My son Noah was eight. The similarities between them tickled me. Both dog and boy loved to run and wrestle everywhere in our house. Both possessed loud voices, one a squeal and one a bark, and both still needed help in being house trained.

Now Scooby is four, or twenty-eight in dog years, and Noah is eleven. These days their relationship is akin to older and younger brother. They love to wrestle and run together, but Scooby has become a protector for Noah more than a playmate. Last week this was solidified in our home. To Scooby, sickness emits the same perfumed scent as bacon. At least that's been our family joke. Whenever I've been sick, Scooby sits with me and loves me. He can tell when I'm not feeling well. But he'd never done this with Noah until Monday night.

Noah came home from school Friday afternoon not feeling well. He was sick all weekend but his cold didn't affect his asthma until Monday. That day he used his inhaler several times. Late that night, I sat on the couch watching TV with Scooby sleeping peacefully beside me. At midnight Scooby suddenly awoke and bounced up with a curious look, even tilting his head as if confused.

"Scooby, we'll go to bed soon," I said.

He jumped down off the couch and left. I thought he was going to his bed. We'd taken it from Noah's room and put it in ours because Noah was sick. Ten minutes later, I decided to go to bed, but noticed Scooby wasn't in our room. I looked around and peeked into Noah's room. Scooby lay cuddled up to Noah's side.

"Scooby, get down," I said. But Scooby wouldn't go. I tried to push and pull him but the dog wouldn't budge. He just stared at me. Scooby had never displayed this behavior before. Noah woke up and told me that he was having trouble breathing.

Thirty minutes later I was on the phone with the doctor and an hour later we were in the emergency room. By the next day, Noah was admitted to the hospital due to a severe asthma attack. Somehow Scooby knew.

Asthma is one of those sicknesses that require judgment calls. You don't know how bad it is sometimes. Monday night, John and I were on the fence about the seriousness of Noah's lungs. Scooby knew and brought it to our attention. Noah spent three days and nights in the hospital while his lungs were fortified with breathing treatments and steroids. A tough patch for our little man, but Noah persevered. And he loved the good food and the hospital bed.

"We gotta get one of these, Mom," he informed me as he hit the button for up and then down. Up and then down again. On what turned out to be our last evening in the hospital, we presented Noah with a surprise.

"Scooby!" Noah yelled as the Puggle ran into his hospital room and jumped on his bed.

Licking of the face and petting of the ears ensued. One of our wonderful respiratory therapists had informed John and me that a visit from our dog would be good for Noah, and wasn't against hospital rules.

I teared up as I remembered Scooby's first day in our family, and how he and Noah had resembled a cartoon twister rolling and tumbling across the carpet, all feet and paws and laughter. As Noah and Scooby snuggled in the hospital bed, my son looked down at his dog and said, "Thank you for saving me, Scooby."

~Robbie Iobst

From Seeing Eye to Saying Bye

Maybe part of loving is learning to let go.
~From the television show The Wonder Years

"**I** could never give him up" is the most common phrase all puppy raisers hear, and I heard it from friends, family, and total strangers. I responded with the same answer that Puppy Raising Supervisor Donna Luchak gave me two years earlier when she first interviewed us: "We wouldn't want our puppies going to anyone who could easily give them up."

With that in mind, my family and I dove into our first puppy-raising experience with Alberta Guide Dog Services. Dudley was the cutest little Golden Retriever puppy we had ever seen. Over the next seventeen months, we poured our hearts and souls into helping Dudley prepare to become a full-fledged seeing-eye dog.

Dudley was a typical puppy. Despite our constant supervision, he managed to swallow washcloths and socks in a matter of seconds, leading to sleepless nights and many trips outside to "Get Busy," the command that encourages him to go to the bathroom. At our neighborhood block party Dudley took advantage of me talking to everyone about him and snuck a beer bottle cap into his mouth. Of course, I didn't notice until it was too late and watched it glow menacingly at me on an X-ray. While Dudley had emergency surgery that night, I should have capitalized on my first chance to sleep through the night in months. Instead, I lay awake, worrying that I would be the first puppy raiser to ever kill a puppy in training.

As part of his training, Dudley and I were constant companions. He came to the dentist, grocery store, sporting events, dance lessons, and many visits to my kids' school. Everywhere we went people would say "Hi Dudley!" Dudley learned to stop and sit at every door, curb, and stairway—important lessons for a future guide dog. He learned to ignore sudden noises, like a dentist's drill, car horns, or electric guitar riffs, and to stay focused on his "work." Of course, when his training cape came off, Dudley had lots of fun, and especially loved romping at the local off-leash park with our Golden Retriever, Bogey. As Dudley had to come everywhere with us, he sometimes cramped our lifestyle, and parts of me yearned for the freedom I had before committing to this 24/7 volunteer position.

After seventeen months, Dudley was ready for advanced training with a Guide Dog Mobility Instructor in Vancouver, British Columbia. Once I got "the call" that Dudley was leaving my family, I realized that none of us, including me, could be there when he left. Dudley was very attached to me and became upset every time someone tried to take him from me. He never allowed anyone else at puppy class to be his handler. I knew that seeing Dudley try and fight his way back to me would be heartbreaking. So I came up with a plan. I got everyone out of the house while Donna, the trainer, who Dudley knew and trusted the most, came and got him. Dudley was happy to go with her, and we did not have to endure a painful goodbye. We came home to an empty house and newfound freedom.

Everything went according to plan. My job was done and Dudley was settling nicely into his new home. After a few weeks though, something came over us. My children began to miss him, and I had to admit that I did too. Was he going to come back to us? Some puppies don't make the cut and are allowed to return to their puppy raiser as a pet. Would we ever see him again? I knew that if Dudley was successful, I would be given the opportunity to conduct a blindfolded walk with him to see firsthand how well he turned out.

So for the next three months, my goal became to see Dudley one last time. I realized that I needed that closure, that chance to say goodbye that I denied both of us.

After four months, I received an e-mail that Dudley was about to graduate as a full-fledged guide dog. Before he went to his new home though, I was invited to do the blindfolded walk. I quickly responded that I would love to come, much to the surprise of the trainers. I was the first puppy raiser in Alberta to have ever done this. Alberta Guide Dog Services' puppy raising program had only started two years earlier, with Dudley being one of their first dogs.

Jaime Arnup, the head trainer at British Columbia Guide Dog Services, met me at the airport. Dudley obediently sat so I could greet him. He didn't realize at first who I was, but once I got down to hug him, he knew me. In fact, when I stood up, he heeled right around beside me as if to say, "Where've you been? Let's go!" Jaime attempted to take over Dudley's leash, but since she wasn't his usual trainer, he wanted me to be the one holding his leash—just like it always had been.

I spent about twenty minutes in a blindfold, with Dudley in his special harness expertly leading me on sidewalks, through crosswalks, up and down curbs, up stairs, through doorways, around parked cars, through a busy mall, and ultimately to a chair at the coffee shop, a place he's apparently quite familiar with. Jaime provided commentary so I knew what Dudley was doing, and thankfully, was able to video this encounter so I could share it back home.

Soon, it was time to go. Even though it had only been a few hours, the past four months had been erased. We were a team again, and I knew that the trip back home would be emotional. As Jaime pulled away at the airport, I could see Dudley jostling for position with the other training dogs in the back of the van so he could see me. The look in his eyes said "Why are you leaving me again?" but I think deep down he knew why I had to go. After all that planning so I could avoid this final goodbye, it happened anyway.

My tears fell fast and furious, to the point where a security officer at the airport asked me if I was okay. "Yes," I replied. I was more than okay. I was beyond proud. I had finally seen what all those months of hard work had led to. I could finally imagine what he was going to mean to his future owner, even though I only experienced twenty minutes of blindness. And I finally had proper closure. Good luck Dudley. We'll miss you.

~Connie Greenshields

46

Angel Dog

Angels have no philosophy but love.
~Adeline Cullen Ray

I t was a stormy afternoon in Florida. I couldn't help feeling disappointed. Time was slipping by like the sailboats we had watched floating along the Intercoastal the day before. There wasn't much vacation left for relaxing in the sun. Suddenly Kati barked. I couldn't help smiling at Mom's fluffy white West Highland Terrier. She seemed bored herself, as she coaxed a pink tennis ball in Mom's direction.

"Okay, I'd say this calls for a trip to Lowe's," Mom announced.

"Lowe's," I repeated, staring curiously at my mother. Thunder rumbled in the distance followed by flashes of lightning across the sky.

"Kati has work to do." Mom smiled, reaching for a pink dog leash. "You'll see what I mean."

All the way to the hardware store I tried to figure out what my mother and her sweet little Westie could possibly be up to. Soon, we were wheeling up aisle after aisle with Kati comfortably situated in a bright orange shopping cart.

"I'm glad someone's comfortable," I mumbled, listening to my soggy sneakers squeaking each time they made contact with the cement floor.

Suddenly an elderly woman shyly approached, "Oh, it's a Westie!

She reminds me so much of my little Sadie. I can't tell you how much I miss my little companion. Do you mind if I pet her?"

"Go right ahead," Mom kindly offered. "Kati loves to be stroked and loved."

I watched with fascination as woman and dog bonded faster than any glue the hardware store recommended. Thanking Mom over and over the woman had just moved on when an employee in a bright red jacket approached.

"Hello there young lady," the handsome man cried, reaching out and stroking Kati's soft white fur. "I have a Westie at home who could be your twin brother! His name's Ambrose and he would just love to play with you!"

I couldn't help noticing the transformation in the young man's face as his frown suddenly turned upside down.

"What's her name?"

"Kati," Mom smiled.

"That figures… Not only does she look exactly like my Ambrose, she happens to have the same name as my godchild, Katie. She was killed in a horseback riding accident a year ago today. I can't help feeling like I've just received a hug from heaven."

Slowly he leaned over and pressed his cheek against Kati's furry one.

"Thanks for making my day easier, Kati," he murmured before moving on.

The storm continued outdoors, but our angel of mercy calmed the storms inside. The ride home later on was blissfully peaceful. I didn't need to ask Mom what Kati's job entailed. Angel dog had already filled me in.

~Mary Z. Smith

47

Second Class Citizen

A man and his dog is a sacred relationship.
What nature hath put together let no woman put asunder.
~A.R. Gurney

He won't admit it but my husband, Bob, who is crazy about me, likes the dog better. I know I'm not alone in this dog-first, wife-second hierarchy. I turned this situation around recently, when Bob was cleaning out the fridge. I thanked him for getting rid of everything in there that was a different color from when we first bought it. He glared at me. Then Gracie, our big adorable golden dog, trotted in.

Bob cooed, "Hey, Sweet Potato. Got a kissie?" He put his arms around the dog while they played. I turned around and tiptoed out of the room, wondering when the last time was that I got as many kisses as the dog. A few minutes later, Bob came into the living room and declared that we have a gender-biased household, which of course, was nothing new to me. Gracie jumped on the couch and whimpered, and Bob soothingly rubbed her fur. (My hairs were bristling, too, but nobody cared to soothe them.)

"It's my job to do all the housework around here, including the fridge," Bob said.

"But I hate doing that," I said.

Gracie went and got her binky which she placed in Bob's lap. The binky is my bra. It once was white, but is now brown, although it has still retained its shape. Gracie not only carries it, inside and out, but she tries to play fetch with the mailman—which he actually does. I watched as Bob picked up the bra and explained to the dog, "Thank you, Gracie. But I'm not angry. Your mother just doesn't do any housework, that's all."

I suggested that communicating through the dog is not good for mental health, but he ignored me and said, "Howdy-do?" to Gracie and she gave him her paw. They sat holding hands while we spoke.

"You're nicer to the dog than you are to me," I said.

"I'm not," he said.

"If the dog..." I started.

"She has a name," he said. "Don't you, Grace-ums?" They both looked at me and tilted their heads in the same direction.

"Okay," I said. "If Gracie complained about how she was treated, you'd jump through hoops to fix it."

"That's different," he said.

"I'd really like to hear exactly how that is different," I replied.

Then they both hung their heads in guilty silence. I wasn't intentionally trying to divert Bob from the housework business, but what the heck?

"You always bring this up," he said, "when I discuss housework."

Now, there are plenty of us who play second fiddle to the family pet. (We're the ones with only half of our faces visible in holiday photos.) This can work in our favor. After Bob had his say about domestic inequity, I made my pivotal move. I knelt beside Gracie and said, "Why don't you tell Dad that I'll do more around the house if he'll start treating you like a dog?"

Bob will never do this, so I'm safe.

~Saralee Perel

"Honey, did you walk the dog?"

Mending Hearts

The life of a good dog is like the life of a good person,
only shorter and more compressed.
~Anna Quindlen

Wind sucked the limbs of the tulip poplar upward, twisting them into painfully contorted positions. Icy spring rain blew into my face as I struggled to close the kitchen window. The yard lit up for one brief moment and I scanned for damage. I struggled to focus my eyes. I was sure I saw a dog huddled against the old spruce tree next to the garage. A window-rattling clap of thunder made me jump. I stared hard at the same spot the next time the lightning flashed, but the dog had disappeared.

After Nemo died we hadn't had the courage to consider another dog. It didn't matter that he had lived more than an average lifespan. That crushing feeling I felt in my middle as he drew his final breath did not abate with time. Bruce and I mourned him as though he'd been our child. Though nearly two years had passed, I still occasionally awakened in the night, aware I'd been dreaming of him, my pillow wet with tears.

I flicked on the spotlights and stood for a moment longer at the window, not certain I'd seen anything. I was concentrating so hard that Bruce startled me when he came to my side.

"I bet he weighs a good two hundred pounds," he said.

I blinked. The shadowy image once again appeared from behind the tree trunk. I reached for the garage door opener, hoping he'd take shelter there, but the noise sent him retreating further into darkness. For a moment, I thought he might be gone, but another flash of lightning reflected in his frightened eyes. Too quick for me to register any wifely concern, Bruce dove out the door toward the garage. I watched from the window as my kind-hearted husband tried every inducement he could think of to coax the frightened creature inside. Unsure, the dog remained within the shadow of the tree, feeling safe and invisible. Bruce returned to the house, T-shirt and jeans soaked and clinging to his lean body.

"Look," I said, nodding toward the garage. Bruce glanced over his shoulder out the door. "It seems he decided to accept our offer after all."

Now within range of the spotlight, I got a much better look at our visitor. The markings of a German Shepherd coupled with the size and thickness of a Saint Bernard. Oversized ears, one erect, the other flopped over, were divided as to which lineage they owed allegiance. An hour later, as rain continued to pound the landscape, I returned to the kitchen and looked out the window. No dog. Figuring he'd moved on, I pushed the button to close the garage door and reached for the switch to turn off the light. I first startled, then recognized the large brown and white form huddled against the storm door beneath the small canopy. I nudged his body gently with the door. He entered and stood as though he expected me to towel him down and wipe his feet. His massive bulk filled the small landing between the stairs to the basement and those to the kitchen. He wore neither collar nor tags.

As I ran an old bath towel over his back, down his legs to his feet, he turned his head to assess me. Sad brown eyes would have me believe he had been abandoned, but legs thicker than my arms, paws the size of my hands and not a rib showing, told me that this boy ate regularly. For one brief moment, overwhelmed by his immense size, I hoped his diet didn't include chubby middle-aged blondes. With damp but clean feet, he confidently strolled through the house checking out each room slowly and in detail. I wondered what personal history that giant nose might be telling him about this house and its inhabitants.

Certain he must be hungry, I surveyed the contents of the refrigerator. Nemo had loved carrots, so I offered a large one. After a brief sniff, it disappeared with a few bites. So did a huge bowl of spaghetti with meat sauce, one vanilla yogurt, another carrot and a leftover hot dog. Polite and grateful, Dog waited patiently to be served each course. As I loaded the empty food containers into the dishwasher, I heard a loud thump in the living room. Startled, I peeked around the corner. Bruce was lying face up on the floor. Dog stood over him, smiling, wagging his tail. After a short tussle, he flopped down on his back in an obvious request for a tummy rub. Bruce looked up at me, our eyes exchanging shared memories. The possibility of keeping him came from both of us at once. But we couldn't be absolutely certain he hadn't run off, and we would never want to take someone else's pet. Reluctantly, I called animal control.

Dog appeared to recognize the city truck as it parked in front of our house. He pushed past the semi-opened storm door as the animal control officer approached the porch. Acknowledging no one, he strode down the walk, hopped into the open cab and sat in the driver's seat. We laughed out loud as the officer hopelessly attempted to shove Dog's massive body across the seat toward the passenger's side. Finally striking a compromise, he drove off wedged between Dog and door, steering left-handed, his right arm draped over the seatback.

That night we talked for the first time about bringing another dog into our lives. Concerned Dog might somehow go unclaimed, I mentioned my plan to call the pound and check on him in the morning.

"If you want to call, go ahead but he won't be there," Bruce said confidently.

"He's not exactly a spring chicken," I said. "Maybe they decided they didn't want him anymore and just dropped him off. People do that even to good dogs, you know. If he stays more than a few days at the pound, they might put him down. I couldn't stand that. He doesn't deserve that," I said, half hoping for the dismal scenario to be true.

"Oh, someone will come for him," Bruce responded. "He's too good a dog to let go."

We talked through all of the "what ifs" until I drifted into a fitful sleep.

I called the pound first thing in the morning. Barely suppressing the giggle in her response, the secretary explained Dog had already been bailed out by his owner. A "repeat offender," he was well known to the staff. Wherever he stayed during his adventures, his temporary hosts always called hoping to get him back.

Dog's visit brought our souls to life again. He taught us that even badly broken hearts have the capacity to mend. Most of all, he helped us summon the courage to risk them again. Circumstances delayed us for another few years, but when a puppy named Alex finally came into our lives, he brought with him the best of Nemo, Dog and more.

~Barbara Ann Burris

My Dancing Partner

Our perfect companions never have fewer than four feet.
~Colette

The oversized Collie wasn't sure what to expect as he suspiciously looked around the house. Adopted from a rescue mission, he had been shuffled from home to home and never for a lengthy stay in any of them. I sat down in my favorite chair and spoke in his direction. "Tyler," I called in a sing-song voice. "Come over here." He looked at me a long time. Then he slowly approached, ultimately plopping across my feet. As I stroked his thick fur coat, I knew we would connect.

According to the workers at the rescue shelter, Tyler had been abandoned, probably pushed out of a moving car and left on the side of the road to die. When he was found, he was starved and sick. Doctors at the veterinary clinic donated their time and resources to Tyler's recovery. However, his experience left him with permanent scars. Though physically sound, Tyler exhibited signs of self-doubt, especially in new situations. He rarely barked, almost as if he was afraid we would get angry and kick him out of our home. For the most part, Tyler kept a low profile, even trying to hide his big body behind the sofa or the bed.

Having been abused and abandoned myself, I identified with Tyler. My past had been sad too. For me, the way to overcome life's hard knocks was to immerse myself in music. When situations or circumstances seemed tenuous and made me fearful, a rousing song with a strong beat lifted my spirits. I danced around the house, singing and laughing. Once when I was harmonizing with an old version of "Light My Fire," Tyler poked his head out from behind a chair to watch. Little by little, he edged around the corner and into the room where I was performing. And then, dropping his usual persona, Tyler started to run around me in circles, barking.

At first, his bark scared me. I even wondered if he might bite me, so I stopped singing. But when I went quiet, Tyler did too. When I began to sing again Tyler resumed jumping and barking, growing more excited with each new chorus. From that day on, Tyler and I fought the blues together by singing and dancing, warding off any fears. We grew closer and our bond became more about the music than about our pasts.

One night when my husband was away, I heard a knock at the front door. Expecting a neighbor, I was surprised to see a man dressed in a delivery uniform. I thought it strange that he would still be on his route so late in the evening.

"I'm lost," he began. "Could you give me directions?"

"Sure," I said slowly, still with misgivings about his purpose. "Where are you headed?"

"Well, actually, it's a little hard to describe," he answered. "How about I just come in and use your telephone to call my office?"

This seemed particularly odd when most delivery personnel have a communication device in their truck or even a cell phone. I placed my hand on the screen door's knob and pulled it tight. The deliveryman grabbed the handle on the opposite side of the screen and pulled. I noted Tyler's position behind the couch. In a very quiet voice, I began to hum the tune to "Light My Fire." As I hummed the man stared at me and demanded use of my phone. We both stood frozen, each with a hand on the screen door handle. I raised the pitch and volume of my song and glanced at Tyler. The man jerked the screen and Tyler took that as a cue to dance. Right to my side he bounded toward us, barking in rhythm to the song.

The man looked at the dog's size — his muscular shoulders, long nose, massive jaw, and the huge teeth revealed in Tyler's smile — and he backed away from the screen, down the steps, and to his truck. I slammed the door shut and double locked it, and then sank to my knees to kiss my singing Collie.

~Elaine Ernst Schneider

Their Trust, Our Privilege

You have to take risks. We will only understand the miracle of life fully when we allow the unexpected to happen.
~Paulo Coelho

The index card at the shelter read "Two-year-old Collie mix. Found as a stray. Shy. Needs loving home." Translation: patience. As the dog peered at me through the chain-link fence, he hugged the side of the cage with his shoulders slumped. The dog inched toward the front of the run but stopped safely in the middle. If he only knew how much I believed in the value of an unwanted dog. Every few moments, he tossed a glance behind him as if searching for lost courage. While his tail lightly tapped the side of the fence, his legs trembled, his body unable to fully accept my goodwill. Perhaps I looked like the person who'd shattered his trust. Or maybe it was merely the stress from the noisy environment, and once in a quiet home he'd be a different dog.

I attempted to picture the real dog beneath the layers of fear and distrust. When he lay down and began to whine, he was asking me to take a chance. Wasn't I asking the same of him? Feeling a commitment to this dog that I'd met only minutes earlier, I extended my hand, and he inched closer. As long as he held a flicker of desire for human contact, I'd wait for him to come forward to claim me. He did.

It took some time for Dexter to trust me. I gave him space,

cajoling him from the dark corners of the house for meals and trips outside, but otherwise letting him decide when he felt safe enough to come around. Every day, he showed more interest in his surroundings and after a couple of months Dexter stopped cowering when I bent down to stroke his head, no longer fearing my hand but welcoming my touch with a nudge of his nose. He began following me from room to room and soon wouldn't leave my side.

Six years later, Dexter, once again, had to trust that I'd nurture him back to life as a cancerous tumor spread within his front right leg. I had to make the painful decision whether to euthanize him or to have the leg amputated. I never considered myself a selfish person, but I wanted to keep him alive for my benefit. Agonizing over the decision, I looked to Dexter for the answer. His tail still thumped and his eyes still showed a zest for life. He wasn't ready to leave me anymore than I was ready to let him go. So I scheduled him for surgery, praying that Dexter would recall his survival skills from living on the streets.

Following the amputation, as Dexter lay motionless on the bedroom floor, I questioned my decision. What had I done? As he groaned and whimpered, even while heavily medicated for the pain, I lay beside him and cried along with him. How many of my tears were soaked up by the nape of his neck? Remarkably, he still wagged his tail whenever I approached, which only added to my guilt. Since Dexter no longer had the balance or strength to stand on his own, my husband and I carried him outside, holding Dexter upright with a makeshift sling in order to take care of his most basic needs. Dexter often collapsed on the lawn, unable to get back inside the house, but we waited patiently. I followed him from room to room, checking on his wellbeing. When he became apathetic and stopped eating, I hand fed him and coaxed him to follow me around the house as he'd done for so long. This dog, my companion for six years, would not wither away on my watch. Within a few short weeks, Dexter began using his nose as a prop to get to his feet and, eventually, started hopping up and down the stairs to go outside. Our family learned about resilience, watching our stoic dog make adjustments for his limitations.

Now, at the age of ten, Dexter often collapses into a heap on the floor halfway to his destination. But we don't pity him. Instead, we wait patiently as he gathers the strength to get to his feet again. The journey is getting harder, and I know there'll be a day when Dexter will be too tired to continue. I may have to show my ultimate loyalty to him by peacefully ending the life that I fought so hard to save. But isn't that why he chose me at the shelter so many years ago? He trusted that I'd bring him no harm.

Knowing the joys of adopting a shelter dog, we recently invited another unwanted dog to claim us. While Penny, our Pembroke Welsh Corgi, enjoyed the safety of a foster home following her rescue from a shelter, her eyes still told of lingering fear and distrust. The transition to our home was a setback for her and, once again, we watched a dog slink from the dark corners of the house for a meal or a trip outside. It has been nearly three months since Penny joined our family and, like Dexter, she no longer cowers in fear at the touch of our hands, and now she regularly greets us at the door upon our arrival home. Our daughter enrolled Penny in an obedience and agility class to bolster her courage, a huge step for a dog that used to flinch with the slightest movement or noise. Dexter and Penny have also formed a bond. She waits for him to navigate to the bottom of the stairs, and he won't return inside the house until she makes her way in first. They watch over one another, just as we watch over them.

Although we'll never know what Dexter and Penny suffered prior to their adoptions, we do know there'll come a day when yet another rescue dog will stand before us with trembling legs and a head held low. With love and patience, the layers of its misfortune will peel back to reveal the dog's true nature: gratitude and loyalty for those willing to take a chance on a dog deemed worthless by another. A dog's newfound trust will be our reward and a privilege that we will cherish for years.

~Cathi LaMarche

Puppy Playdates

Dogs love company. They place it first in their short list of needs.
~J.R. Ackerley

A white Poodle with beige ears showed up the night before Christmas on our doorstep. We advertised and put up notices so that the rightful owners could claim their dog. When no one claimed him, we kept him. My daughters were sure that Santa must have brought him to us. After all, it was Christmas Eve and they wanted a dog! The first night he was in our house he went directly upstairs to the bedroom where my two daughters slept and jumped onto one of their beds. Since it had been snowing outside, the dog was wet.

"He looks just like a wet noodle!" said Nell, laughing as she petted him. "Noodles" was his name from that moment on.

Noodles adjusted well to his new home. He had many health problems but we learned to care for him. He loved the girls, and Hope, my younger daughter, claimed him as "her dog." He also adjusted well to the female dog, Wendy, who lived two doors away. Wendy and Noodles had a love affair, which resulted in Pepper, who ended up being adopted by some neighbors.

Noodles, Wendy, and Pepper weren't the only dogs in the neighborhood, and it wasn't long before Noodles met them all and became friends. They would go on daily jaunts around the neighborhood. There were at least six of them that went walking together every day, and, no, they didn't take a human with them. Every morning at 10 o'clock, Pepper would come and knock on our door. Noodles would come prancing to the door. He could not wait to go outside with his son. The two of them sniffed each other and started walking off toward Wendy's house. She left her yard and went with them as they started up the hill to pick up other neighbor dogs.

When Noodles got older, he would be the last to be picked up by the "gang." Pepper and his friends would come to the door for Noodles almost every day at ten o'clock in the morning, and it was always Pepper who knocked on the door.

Over time, Noodles' early health problems caught up with him, and he was also hit by a car. His neighborhood buddies still came around and we still let him go out because we knew Pepper and the other dog pals would watch over Noodles. Wendy wasn't around anymore, which was sad, but the others still came. Pepper knocked on the door at 10 o'clock every morning.

After thirteen wonderful years with Noodles, he finally passed on one day. The next day there was a knock on the door. I knew who it was and didn't know if I could handle it or not. I opened the door and began to cry. It was Pepper, of course.

I went outside and sat down on the stoop. I petted Pepper and told him what had happened and that Noodles wasn't here anymore. I told him how much Noodles loved him and cried into his big shaggy body. Pepper looked sad and I am sure he knew what I was telling him. He didn't leave until I got up, brushed myself off, wiped my eyes, and went back inside the house.

The next morning at 10 o'clock, the silence was louder than any knock I had ever heard.

~Lynn Hartz

"Who's Spike? Who's Pitzi? Why are we getting all these RSVPs from people we didn't invite?"

52

When Darkness Fell

One can never consent to creep when one feels an impulse to soar.
~Helen Keller

The tiny Schnauzer pup slumbering in my lap was on the most important journey of her life. Destination: her forever home. "That's it," I squealed.

"What's what?" fussed Jerry, my husband, as frenzied Dallas drivers darted about in all directions.

"We're on Shiloh Road. Isn't Shiloh a beautiful name for this little gal?" I cooed.

Shiloh's youth was filled with gleeful days. She romped, played, and thrived, learning new words and tricks. She never showed aggression or anger. Perhaps it was absent from her gene pool. She was a true love bug and adored anyone she met, be they human or canine.

But one day, Shiloh careened into our recliner, hitting it hard enough to evoke a yelp from the rough-and-tumble gal. I had tossed her a tennis ball to fetch seemingly a million times before. Gently I lifted her up and cradled her in my arms. She had missed catching her ball a few times recently, and I had blamed myself for a bad throw or the glare of a lamp in her eyes. Now I knew without a doubt that Shiloh was losing her vision.

Within days a specialist confirmed my diagnosis. The condition was hereditary, had no cure, and would progress rapidly. I grieved for my feisty, five-year-old Schnauzer the same as if she'd lost her life. I considered vision crucial for a dog's cheerful existence, and it was about to vanish. I envisioned her growing old before her time, each day filled with depression in a fearful, dark, and strange world. Grief gnawed at me and I dwelled endlessly upon a hopeless situation. Depression took a mighty toll on our family. Rapidly the tiny amount of vision that remained was gone and Shiloh became a recluse under our bed. I wanted to snuggle and console her but she had no desire. Thus, we grieved separately, which nearly undid me.

The prior year, Hank, a white Schnauzer, had joined our family and fun-filled chaos reigned from the moment he pranced into our lives. He and Shiloh wrestled, played tug of war or chase from morning until night. Not even a young pup could outshine Shiloh's energy and grit. She was a whirling dervish even when pitted against a pup. When finally exhausted, they slept side by side.

It was Hank who eventually coaxed Shiloh from under the bed and back into the real world. He instinctively transformed himself into her personal guide dog. Fetching a favorite toy, he would dangle it under her nose until she'd grab hold. Tug-of-war games continued as well as wrestling matches. When mealtime rolled around he not only brought his dish to the kitchen, but Shiloh's as well. Being a true Texas gentleman, he was devoted to his needy charge.

Following Hank's lead, I devised different sounds and commands that Shiloh learned rapidly. After several months of trial and error, any stranger entering our home had no idea the beautiful black-and-white Schnauzer was sightless. I purchased new toys that played tunes or talked for lengthy amounts of time, long enough that Shiloh could locate them. She knew and trusted that I would only toss them into furniture-free areas. I could see her pride and excitement when she realized that she could retrieve once again.

Her newly-acquired skills were tested in earnest on a visit to my dad's home. Shiloh pranced into his house and zoomed by each piece of furniture on her quest to inspect the guest room without bumping into anything. Then she zoomed by me while I fumbled with the baby gate I was about to erect at the top of the stairway leading to the basement. I watched in horror as Shiloh was already halfway down. She didn't miss a step nor slow her normal pace. She stopped on the bottom step, looked up, and anxiously waited for someone to open the door. It was time to visit Dad's sump pump, her absolute favorite amusement in life. Those steps were programmed into her mind like a keyboard is burned into a typist's brain. No longer able to peer into the depths of the sump hole, she'd stand at the edge with her head lowered and sniff the musty aroma. Should the pump kick on, her tail wagged at double speed. Shiloh required several treks a day for pump inspections, the same as in her sighted days.

The last five years of Shiloh's life appeared so normal that I wondered if she assumed the lights had gone out for all of us. When Shiloh's blindness struck, I grieved for our dear girl, but it was Shiloh who taught us so much. Her resilience and ability to adjust to her handicap was staggering. Overcoming that black, ominous roadblock, regaining her self-assurance and love of life seemed an unimaginable burden for any animal born sighted. But Shiloh seemed to handle anything that was thrown her way, and our little Southern beauty never failed to make our lives richer.

~Kathleene S. Baker

My Dog's Life

Leader of the Pack

53

Time for a Walk

What really helps motivate me to walk are my dogs, who are my best pals.
They keep you honest about walking because when it's time to go,
you can't disappoint those little faces.
~Wendie Malick

Sitting on the edge of the bed, I reach down, slip off my sandals, and quietly place them on the floor. I am moving with exaggerated slowness, trying to make as little noise as possible. I put on my sneakers as quietly as possible.

As I move, the bed creaks. I hear a jingling sound from the living room. Despite my best efforts, the dog is stirring. Last I saw him he was asleep on the couch, and I had hoped to change my clothes without alerting him. I hear a solid thump and the click-clack of his nails on the wood floor. Soon, he is heading full speed down the hall. He skids to a stop right outside my room. Peering at me, he cocks his head, brown eyes full of expectation. I can see the question in his eyes. Time for our walk?

My smile is all the encouragement he needs. He comes over and bumps my leg with his wet nose. When that doesn't get me moving, he starts to whine and pushes his face into my lap. Ruffling his ears, I stand up. This is his indication that it is time to start the pre-walk dance. Up and down the hall he prances, turning in tight little circles, barking at me to hurry. This is why I try to be quiet when I change, to avoid getting him worked up until I am ready to leave. Even so, this display never fails to make me laugh. I walk over and grab his leash.

Now, comes the second and hardest part of our ritual—convincing him to come and put his harness on. I need the harness. He is a big dog—part Labrador, part Brittany Spaniel—and without the harness he is the one walking me.

He dances around me, just out of reach. He hates the harness. No matter how many times we have walked, each time he tries to convince me he doesn't need the leash. Even though he has worn it every time we have taken a walk over the past ten years, each time he thinks that this time he won't have to.

We've logged hundreds of miles together. I rarely walk without him, and the few times I have I felt naked. Without him my arm just dangles uselessly, instead of firmly coiled around his leash.

I call to him using my best "good dog" voice. No dice. He stays five feet away from me. Next, I try to cajole him to stand still so I can put on the harness. He is wise to all my tricks and stays just out of reach. Then he runs around the house. I try to fake him out and trap him between the table and the wall. As usual he outsmarts me and dashes under the table. Frustrated I finally threaten to go on the walk without him. He calls my bluff. I have to actually step over the threshold of the door and call him one last time before he will submit to the harness. I step through the door and wait patiently. Sensing he's lost yet again, he slinks over to me and drops his head. I gently slip it over his head and snap it closed. Head down and ears back he looks at me with sad dog eyes. He hates wearing it. I carefully tug his floppy ears to make sure the harness doesn't rub against them.

Once we are out the door he is all business and ready to walk, such a change from the roly-poly puppy that I brought home. Our first walk together—just a short walk around the block—ended with him sitting down at the corner, unwilling to take another step. I had to pick him up and carry him home.

Now as we start down the street he is in the lead gently tugging me along. His tail is curled and there is a spring in his step. As we walk I remember how much I missed walking with him during my pregnancy. I was hugely pregnant with twins and the doctor ordered bed rest. It was a beautiful summer and the dog and I were stuck in the yard—no walks for us.

He helped me bounce back from the pregnancy pounds. Each morning I would wrestle him into the leash. After I got him ready, I packed both babies into the stroller and we would walk through the neighborhood. It has many hills and those first few weeks I relied on him to help me get the enormous, heavy stroller up each hill. By the end of the summer, both of us were fit once again. The kids are way past stroller age now, so when we take family walks the kids take turns holding his leash.

I can't imagine taking my walk without him. He is getting older, but the vet assures me that walking him is the best thing to keep arthritis at bay. Doctor advises the same thing for me. Good thing we have each other.

~Jennifer Flaten

54

My Dog Ate My Homework

We derive immeasurable good, uncounted pleasures, enormous security,
and many critical lessons about life by owning dogs.
~Roger Caras

My husband and I came home from our errands one day and opened our bedroom door to let out Sunny, our six-year-old Greyhound. Gary opened the door to the backyard while I entered the bedroom.

"Oh no!" I yelled, looking at the scraps of paper all over the floor. I realized that they were from a book my counselor had assigned me to read. I was seeing someone because Gary and I were at odds about starting a family. I was apprehensive, while Gary had been ready soon after we were married. I felt that I needed to talk with someone to process why I didn't want to move forward, especially since when we were dating I thought I was certain that I wanted a family.

In the two years since we had adopted Sunny, we had developed a regular routine for leaving Sunny alone at home. During short errands of less than an hour, we would let her stay in our room, her favorite place in the house. She loved lying on our bed soaking up the sunshine. When we knew we'd be gone longer, we had to put her in her kennel. Ninety-nine percent of the time she didn't shred things when we were only gone a short time. However, unfortunately, this time my homework was the victim of one of the one percent episodes.

Choosing a Greyhound for a pet was an unusual selection for both Gary and me. Our parents both had hunting dogs. When I was a girl, I would look through dog breed books and plan what kind of dog I wanted when I was on my own. I had never considered a Greyhound, but when we decided to get a dog early in our marriage, Gary wanted an unusual breed. We read a newspaper article about a retired racing Greyhound adoption network. It piqued our interest so we attended a Greyhound showing at a local pet store. We met Sunny, an elegant brindle-colored lady, whose racing name was Sparky's Sunbug. We fell in love with her.

After bringing Sunny home, we discovered the advantages of owning a retired racing Greyhound. Sunny was completely housebroken, and, in general, was easily trained. One "no" after she climbed on our furniture and she never tried it again. Once I caught her putting her front legs up on our kitchen table to try to mooch Chinese food off a plate, but after one reprimand, she never did it again. Since she was shorthaired, she shed very little, and she was quiet, only barking when she was in a playful mood. Sunny did not slobber either. Her means of affection was more like an Eskimo kiss. She would gently make contact with her nose instead of trying to lick your face.

In human years, Sunny was well into her adulthood when we adopted her. Although, she had her child-like times, often she seemed like an old soul. Sunny would stick close to me whenever she sensed that I was troubled. When there was a vibe of stress in the house, she picked up on it, would stand near one of us, and lean against us. She seemed to know when I was worried, since in her soulful eyes was a sage, grandmotherly look that conveyed, "This too shall pass, dear."

At the time of the homework shredding, I was anxious about the idea of starting a family while maintaining a job that at times required working fifty to sixty hours a week. I couldn't imagine raising a child under those circumstances, although I knew women with careers who managed it somehow. I was approaching a milestone that would require me to make some life changes, and I didn't want to. I liked the familiarity of the life that Gary and I had.

I didn't know it then, but letting go of worry and restlessness was the lesson that I needed to learn. Sunny introduced me to the idea of appreciating simply what I had at the moment—a home, a good marriage, and a secure lifestyle. She was helping me settle into the kind of home life that was needed for welcoming a child.

Gary and I were in our late-twenties when we adopted Sunny. We enjoyed traveling and going out to restaurants and concerts, but after we adopted her, it meant staying home more. It also signaled to me that it was time to move beyond simply owning a house to making it into a home. Slowly I made attempts at modest decorating—well, painting anyway—and staying home to cook a meal rather than going out. Over time I came to enjoy cooking and developed a repertoire of Italian and Asian dishes. This was all a prerequisite, the true homework that I needed to complete before I could be ready for parenting.

When I reflect on the ripped pages of the counselor's homework, I see the lesson that Sunny presented to us: to simply be there for her and give her more attention. I really didn't need the counselor. Her conclusion after a couple of sessions was that I needed to give myself more time. Although it would take us two more years to take the plunge, Sunny was conditioning me for parenting.

Sunny delivered the lesson that day with ironic flair. When I knelt down on our bedroom floor amidst the snippets of book pages, I read the shreds to Gary, "kindness," "time together," and "loving attentiveness."

I pictured Sunny with an uncharacteristic rebellious look in her eye, ripping up the book.

"I guess she showed us," Gary said.

~Colleen Ferris Holz

55

George, the Lithuanian Fish-Finding Dog

A hungry dog hunts best.
~Lee Trevino

"**W**hat a cute little dog. What kind of a dog is it?" asked the woman fishing top water lures out of the antique Skeeter bass boat next to us. That's not exactly what my husband, Roy, our Yorkie, George Mutt, and I were expecting to hear as we broke out of the Cypress trees and undergrowth swamp we had been paddling through. We were on Caddo Lake during our annual Easter trip with the Houston Canoe Club, and according to our map, we thought we'd be in a quiet clearing not far from camp.

On the trip we were reenergizing our souls and George Mutt was looking for an excuse—any excuse—to jump in the water on his own fishing expedition. George loved the water, and if I wasn't paying attention, he would be out of the boat and into the lake trying to snap up fish, reminiscent of Jaws. Roy and I were looking for our own place to fish since we had not had as much luck as George in finding fish that day. We were on the hunt for a good bream hole so we could have our traditional fresh bream and scrambled eggs for breakfast in the morning.

George was busy running around on his "Mutt Butt Board," his place in the canoe that Roy had fashioned out of plywood and outdoor carpet that fit between the thwarts of our red canoe. If you live right, and you're really lucky, you might be blessed with a dog like George at least once in your life. He had a human personality and never met a stranger.

So, when Roy and I greeted the other couple in the Skeeter, George ran to the side of the canoe closest to them. He offered his characteristic "smile" and tail wag. He knew an audience when he saw them, and George was always a ham.

Roy and I asked them how fishing was. The man told us that they'd had a couple of bites, a bream or two and a barely-legal bass. So the fishing wasn't good, but the couple was friendly and we struck up a conversation. George, of course, was not going to be left out, and he barked and wagged, his insistence to be noticed—hence the lady's question, "What kind of a little dog is that?"

In our canoe club, there was another couple who owned an unusual dog who often went paddling with them. He was a beautiful soft gray dog with unknown parentage, but he looked so good he should have been an official breed. His owners were often asked what kind of dog he was so, on canoe trips, they made up a breed for him, a Lithuanian Canoe Dog. So when we were asked what kind of dog George was that day I glibly answered, "Oh, this dog is a Lithuanian Fish-Finding Dog."

"A what?" asked the surprised fisherman at the controls of the Skeeter.

All my life, I have thought that fishing took talent and just the right timing. This situation was no exception. At that moment, as if it were planned, George ran up to the gunnels of the boat, smiled, and pointed with his paw to a location just in front of the bass boat.

I guess we had been married too long because Roy picked up my line of thought, and replied, "Yeah, a Lithuanian Fish-Finding Dog. See, if we pass by someone who's fishing, and George likes them, he'll point to where he sees the fish—like a Pointer shows where the birds are. Look, he's on point now."

"R-i-g-h-t," said the doubting fisherman, noting George's posture, "and where's that dog pointing to now?"

Roy wasn't about to give up on a good tale, so he quickly shot a line down George's paw, and using his best fisherman's instinct, searched for a likely place in that general direction where a fish could be hiding. He saw it and just as the lady fisherman drew back her rod to cast, Roy instructed, "Tell your wife to cast to that Cypress stump on your left."

She looked, shrugged her shoulders and cast her top water lure directly over the Cypress stump in question. As the lure snaked out across the water between the boat and the stump, everything began to move in slow motion. The lure started its descent to the stump, and an eight-pound black bass exploded from the lake engulfing the lure, which never even had the chance to hit the water. George excitedly barked his approval as the lady reared back, screamed in delight and set the hook. Then the war was on. The lady reeled for all she was worth and that bass, who never saw what hooked him and never had the chance to go down, tail walked, gills flaring and water splashing, all the way back to the Skeeter boat. She had just landed the catch of the day.

Sometimes, truth is stranger than fish tales. Those of us who witnessed the event sat there in stunned silence for a minute. After all, we were just telling tall tales. The man in the Skeeter bass boat went slack-jawed and said, "How much do you want for the dog? I want to buy that dog!" George, our loveable fish-finding dog, made believers out of a couple of fishermen. I'll bet to this day that there is someone in Uncertain, Texas still looking for a Lithuanian Fish-Finding Dog.

~Janice R. Edwards

56

Because of Barkley

You enter into a certain amount of madness
when you marry a person with pets.
~Nora Ephron

T o be honest, I wasn't much of a dog person when I first met Barkley, Jim's four-year-old black Lab. Jim and I had barely been dating a week when he brought me to his house for the first time. We were coming home from a nice dinner and were greeted by the competing smells of I-better-clean-my-house-to-impress-this-girl Lysol and diarrhea because Barkley had had a tummy ache. Normally, I would have plugged my nose and waited outside until the mess was cleaned up, but the look on both of their faces somehow convinced me to stay and help. Jim was horrified, and Barkley was ears-back, tail-between-his-legs embarrassed. He slithered away to hide in the next room, and Jim and I threw first impression etiquette to the wind and picked up our mops.

It was putrid and disgusting, but as we dry heaved and plugged our noses together, I got a glimpse into the special bond between the man I was falling for and the dog he loved so much. Jim knelt down to pet Barkley's face, and told him he wasn't mad. He kissed him on the nose, and then turned to me, smiled sheepishly and said, "Well, welcome to our home!"

That was the beginning of my crossover into becoming more of a dog person. It wasn't easy though. For the first four months, I couldn't be around Barkley for more than a few hours before the itchy, watery eyes and incessant sneezing started. I hated the shedding, and one day he drooled a puddle into my favorite running shoes.

I thought the dark floors and black couches, sheets and towels were a bachelor thing, but when I tried to brighten up the place once we started talking marriage, Jim refused to let me get a beige rug because Barkley would shed on it. It was a bit trying when we couldn't go on long trips because Barkley couldn't be left for too long. We couldn't walk on certain "no dogs allowed" paths because Barkley couldn't come along, and we couldn't stay out late because Barkley had to be let out. Literally, everything Jim did considered Barkley. Though it was frustrating, and I didn't always understand it, I knew that I was falling in love with Jim partly because of the way Jim and Barkley loved each other.

The first time I saw Jim cry was because a conversation somehow moved in the direction of discussing a time when Barkley might not be around anymore, and our first domestic fight happened when I tried to clean a little clutter off Jim's kitchen counter by putting Barkley's treat canister up in the cupboard.

"That has to stay on the counter," Jim pleaded. "That's Barkley on the front of it."

"No it's not, babe. It's a picture of a dog that looks like Barkley," I said, trying not to hurt his feelings, and genuinely believing that a thirty-three-year-old man wouldn't know that sometimes companies use pictures of black Labs for marketing material.

"Yes, it is, I promise you! Look, he has the same collar and tags," he explained, pointing. "It took me a long time to save up the UPCs so I could get a tin with his picture on it!"

Before I came along, Barkley and Jim had traveled the country as a physical therapist and therapy dog team. Most of the time, they were each other's only companions. They had been through endless adventures and incredible challenges together, and had formed an incredibly close bond. Barkley was a best friend, cohort, and coworker. They were a team, a package deal, and a dynamic duo, and I was beginning to see that the only way I was going to make it into the family was if I found acceptance through Barkley too.

Jim was gracious and let us gently warm up to each other. When I had the flu, he left Barkley with me so I would have someone to watch movies and take naps with. When I was sad, Jim and Barkley cuddled with me on the couch, and when Jim had to go out of town, I got to watch Barkley so that he could keep me safe and make me feel protected. Little by little, Barkley and I accepted each other.

Nearly one year after the night we mopped the floors, Jim asked me to marry him. The three of us were hiking one fall afternoon and Jim called Barkley over to his side. He reached into a little backpack Barkley was wearing and got down on one knee. As Jim popped the question, Barkley sat by his side, staring up at me, and wagging his tail. At that moment, I knew that Barkley was asking too, and I was joyfully saying, "Yes!" to both of them.

Looking back, I can see that I had fallen in love with Jim because Barkley had, in his own special way, taught me that he was a man worth falling for. That first night that I decided to stay and clean, Barkley showed me that Jim had a heart of gold and did not get mad easily. He demonstrated that he would stick around when things got messy, and would love and console us when we didn't feel well. When Jim and I argued about the treat canister, Barkley taught me that Jim wanted to display his love for us to the world instead of hide it behind a cabinet door. I knew that I could trust Jim because Barkley trusted him, and I knew that I would always be taken care of because Barkley was taken care of. The adoration in Barkley's eyes confirmed that Jim was a man of character, strength, and kindness, and I can see now that life is so much better because of Barkley.

~Kara Johnson

"Mark, when I said I wouldn't mind if your dog came over, that was assuming you were coming with him."

57

Wherefore Art Thou?

I wonder if other dogs think poodles are members of a weird religious cult.
~Rita Rudner

"**W**ho let the dog in?" I asked from our second floor, surprised that one of the kids actually opened the door for our black Standard Poodle. The pitter-patter of Romeo's feet up the stairs coincided with a chorus of "not me" that resonated through the bedrooms where two sons and a daughter dressed for Sunday Mass.

"How did the dog get into the house?" I asked as I ran down to the patio doors in the kitchen. The screen flapped in the breeze. Our eighty-five-pound Poodle had let himself in. He walked right through the screen door. Repairing the screen door did not thrill my husband, Dave, but he loved the dog nevertheless.

Since the day Romeo joined our family as a pup, he had entertained us and kept our family laughing. Our daughter, Cabrina, had been studying *Romeo and Juliet* the semester we found the ad in the paper for our Romeo, and that was how he got his name.

One of Romeo's favorite games involved our younger son, Mark. When Mark sat on the floor in the family room playing, Romeo would grab nine-year-old Mark's pant leg at the ankle and drag him around the room. Unable to pry the dog's mouth open, Steve, fourteen, would warn Romeo: "You better stop it. Mama's coming." With that, Romeo would relent, run to the hallway, look up the staircase, and when he realized that I was nowhere in sight, he would race back to the family room and to Mark's pant leg. Cabrina, thirteen, would run up the stairs to give me the lowdown. Down we would speed to rescue Mark. All I had to do was stand in the family room archway, place my hands on my hips, make my eyes small, and stare. Immediately, Romeo would stop and run to me, expecting a pat.

"Romeo! Go in the kitchen," I would say.

He would slink in there and take a nap beneath the table.

Wintertime and snow brought a continuation outdoors. If Mark fell during a game of chase, Romeo gripped that pant leg and gave Mark a ride on his behind around the backyard. Mark loved it.

When my parents visited from Michigan, there was enough of Romeo to satisfy both my dad and Uncle Louie. Dog lovers, they each wanted the dog to sit beside them on the couch. Dad sat on one end, patting Romeo's head that snuggled on his lap. Our giant Poodle scrunched his body along the extra long couch to leave space for Uncle Louie who sat on the other side. My uncle rested one arm on the dog's thighs and scratched his back with the other. All three shared bliss. My parents thought I was joking when I told them that Romeo had a favorite television program, *Northern Exposure*.

No matter where our pooch was snoozing in the house, when the theme song sounded, Romeo came running. He remembered that a moose would cross the screen. He stood before the TV, blocking everyone's view and waited for his buddy to appear.

"Sit down, Romeo. We can't see through you," my dad said after a bit.

Romeo jumped up on the love seat and watched the entire show, hoping for another glimpse of the moose.

While my parents struggled with ailments in Michigan, I could brighten their day with a phone call about Romeo's latest shenanigans. They looked forward to our visits to their house and to showing off their grand-dog to their neighbors.

When Steve went off to college, Romeo searched the house. He ran up to his bedroom, jumped up on the bed, knocked the pillows on the floor, hoping to find Steve hiding beneath them. When Steve phoned, I placed the receiver against the dog's ear. Poor Romeo couldn't figure it out. He ran to the front door, thinking Steve was outside.

Romeo loved to sleep on his back in Cabrina's bed. "Mom, hurry," she called from her bedroom one morning. Romeo had slipped between the mattress and the wall. With his legs in the air, he struggled, wedged. I feared if we moved the bed, he would fall on his spine and injure himself.

So, there she and I stood, our feet sinking into the foam and springs. She held his front legs while I gripped the other two. We yanked, struggled and pulled. He grunted. Finally we freed our poor dog.

Romeo visited all three kids when they went to college. He accompanied us not only to Michigan, but on a road trip to Savannah and Charleston and gave motorists a chuckle.

"Why do people in the passing cars laugh and turn to stare at our van?"

Dave glanced in the rearview mirror and chuckled. I twisted toward the back.

"Oh, how funny you boys look." There they sat, our two tall sons, with the dog sitting erect between them, towering over their heads. Cabrina had curled herself up in the third row. That explained the other drivers' mirth.

It's been about twenty years since we lost our wonderful dog to liver cancer, but his memory lives in our thoughts. When I share Romeo stories with our grandchildren, their parents chime in with other remembered antics. Time seems to melt as we all laugh and relive those years. Our grandchildren have learned to love animals through their parents. They have dogs with personalities of their own. Now our children and grandkids share their funny pet stories with us, as I did with my parents.

When I'm alone, I smile. There will never be another Romeo.

~Toni Louise Diol

Sandy's Gift

The kind man feeds his beast before sitting down to dinner.
~Hebrew Proverb

Every dog offers you a special gift. Our dog Sandy gave me the gift of cooking.

Sandy was already a member of our family before I was born, so she was more my mom's dog than the family pet. She gave me kisses and was gentle and tolerant of my attempts at "playing nice." But she wasn't a young playful pup by the time I came around. Still, I considered her my best friend, and as my best friend, I thought she should play with me. In fact, I was determined to make her play with me. I soon realized that the way to this dog's heart, or at least her cooperation, was through her stomach.

"Want to play parade, Sandy?" I asked, handing her a piece of chicken.

"Want to play dress-up in Daddy's work clothes?" I said, offering her a tidbit of cheese.

As long as food was involved, Sandy was game and she'd follow me.

Since Sandy was so much fun to play with, I wanted to reward her for her companionship. I asked Mom if I could make her dinner. "Making dinner" for Sandy initially involved adding an egg or two to her dog food. But it wasn't long before Sandy's dinners became gourmet meals, or at least, what I thought were gourmet meals. In reality, I was cooking canned dog food on the stove and adding spices to it.

I have since learned, from my parents, that there is nothing worse than the smell of canned dog food being slow-cooked on the stove. All I knew was that I had one very satisfied customer. Sandy eagerly devoured my every creation, and she gave me kisses as tips. Other little girls may have made tiny cakes in their light bulb-powered ovens, but I cooked real meals on a real stove. I proudly vowed to Sandy, "When I grow up, I'm going to write a doggie cookbook."

I was only able to cook for Sandy for three short years before she succumbed to a cancerous tumor. Even toward the very end, when her voracious appetite had dimmed, she remained my best customer. For her last meal, I didn't serve her cooked dog food. I made her chicken. Her kisses were the sweetest tips I ever received.

After Sandy died, even though I had lost my favorite customer, I kept cooking. My two younger sisters didn't give me kisses, but their hearty thanks kept me experimenting in the kitchen.

Today, I am a food writer, recipe developer, and cookbook author. Though I have yet to write my own doggie cookbook, I still feel Sandy's presence whenever I am in the kitchen. My first book, about cheese, even contains a recipe for cheesy dog treats, a tribute to Sandy's legacy. I will be forever grateful to her gift of cooking, which changed the course of my life.

In her memory, here are Sandy's Everything-But-The-Kitchen-Sink Biscuits:

1 ½ cups whole wheat flour
1 ½ cups of leftover cheese, meat, cooked veggies, canned tuna
        or any such combination
1 tablespoon canola or olive oil
½ cup water

Preheat oven to 350 degrees. In a large bowl, combine flour with filling and oil. Add the water a little bit at a time. Depending on your choice of leftover ingredients, you may need additional water, or, if you're using tuna, for example, you may use less.

You want the dough to be malleable, but not overly wet, and you want all the ingredients to be mixed together. Wet your hands, and then roll ingredients into little balls, about the size of a quarter or a half-dollar, depending on the size of your dog. Makes about 24 to 34 treats. Bake for 15 to 20 minutes or until hard.

~Jeanette Hurt

Pointy Ettas

I've seen a look in dogs' eyes, a quickly vanishing look of amazed contempt,
and I am convinced that basically dogs think humans are nuts.
~John Steinbeck

So here's the deal. I'm not the one who writes the holiday letter. I'm the dog, Kirby, the smart one in the pack. The female human, the human that the others call "Mom," is busy. She says she's doing holiday stuff, but between you and me, she's suffering from severe cookie overdose.

Look, it's been a stressful season. First of all, there's a dead, fat guy dressed in a red suit on the lawn. Now you'd think the humans would be upset, but each morning when I go out to bark at him, the female human yells, "For Pete's sake Kirby, it's just deflated." Believe me, I know dead, and that guy in the red suit isn't just deflated.

But here's the real problem. The dead guy comes back to life every night. And he looks really happy about it. There's a bunch of little skinny guys with him. I don't know much about fashion, but I wouldn't be caught dead in their pointy shoes. Anyway, being the defender of the home, I run outside when the dead guy stands up. And what do I get for it? I get yelled at. Even the wannabe-alpha male called "Dad" (my favorite human because he shares something called "fries") yells at me.

But you know what? It gets worse. The dead guy is bad, but there's also a deer out there. And that deer is really, really sneaky. He stands completely still all day long and then at night he lights up like

Vegas and starts lifting his head up and down. I bark at him, too… but from a safe distance. Take it from me; you don't want to mess with a deer. Horns hurt.

Oh, and that's not all. There's also a huge pink bird out there that waves its head. It wears a hat like the dead guy and drags around a sleigh. Yeah, I don't get it either. I don't go anywhere near that pink bird. It scares me.

Inside there are all these red flowers around called Pointy Ettas. We had a really nice big one that looked and smelled good. So I ate it. It was all soft and chewy—not like the stinkbugs or mice I usually eat. But after I ate it I didn't feel so hot. Kind of like that one time I ate too many stinkbugs and threw up all over the couch. The female human saw the remains of the Pointy Etta and started freaking out and I ended up in the car. Fortunately I barfed up the Pointy Etta right as I got onto the leather seats, so I got to get out again.

After that I decided that if it smelled nice, I wouldn't eat it. So that's why I ate berry-looking things that were on the Christmas tree—which, by the way, isn't a real tree. So I ate those red things and they turned out to be something called Styrofoam. Then Dad said something about it "expanding in my stomach." I had to get in the car again. But don't worry, I barfed it up. This time on the female human. The female human said that she was really happy that I was okay, but her eyes were leaking water.

Just between you and me, it smelled really good in the car.

~Laurie Sontag

Rudy to the Rescue

Most owners are at length able to teach themselves to obey their dog.
~Robert Morley

When I retired I decided that I wanted a dog. I searched the Web and decided that a Shetland Sheepdog was the right breed for me. They are natural herders and "Lassie" look-alikes, but shorter and more compact. The breed possesses a companionable temperament which was what I wanted. I found Rudy's picture on a Sheltie rescue website and went to meet the black-and-white dog with the thick Collie ruff. When I looked into his soulful Rudolph Valentino eyes, I fell in love.

My life with Rudy fell into a comfortable routine. We were a familiar sight walking in our urban townhome neighborhood, his leash stretched taut as I tried to keep pace. With months of loving care Rudy blossomed into an enjoyable canine companion.

One morning, much earlier than usual, I took Rudy out for our morning constitutional. We walked our route and had the streets to ourselves in an eerie way. The rising sun was barely visible behind the trees and buildings.

Without warning, Rudy stopped walking.

"Come on, Rudy, what's the trouble?" I asked. "Let's go."

Rudy stood staring fixedly at something only he could see.

"What is the matter with you?" I repeated.

Pulling the leash had no effect. His feet didn't move. I touched his back in a familiar way but only for a moment. His body was so rigid with tension I pulled my hand away.

Trying a placating tone, I said, "Now Rudy, what's the trouble, boy? What's on your mind?" Still he stared, unmoving.

I dropped the leash on the sidewalk thinking he would turn around, but he didn't stir.

"Okay, Rudy," I said.

Using the angle of Rudy's head as a guide, I moved in slow motion toward a small grassy yard, surveying the gloomy porch and darker side of the townhouse. I listened hard, swiveling my head to see if Rudy had moved. He had turned to stone.

Was there a sound or did I hear my own blood thumping in my temples? I moved closer to the side of the townhouse. While wet grass brushed my ankles, I noticed an open window. I moved closer, listening hard. I heard a faint whimper, like an animal in pain.

"Yes?" I whispered. "Yes?"

"Help me, help me," a female voice moaned.

I called out softly, "My name is Jane and I can help you."

The weak woman relayed the code that I needed to get into her locked door. It was her birth year, 1925. When I entered I saw that she had fallen in the kitchen. She had been on the floor all night.

She told me that her name was Betty, and that she had spilled her dog's water and then slipped on it, falling next to the dishwasher. She had attempted to right herself by grasping the open dishwasher door but couldn't. Her legs were crumpled under her body, and she begged for a pillow to relieve the pressure to her slight frame. Her dog Winston stood near her. She was anxious about Winston, who needed to be let out.

Her injury looked serious, and because she was in extreme pain I was reluctant to try to move her. She gave me her daughter's name and number and I called both her and the rescue squad. They came quickly. Once help had arrived and they were working with her, I remembered Rudy. I left the townhouse and found Rudy sniffing a lamppost.

I picked up his leash, and said, "You did it, boy. You were right."

I think he knew.

Betty's daughter called a few days later with news of her mother and to thank us. Betty had broken a large bone in her leg and had a long recovery ahead of her. Several months passed before Betty was able to return home with a caretaker. I visited one day but she did not recognize me nor could she clearly remember what had taken place. Our townhouse community knew, though. To them and to me Rudy was nothing short of a hero.

~Charlene Dickinson

61

Cairn Mind Meld

You're suffering from a Vulcan Mind Meld, Doctor.
~Captain Kirk, Star Trek

Spock and Captain Kirk practiced the Vulcan mind meld. Dealing with my Cairn Terrier, Chip, required the Cairn mind meld. One of a litter of five males, he was the last of the larger pups available when I looked them over. They were enclosed in a makeshift playpen of wire mesh in a spare room in the breeder's home. When all three available pups were let loose so that I could observe them, one of the small ones came right over and licked my hand. The larger one ignored me, preferring to explore the perimeter of the room and chew on an electrical cord.

Instead of picking the affectionate one, I chose the independent one because I thought he displayed the proper Terrier attitude. I had no clue that I had chosen the alpha of all alpha males and attitude was something he had in spades. I tried teaching him the "come" command and the boundaries of our property. Most of the time, he came when called and stayed within bounds—"most" being the operative word. Has the earth ever been home to a Terrier who obeyed all the time?

One time when he ignored my calls, he wandered up the street to where some neighbors were on their front porch. I hustled up the sidewalk to get ahead of him. When I blocked Chip's path, he gave me a look that said, "Yeah, what do you want?"

I glared into his eyes, raised my arm, and pointed toward home.

He stood his ground and growled. One of the neighbors called out, "He has attitude."

"Tell me about it," I shouted back with a smile.

Praying I would avoid further embarrassment, I locked eyes with Chip in silent communication before raising my right arm and pointing. He reluctantly sauntered toward home, not taking a direct line but a forty-five degree angle to the curb where he raised his leg and blessed a sweet gum tree. He looked back at me as if to check my reaction to his delay tactics.

"Go on," I said, pointing again toward home.

He growled louder than before, then slowly turned in the right direction and moved on. I'm not sure what that growl meant, but I imagine it was something like, "Don't be so impatient. You and I both know you can't make me do this, but I'll humor you—this time."

It took one more growl and point exchange before we reached home. If we encountered another dog on one of our walks, Chip ignored most of them no matter how much they barked. Only German Shepherds and Portuguese Water Dogs merited his retort, and they always deferred to mighty Chip.

While visiting my mom one weekend, she joined us on our walk. A loose Rottweiler ran toward us. Chip barked furiously and lunged at the Rottweiler when he came within range, biting his side. Mom screamed and the Rottweiler's owner came running. The Rottweiler stood still, staring at his twenty-one-pound challenger. The owner apologized and took his Rottweiler home.

When Chip developed an ear infection, the vet prescribed a solution. Once a day, I was to put a few drops in the ear, gently massage the base of the ear, and wipe it out with a wad of cotton. Easier said than done. When he saw the bottle approach his ear, he growled. I tried again with the same result. I put the bottle down, cradled his head in my hands, looked into his eyes and said firmly, "Chip, you know your ear has been bothering you. I'm not trying to hurt you. This is going to help you get better." I held his head and looked into his eyes for several more seconds while sending him silent, comforting thoughts. He let me complete the procedure without complaint.

He never protested spending the weekend with my husband and me on our sailboat. While we packed, Chip followed us everywhere with perked ears and wagging tail. Our boat was docked near the head of the pier where few people or pets would walk by and disturb Chip. Whenever I took Chip for a walk, we had to pass by a boat with a nine-month-old Jack Russell. The pup barked constantly until we were out of sight, but Chip never even looked at him.

The pup's owner, who never attempted to stop the barking, seemed to delight in saying, "Look, the other dog is scared." I knew better and ignored the comment.

One day Chip and I were almost off the pier when I stopped to talk with friends. We heard a shout farther out on the dock and turned to see the Jack Russell charging in our direction, barking all the way. He must have jumped off the boat. As the impudent pup neared, Chip merely turned around with his tail pointed straight up and stared at him in silence. The pup stopped short four feet away, stood, cowered, then retreated.

"Good job, Chip," I said. Unlike humans, dogs avoid escalating a confrontation beyond what is required. Well, at least intelligent mature dogs like Chip do. After that, the Jack Russell and his owner remained silent whenever Chip and I walked by their boat.

Many dogs bark when left alone inside a boat. When Chip barked the first time we tried to leave him, I walked back, told him to be quiet, and stared at him in silence while sending reinforcing thoughts. He stayed quiet. The stare worked every time for me but never for my husband. I told him it was the Cairn mind meld.

I developed a sense of pride about my superior human-canine communication ability and the special bond we shared. Then one day, I did my usual routine before leaving the boat but Chip began barking before I left the dock. I paused to see if he would stop, but no luck. Annoyed and wondering if I had lost my special talent, I marched back to the boat. I opened the hatch and stared down at him. Instead of returning the stare, he just sat in a relaxed posture and looked at me.

"Chip, be quiet," I scolded, stared, and shut the hatch. Before I got off the boat, he barked. Again I opened the hatch, yelled at him, and gave him the stare, my eyes bulging in frustration. Again, he just looked at me. Then I realized I was wearing sunglasses. He could not see my eyes. When I took off my dark glasses, he sat at attention, we locked eyes and I said calmly, "Chip, be quiet." After a mutual stare interval, I closed the hatch and he stayed silent. I breathed a sigh of relief.

Later when I returned to the boat, boaters in the slip across from ours confirmed that Chip remained quiet while I was gone.

"How do you keep him from barking?" they asked.

I just shrugged and said, "I tell him to be quiet." If I tried to explain about the Cairn mind meld, they would probably think I was weird.

~Janet Hartman

"Do you think those sounds they make are some primitive attempt to communicate with one another?"

62

Personal Trainer

*A dog is one of the remaining reasons why some people
can be persuaded to go for a walk.*
~O.A. Battista

"Sit!" I commanded my overexcited West Highland Terrier. "Sparkle, I won't put your leash on with you jumping about." It had been weeks since she'd been for a walk. First she'd been recovering from surgery for a "mass removal" below her tail. Then she somehow injured her knee. It was finally time. I knew we had to start slowly so we walked up and down our street just a few times while I watched her gait for any signs of a limp.

"How you doing, girl?" I asked and Sparkle wagged her tail.

Her physical therapy was sporadic. Some days we missed it. I didn't want to overdo it and have her limping around or needing knee surgery. Soon, she could make it around the block, skipping all the little dead-end streets along the way. Little by little, I extended our walk. Occasionally, Sparkle lay down in the middle of the sidewalk.

"What's wrong? Tired?" I asked. She looked at me, rested, and then we were on our way.

Sometimes, we would walk in the morning when I returned from the morning school drop-off. Other times, she had to wait until I came home after a day substitute teaching. Here and there, we'd miss a day. My body was getting used to the exercise as well. I started taking her out on weekends, usually sometime before noon. Our walks grew longer, exploring beyond our block, taking nearly an hour sometimes. When Sparkle got tired, she had a new trick—sniffing. She stopped and smelled a tree or a flower or the grass.

"Come on, Sparkle. We're almost home," I said.

Finally, she could keep pace with me, and sometimes she walked a little ahead. As a bonus, being her trainer meant I was getting much needed workouts. There were times we arrived on our street with Sparkle's tongue hanging out of her mouth, her pace dragging. I thought maybe I had overdone it, but then, as soon as we got to our lawn and I unhooked her leash, she ran like a maniac on our grass, around our neighbor's tree, and then back to our grass for a good roll.

To me, the schedule was random, but Sparkle found a routine in it. Whenever I came home, whatever the time, she'd come to me, spin in a circle, and scratch my pant leg with her paw. She was saying, "Let's go for a walk." If I ignored her, she'd run to where we kept her leash, scratch there, dance around and then come back. Sometimes, she'd do an imitation of her excitement when we were leaving for a real walk. Looking at her meant all was lost. She knew she would be getting that walk. She didn't care that I was tired from sitting all day or pacing up and down a classroom. It didn't matter that there was dinner to get on the table or a house to clean. I'd look at the clock.

"Twenty minutes," I said. "I can spare twenty minutes for a short walk around the block." To make up for the shortened time, I put on ankle weights. However, once I was out there, my body wanted more. Sparkle seemed to know the way. She would pull me across the street. That meant our longer route. Her eager eyes silently compelled me to walk with her, to get both of us in shape. My pants fit better. More importantly, I felt better. I hadn't planned to create a routine when I'd embarked on my path to rehabilitate my dog, but she had taught me more than any personal trainer ever could, and she never yelled. She pushed and cajoled and persuaded with her relentless loyalty.

"Thanks, Sparkle." I hugged her as we returned fifty minutes later. She was tired and content. I was energized and ready to face the rest of the day.

~D. B. Zane

Chapter
7

My Dog's Life

These Old Bones

Old Dogs, Best Friends

Blessed is the person who has earned the love of an old dog.
~Sydney Jeanne Seward

ld dogs make the best friends. I feel a slight twinge of guilt as I write these words, because I think all animals are wonderful. I love how puppies make me laugh as I watch them explore the world, the yard, or even their own food dish. Everything is new to them and there is so much to learn. I love the young, proud dog that runs fast and looks lean and beautiful as it moves. You can see the vitality and pride radiate from its body. But today, my best friend is an eleven-year-old Jack Russell Terrier, and as I stare at her loving face, I know for a fact that old dogs make the best friends.

My old friend came into my life shortly after I had to say good-bye to another loyal friend, an eight-year-old Chow Chow named Tai Pan. We had been through so much together, but try as I might, I couldn't save him from cancer. I was angry and hurt when Tai Pan passed. I felt like I had run as fast as I could into a brick wall, and all the joy had left my body.

The universe saw my pain and sent healing my way. It came in the form of a wild, happy, Jack Russell puppy. She didn't come to replace Tai Pan, she came to help me heal. Once she entered my life, I didn't have time to feel sad. The first day she came into her new home, she tucked her tail and took off running through the house. She showed no fear, no hesitation, just a wild exuberance in exploring her new surroundings. She had such exuberance for life that I named her Zooby.

Zooby wasn't like all the other puppies that had shared my life. I was used to a good round of running and playing, and then the pup would collapse in exhaustion for a nice nap. Zooby never napped. She had things to do. And so began our adventure, with me running after her, trying to keep up. I didn't sit down much that first year. Whenever I did, Zooby would come streaking by with the television remote, a pair of my underwear, or whatever she thought might get me up off the couch. Somehow, she always knew the right thing to do to get a rambunctious game of chase going.

After only a few weeks, I became painfully aware that Zooby could outsmart me. One day she watched my cat jump from the back of the couch onto the counter. I walked away for only a few moments, and when I came back, I saw Zooby standing in the sink licking a dirty dish. She looked up at me and had a huge smile on her face. She was so proud of herself. That afternoon I rearranged the furniture and signed us up for an obedience class.

The day of our class came. Our first lesson was to learn the "long down." This is where the dog lies down on command and remains calm and submissive until released. We were instructed to gently step on the dog's lead until it lay down and then as it submitted, release a little of the lead. The other dogs had no problem with submitting, but Zooby knew I needed more than a submissive, whatever-you-say-goes kind of girl. She went down and then she rolled over and over and over. She was squealing and growling and chewing on my shoe. The instructor went on with the class, and very firmly told us to continue with the long down technique until we got it. We eventually got it, but not that night.

The years have flown by. Zooby is my constant companion. We spend our time traveling, training, walking, exploring new places, sleeping, and expecting joy and wonder every day. We have a history together. We trust and love each other. As I sit on the couch with

Zooby by my side, I reminisce about all the antics she pulled. Jumping up to say hi to a salesman, only to hit him in the groin and drop him to his knees, then licking his face and dancing with delight when he was down on her level. The night I called her inside the house, only to find her standing in a puddle, covered from head to toe with mud. Or how she would get jealous when the other dogs in her agility class ran through the tunnel. That was her favorite obstacle.

Zooby always had a smile on her face and she still does today. So do I. This little girl brought healing, exuberance, and joy into my life and she reminds me that life is good, today and every day. I look at her black face, her muzzle filling in with gray, and I smile. She has always known what I needed even when I didn't know. Yes, old dogs do make the best friends.

~Jamie Lee

Who're You Calling Old?

Age is an issue of mind over matter. If you don't mind, it doesn't matter.
~Mark Twain

I t was raining hard the day my Lotka finished his Advanced Rally title. The trial that day was in a livestock pavilion with a dirt floor and a tin roof, open to the weather on three sides. When it rained hard, the sound of the downpour on the metal roof was deafening, and when the rain slacked off, a mist blew in on a cold wind. But Lotka couldn't hear the pounding rain. At fourteen, he was almost completely deaf. Nor did the cold bother him. A five-pound Papillon with enormous fringed ears and tremendous attitude, he fit neatly under my jacket. But despite his size and the warmth I offered, he wasn't content to cuddle up and be still. He would whine to get down so that he could leap into some bystander's lap, and then jump into the lap of the next person, and then the next. He loved people. All his life, his motto seemed to be: "So many laps, so little time!"

Lotka was my first dog. All my life until I got him, I was painfully shy. Nobody who met me now would guess that, but it's true. Lotka changed my life. After I got him, as long as he was with me, I enjoyed being the center of attention. It was like magic.

When I had Lotka with me, it seemed perfectly reasonable that total strangers would come up to me on the street to tell me how cute he was or ask, "Did you train that dog yourself?" I loved to show

Lotka off, which is probably why I taught him to do so much—sit, down, stay, spin in circles, leap through a hoop of my arms, all kinds of things. I taught him hand signals for everything because it was easy and impressive. I could take him into a bookstore and silently give him signals to lie down and stay, then wander off to browse the shelves thirty feet away. He was so adorable and well-behaved that nobody ever suggested he shouldn't be there.

Now that he was older, I was showing Lotka in Rally just for fun. Lately I had been busy training and showing my young Cavalier King Charles Spaniels in Obedience and in the breed ring. Long retired, Lotka was left behind... and left behind... and left behind again, every time I took other dogs to a show. Lotka would tremble, dance, and whirl in excited circles when I got out a suitcase, then wilt with unhappiness when he didn't get to come. It was hard leaving him. I knew he wasn't getting any younger, so that spring I decided to take him and show him in Rally.

I was pretty sure Rally would be easy for Lotka and I was right. He'd earned his Companion Dog title years earlier, and although I'd hardly done any work with him since, he hadn't forgotten anything. It's a mystery to me how a five-pound dog with a brain the size of a walnut can do that, but I barely had to remind him about heeling and hand signals.

In Rally, the signs are laid out in a course, and when you and your dog get to each sign, you do whatever it says. Your dog might need to lie down while you walk around him in a circle, or take a jump, or heel in a figure eight while ignoring a tempting box of toys set out as a distraction. Some of the Rally exercises require many movements, but at fourteen, Lotka could almost read my mind.

That last day, the bad weather caused a problem for most of the dogs because it was so loud and distracting. One man with a Sheltie instructed his dog to sit, but the dog couldn't hear him. Another dog could hear but was too upset to work because of the noise. The weather made no difference to Lotka. He showed just like he had as a young dog. He danced from foot to foot while waiting to go in the ring, he whined and quivered when I asked him to stay while the other dogs had their turns. When the judge said, "Ready? Start!" he went through the course with his usual delight, taking tiny hand signals for Sit, Down, Stay, Heel, and Jump. Since he was watching for signals, he never took his eyes off me and he never got distracted. He finished his Rally Advanced title with a score of 99 out of 100.

He ended his show career on a high note, which I am thankful for, since four months later he was diagnosed with inoperable cancer. A month later he was gone. I don't claim that the world trembled when my Lotka died, but it should have. It's been a year now since I lost Lotka. I'll always be so grateful that I decided to show him again, even though he was deaf and I was busy with young dogs. I'll always be grateful that he got to travel with me, pester bystanders for attention, dance his way through the ring, and show everybody how brilliant he was.

~Rachel Neumeier

On the Floor

My dear old dog, most constant of all friends.
~William Croswell Doane

"Please, dear," she pleaded, "You're young and she'll make a great companion. She's such a good girl, really she is. If the retirement home allowed pets, I wouldn't dream of leaving her behind."

Her white hair shone brightly in the sun as we stood in the backyard that had just become mine.

"No," I insisted. "I'm sorry but it's just too much responsibility for me right now. I've started a new job and now I have this house to look after and... please understand. It would be best if you found somewhere else for her to live."

Finally, her friends agreed to take her beloved dog, Midnight, once they fenced in their yard. Reluctantly, I agreed to keep her just until then.

Since none of my furniture had arrived yet, the first several nights in my new house were spent on the floor in my sleeping bag. It was just me and Midnight, a gentle black Lab, whose owner had suddenly vanished. Looking understandably worried, she lay next to me, a complete stranger, who was also overwhelmed by the many changes in her life. Sleep didn't come to either of us for hours. During those hours we lay together providing one another with warmth, both physical and emotional. Me and a quiet loving creature, who would soon have a different home with a newly fenced yard.

When the call came two weeks later, I was unprepared. I'd completely forgotten about the conversation I'd had on the day I moved in.

"Hello, dear. Hope you're loving the house as much as I did. And how's my sweet girl, Midnight? Gosh, how I miss her! Listen, dear, my friends just called and the fence is finished. They're ready to take her. I thought I'd give you their number and you can make arrangements for them to pick her up."

I'd never consciously changed my mind but clearly it had been changed drastically. In spite of my initial resistance, Midnight's wet kisses and playful greetings had gotten under my skin and into my heart.

"I'm sorry," I said, "but it's too late now. I want her to stay with me. I love her so much and I need her. I'll be good to her, I promise, but I can't give her away now."

Even I was surprised by my reaction, but clearly, without realizing it, I'd grown accustomed to the wonderful companionship of this mellow, loving dog. MY dog.

After a brief silence her voice calmed my fears.

"Well, to be honest, I was hoping all along it would turn out this way, dear," she said. "Something told me it would be good for both of you. I'll explain things to my friends. You two girls just take care of each other, okay?"

And so we did, during our long journey together.

As my career took off, so did the number of hours I worked. In between business trips, I could work from home. Often, camped out at my desk, buried deep in deadlines, the soft nudge from a damp nose or soft paw reminded me it was time to give, and receive, love. As the years sped by, filled with pressures and promotions, my calm, gentle Midnight was the one sane constant in my life.

Everything has its price, and success, for me, proved costly. After looking after the bottom line, but not myself, for years, my health gave out. Crippling arthritis slowed me down, but by then my dear Midnight had slowed down too. We took shorter walks and on extra cold mornings, skipped them entirely. Whether I napped for hours or sat up crying in pain, fearful about my future, she stayed nearby, snuggling close.

Right around this time, her seizures started to occur frequently, often waking me in the middle of the night. The first time it happened, I was sure it was an earthquake. In fact, it was Midnight on the floor against a glass door, shaking so violently it rattled, waking me from a deep sleep. Moving gingerly, I lowered myself onto the wooden floor to provide comfort during the disorientation that followed each episode. I would stroke her smooth coat and reassure my sixteen-year-old companion in a language I knew she could still comprehend. Between her declining motor skills and my arthritic legs, getting up from the slippery wood floor proved treacherous. We'd stay that way for a long time, sometimes hours. The end was very much like the beginning; both of us needing and providing comfort and love to one another... on the floor.

~Linda R. Frankel

The Gift of Life

Dogs are miracles with paws.
~Attributed to Susan Ariel Rainbow Kennedy

I t was a typical blustery early-spring day in Michigan when all low-hanging clouds carry the promise of another cold rain. That overcast morning my friend Laura and I stood shivering in line at the local "Meet Your Best Friend" adoption event. Laura's heart was set on a big-hearted slobbery St. Bernard. She had hoped for months to find one.

Dozens of tents were lined up on the rain-slicked asphalt. Their multicolored canvas enclosures snapped noisily in the harsh wind. Blue-clad volunteers scampered about, their wool mufflers flying while rescued animals barked out a chaotic symphony. I knew the heartache this kind of event could cause, but by carefully compartmentalizing my role as a supportive one, I felt emotionally prepared. After all, Laura already had a breed picked out. We would be done in no time. We peeked in hundreds of crates but found no St. Bernards.

In the last row of now empty crates, one unwanted, older dog remained. Mike, a top-notch used car salesman and weekend shelter volunteer, whipped the crate open before we came within ten feet.

"Isn't she a beauty? She shakes hands, knows how to heel, sit, lie down and is completely housebroken," he said. He was right. She was a beauty, a perfect cross between a black Lab and Golden Retriever. Laughing, chocolate-brown eyes, a lolling, happy mouth matched with long, soft fur and a gently waving tail.

"Abby" needed a home with older children only. She had shedding issues, and being older, would require medical attention sooner rather than later. The reason she was surrendered was because there was a new baby in the house. Her stay at the shelter was up the next day. She was out of time.

The next time I came to, I was driving home with my newest friend, Abby. I was in shock and panicked. How was I to explain this to my roommate who helped care for my other dog? How would the two dogs get along? What about the shedding? How bad was this going to be? My cover story was that I was dog-sitting for a friend. This would buy me a week to hatch a new plan. The week passed, the friend never materialized, and the inevitable question dropped on the table like a twelve-pound frozen turkey.

"Tell me you didn't adopt this dog," said my roommate.

"I did, but, I adopted her for another friend who recently lost his dog. I am positive he will love her," I quickly replied. But not long after, this friend took one look and backed out. Abby was a sorry picture of canine health. She had kennel cough, labored breathing, and her eyes and nose oozed with a thick, green discharge. What had I gotten myself into? Agonizing weeks ensued. Abby slowly improved after several weeks of quarantine and heavy medication. The pecking order among the dogs was decided with surprisingly little bloodshed. My roommate gradually relented and I began buying vacuum cleaner bags by the crate.

Two and a half years passed quickly. My beloved fifteen-year-old Afghan Hound lost his fight with congestive heart failure. I was on autopilot for months: Work, home, eat, sleep, and feed Abby was the order of the day. After I moved into a new home I decided to have a small housewarming party to alleviate some of my sadness. The new house was a lovely, 1,700 square foot, four-bedroom ranch on a large, wooded lot. The kitchen and Abby's room were ideally situated at one end of the house, and the bedrooms were on the other side at the far end. With a big meal prepared, the house soon filled with music and laughing friends gathered around a crackling fire. Clean-up the following day was fun as I relived the laughter and fond memories from the night before. The last order of the day was to turn on the self-cleaning oven and fall into bed. I was happy for the first time in months.

By 1:30 a.m. the house had filled with a thick, greasy smoke. Oblivious to the screaming smoke detector in the kitchen, I slept on. Two latched doors away Abby began to frantically claw at the first solid wood door. Her paw caught the door handle. Then she did it again. Groggily I awoke to her repeated barks at my bedside. A three-foot thick layer of acrid, roiling smoke shrouded the ceiling. I quickly crawled to the kitchen, shut off the oven and opened all the windows and doors.

Until that night I always believed that I was Abby's hero. I had often wondered what had worked to soften my heart that day. Abby did more than save me that night. She restored my faith in a higher power way beyond my self-centered fast-paced life. Quietly, on four furry, padded feet, in the middle of my darkest hour, she lovingly returned the gift of life.

~Dawn M. Hesse

Someone to Watch Over Me

It is not so much our friends' help that helps us,
as the confidence of their help.
~Epicurus

Gracie, my beautiful fourteen-year-old Shepherd/Collie mix, has found her purpose. Seven years ago, when I came home from a Boston hospital after my spinal cord injury, I was wearing a large brace that went from my chin to the middle of my chest. When my husband, Bob, helped me to our couch, Gracie hopped up to give me her usual three million "Yippee you're home!" kisses. But before she landed her sloppy tongue on my face, she stopped herself upon seeing my brace, and, I believe, sensed my pain. And in that instant, I was no longer her caregiver. I was in her care. Ever since then, Gracie's reason-to-be has been to watch over me. When morning comes, Gracie won't leave the bedroom until I'm up, even when our other pets are noisily having their breakfasts. I am her charge. Her mission is to keep me out of harm's way.

Although she's nearly deaf now, she feels the vibration on the floor when I get out of bed, and she rouses herself from her heated doggie bed. As I head to the bathroom, she leads the way, as if saying, "I'll protect you, Mom. Just stay behind me." If there is anything in my path, like a slipper, she will stop, turn sideways to block me, and then wait until she's sure I've seen the obstacle. I have had to re-learn how to walk, and just recently I made my first trek with her to her favorite spot, a woodland path around a pond. I used to walk there with her every day before I was hurt. It is emotionally brutal to see my old dog amble so lamely sometimes. With her head down, she tries her best to walk a straight line, but sometimes she can't.

One day during our walk something wondrous happened. A dog about thirty pounds heavier and years younger than Gracie raced in my direction. I was terrified. If a dog jumps up to greet me, I lose my balance and fall. Gracie seems to know this. She barked, moved as fast as she could to shield me, and then she planted her old, weak body right in front of me as a barrier. Somehow renewed, she was alert and purposeful in her ever-vigilant role as "Grand Protector of My Mom." She faced the large, spirited dog, and barked again. The dog tried to get around her to reach me, but Gracie growled, something I had not seen her do in ten years. The dog backed off.

Gracie has shown me something I had not known was possible before I became disabled. That she would give up her life for me. I said to a friend, "Gracie has become my caregiver." I could barely get the words out. "She won't be on this earth much longer. Do you think that having her is worth the pain of losing her?" She replied, "Oh yes. Your sadness is so deep only because your love is so deep. What is a life without love?" I knelt on the floor next to my Gracie.

"Thank you for protecting me from all of the evils you think could ever come my way," I said and rubbed her bony hips and shoulders. "You have done a great job." I kissed her golden forehead. "I will always love you." She sighed, tired from a long day of watching over me. I whispered, "You are my true friend."

~Saralee Perel

Hair Today, Hair Tomorrow

Gorgeous hair is the best revenge.
~Ivana Trump

An evening breeze ruffles Buddy's fur as he trots down the sidewalk, head held high. He owns this street, but life hasn't always been so good. A few years ago, he suffered the emotional pain and embarrassment of hair loss.

Buddy's follicles began to fall out when he was eleven years old, first thinning along his backbone, and then spreading to his sides and back legs. Only the hair around his neck remained thick and soft. After three months, most of his downy coat was gone, leaving naked gray skin. At first the gray-and-white Chihuahua denied the increasing shine on his back, avoiding mirrors and his reflection in the back door. A comb-over is no option for a shorthaired dog. When his baldness became too obvious to ignore, Buddy tolerated hairless Chihuahua jokes and the dry skin and itchiness with good humor. Inside, however, he was confused and self-conscious. He kept in shape by chasing squirrels, ate specially formulated dog food and slept well—at least twenty-two hours a day. He still had most of his teeth.

Why did he suffer from this telltale sign of aging? Trips to the veterinarian yielded little relief. He endured expensive blood tests ruling out thyroid disease, Cushing's disease and mites, and suffered through painful steroid shots for seasonal alopecia. His hairline continued to recede. When referred to a specialist, Buddy felt a glimmer of hope. Hair growth medication? A transplant? Maybe weaving?

Dr. Garfield's office was located on the first floor of a four-story building devoted to veterinary specialists. A Dachshund wearing an eye patch and a Sheltie with a plastic cone around his neck stared at Buddy as he entered the lobby. Buddy couldn't stop trembling as he waited on the plastic and steel chairs in the specialist's office. The veterinary assistant looked pitifully at him as she led him to the examining room. Shivering, he stood on the crackly paper covering the table. Dr. Garfield gently examined Buddy. He ordered more blood tests to rule out other rare diseases. While awaiting the results of the tests, Dr. Garfield asked, "Would you mind if I took Buddy's picture? I travel throughout the state speaking to other veterinarians about animal skin diseases. He is an excellent example of hair loss."

Complete humiliation. For the advancement of science and with the condition that his facial features be digitally altered, Buddy stood tall for the photograph.

"I have good news," Dr. Garfield said after reviewing Buddy's tests. "Buddy's hair loss is not caused by disease but by color dilution alopecia." Also known as blue balding syndrome or blue Doberman syndrome, CDA is a genetic disorder most common in dog breeds with gray coats. The affected hair thins along the backbone and on the haunches, but white or tan fur is not affected, he explained.

"It's only a cosmetic problem. Buddy is a healthy dog," Dr. Garfield said. No messy creams? No painful surgery? No hair forever? Buddy needed to know.

"There's one thing you might try," Dr. Garfield said. "You can purchase a natural remedy at the health food store for just a few dollars." That evening, Buddy took his first tablet wrapped in a bread ball. A few weeks later thin fuzz appeared on his backbone. Soon the fuzz grew into the soft gray fur of a young dog. Buddy began answering to new nicknames: "Fluffy," "Blue Velvet," or "Bigfoot." Young female visitors loved to pet his smooth fur. Older male visitors asked, "What was the name of that pill?"

After two years, Buddy still sports the coat of a much younger dog. Buddy wants to start the Hair Club for Dogs. As president and client he would star in late night infomercials, riding in a convertible with the wind in his ears, chasing a stick into the pounding surf, or maybe just resting by his lady friend, as she strokes his gray fur.

~Nancy Lowell George

"So he's not self-conscious."

Escape Artist

A door is what a dog is perpetually on the wrong side of.
~Ogden Nash

If you happened to go by my house this morning, you might have seen me climbing out a window. My home has two very usable doors, but instead I removed a window screen and crawled outside. The reason for my behavior has to do with my dog.

I am the owner of a nine-year-old yellow Lab. I will never forget the day my husband told our three young daughters that he was bringing home a surprise. He took out from his jacket a little bundle of golden fur with a tail that would not quit wagging, and from that moment on, Sundance stole each of our hearts.

Sundance loves to be a part of my daily activities, and has learned by watching me just what the day may hold. If I have my work shoes on, chances are I will be working in my garden and he will be living up to the retriever part in his name by catching the weeds I pull and throw. If I am barefoot in the summer, he seems to know I intend to sit in my swing and read or write, in which case he will pant next to me, napping, instead of enjoying the comfort of air conditioning.

However, I think Sundance's favorite activity is running with me. When I tie on my running shoes his ears perk up, he wiggles his bottom, and he stays at my heels until we are out the door. In his youth, we would go four miles together, but he has aged and now his limit is two miles, which isn't bad considering in human years he is over sixty years old.

I often go the two miles and take him with me, but occasionally, I like to run three or four and therefore leave him behind. When I get back, he follows me around with a droopy tail and sad eyes which seem to say, "What did I do wrong? Why didn't you take me along?"

Since I cannot bear to hurt my buddy, I have tried to trick him. He sleeps in our laundry room, which is also one of the entrances to our home. If I leave soon enough in the morning, I can sneak out the front door and get back before he gets up. Lately though, he has caught on to the sound of the front door opening and barks and whines until I get back. Then he proceeds to pout for hours. Fortunately, the window has been working just fine, as long as I change my incriminating clothes before I greet him.

Some people wonder why I would go through all this trouble. After all, Sundance is "just a dog." Well, he is more than just a dog to me. He has become one of my most perceptive friends. He senses when I am having a bad day and quietly stays by my side or puts his chin on my lap. He is aware of my good days and the mood changes as we wrestle and play. My loving Lab does not care if I do not wear make-up, have bad breath, or suffer a bad hair day. He does not notice if I sing off-key or judge me if I swear; he just faithfully stays by my side.

I have learned much from my loyal Labrador Retriever. Too often I have judged others or held back affection because of looks, smell, or actions, all the time never considering the circumstances in their life. Thanks to Sundance, I have come to realize two of our basic human desires are to be loved and enjoyed. My finest days are when I have been with my best friends who love me and want to be with me. My best friends come in the form of: my husband, special women, my family members, and yes, Sundance.

So, do not be alarmed if you happen to go by a house in the wee hours of the morning and see a middle-aged woman escaping through a window. She is just protecting the feelings of a beloved friend.

~Sheri Bull

Running Free

It takes a long time to grow an old friend.
~John Leonard

It's late afternoon and Bo and I are sitting on the steps, enjoying a cool breeze. My eyes fall on his gray muzzle and I smile, realizing that my hair too has turned gray. Why, we've grown old together!

We still go for walks, but I notice the heat bothers him. He's slower than he used to be. Like me, he's stiff when he gets up. Arthritis is setting in around those once broken bones. We have a routine in the morning when I take my medication. As soon as Bo hears the rattle of the pills, he's at my feet. He knows he has pills to take too. Afterwards, he gets a treat and I get coffee.

Fifteen years have flown by since he first picked me. I stood perplexed in the pen, wondering how on earth I could possibly choose from among thirteen adorable Golden Retriever pups. While laughing at the antics of the puppies, one of them waddled over, plopped down, put his head on my foot and looked up expectantly. How could I resist that? And, so Bo became the delight of my heart.

The roly-poly pup grew to be a fine strapping dog. Bo's coat darkened to a deep red, more the color of an Irish Setter. It was luxurious and thick and he carried himself in a regal manner. This king, however, had a playful streak. Tug of war with any stick was one of his favorite games. In spite of my superior weight, he always held on the longest.

One fateful evening I arrived home to find Bo missing. I called and searched. I checked ditches with my heart in my mouth, but no Bo. I repeated the routine the next morning, but to no avail. Two days of searching revealed nothing. Disheartened, I sat on the porch swing and prayed for God to help me find Bo. It was a quiet evening, not even any insect sounds, a storm brewing in the distance. A tiny whimper reached my ears. "Bo?" I whispered. "Where are you?" There it was again. I traced the sound to a spot under the house below our kitchen sink. Sure enough, my Bo was lying there with the most pitiful brown eyes.

How to get him out? No amount of coaxing worked. There was latticework nailed up at the kitchen end of the house. The only way to reach Bo was to crawl under the deck and then under the house from the other end. Ugh! No telling what I would encounter—spiders for sure and snakes were a distinct possibility. By this time, lightning was flashing and thunder rolling. Bo was frightened. So was I. Nothing to do but suck it up and start crawling.

Under the deck I went, praying all the while. I got to the section where the house and deck connect and remembered that there were two-by-fours along the edge of the house to discourage armadillos from digging. Out I came and went searching for the crowbar. Taking a very deep breath, I once again wiggled under the house, still praying, juggling a flashlight and the crowbar. By this time, it was raining and water dripping through the spaces in the decking made the rescue even more uncomfortable. One final jerk and the two-by-four came loose.

Slithering on my tummy to a Bo whose eyes had never before been so enormous, I began to tug at him. I expected him to snap since he was in pain and frightened. But, he licked my hand and I saw trust in his eyes. Little by little, we inched out. Clearly, I had to get him to the vet, but how would I get him in the truck? He had always been a big dog and now he was deadweight. I spied a piece of plywood and decided to make a ramp. I never heard a complaint from my valiant Bo as I dragged him into the bed of the truck.

A broken pelvic bone and hip, probably the result of being hit by a car, was the diagnosis. The injury was so serious, I was told, that Bo needed to be sent to the local veterinary teaching hospital. Surgery, expensive and extensive, was the suggested course of action. Did we want to proceed?

"Absolutely," I responded immediately. Bo and I both had struggled too hard to get him to this point not to go forward now.

Bo's bravery evoked the sympathy of the technicians where his surgery occurred. He received special attention, sleeping on a waterbed, having treats sneaked to him. We inundated him with squeaky toys. Recuperation was slow and sometimes I wondered if I had made the right decision. His foot turned under and walking was tough. Yet his tail always wagged in greeting and he accepted this problem as just the way things were. We all laughed at how he elicited commiseration from us, inching over until his nose touched one of us.

Who would have thought that a dog that could barely hobble after surgery would be able to run again? But, much to my joyful delight, he could. It all began with a game of tug of war. I was gentle and let him win, my heart full of sympathy for my injured, broken pet. But one day, he pulled the stick from my hand with such energy that I stood open-mouthed with surprise. Then he ran a few steps, inviting a game of keep away. He was clearly pleased with himself.

Thus, began our daily dog therapy/game sessions. Although he still limped, nothing kept him away from that stick. Soon, I quit letting him win. Each time he won the prize, he would stand a few feet from me with a sparkle in his eyes, grinning and panting. He was in heaven fetching sticks from the pond. Within six months, he was racing full speed down the pier, stretching out as he flew through the air, making the jump as long as possible. He landed with a resounding splash that I'm sure frightened the fish, frogs, turtles and other critters that lived there. He quickly found the stick, paddled feverishly to shore and never failed to shake off on me, ready to do it all over again.

~Nancy Baker

Angel Sighting

*With an endless assortment of children and animals living under one roof,
there was always some absurd crisis that gave comic relief to my problems.*
~Sally Jessy Raphael

That morning everything was moving on schedule, which means the household was a chaotic mixture of grownups getting dressed, kids waking up, and dogs eating breakfast and heading outside. Our family has two dogs. As usual, Frisbee ate faster and headed out first. Angel savored every morsel in her bowl, got a drink of water and licked her bowl again and again to make sure she hadn't missed the tiniest trace of kibble.

Angel is an unusual wild-looking dog. Found as a stray, the vet's best guess was that Angel was a mix of Australian Cattle Dog and Weimaraner. Whatever her genetic heritage, she looks like a golden-eyed, light gray coyote, and she doesn't bark or growl. If she has something to say, she makes a high-pitched singsong wailing noise, like a cross between a Husky and a leaking balloon. Luckily, she's not much of a talker. When she's ready to come in, she waits patiently and silently by the door. I hurried Angel outside and turned back to the kitchen to make sure the kids ate something before they left for school. Mission accomplished, I heard Frisbee bark at the back door, waiting to come in. Angel wasn't back yet, but since she was second to go out, that was normal, too.

I took a stab at the crossword puzzle in the newspaper while my husband finished his cereal. From my vantage point, I could see the sliding door to the backyard. Still no Angel. Finally, I pushed back my chair and went to get a pair of shoes so that I could go outside and look for her.

Twelve-year-old Angel wasn't as sure-footed as she used to be. She had been severely epileptic all her life, and that contributed to her unsteadiness. She lost the ability to back up a year or so earlier, but it didn't seem to bother her and she still enjoyed dogging around outside. We have a fenced-in backyard and sometimes Angel sat down before completing the entire patrol of the perimeter. When this happened, one of us had to lift her up and urge her on or she would nap happily outdoors, oblivious to our schedule. I expected that was the case this morning. I went outside and scanned the yard. Our yard is a typical suburban space with a row of bushy evergreens along three sides of the yard. Good for birds and privacy, and lots of good places for a dog to hide, too. I looked and looked. No dog. I sighed, knowing Angel was probably lying under the overhang of a bush or in my perennial gardens. I scouted her favorite haunts.

"Angel!" I called. She wasn't talking.

I checked both gates to the yard. They were still latched. Besides, we would have heard if anyone had tried to come in. Frisbee more than makes up for Angel's lack of barking, and won't let anyone set foot on the property without raising the alarm. From experience I knew that Angel's gray fur blended perfectly into the shadows. Shaking my head, I realized I needed to take a more methodical approach. Starting by the house, I worked around the yard, peeking under every bush. By the time I got back to the start, I was panicked. How could the dog vanish? I ran inside to catch my husband before he left for work.

"I can't find Angel!" I said.

"I have an early meeting," Dave said. "Give me a call at work, and I'll come home after the meeting if you still can't find her." I headed back outside.

"Go find Angel!" I told Frisbee. Frisbee raced off, distracted by a squirrel. She wasn't going to be any help. I started to retrace my steps.

"Angel! Where are you, Angel?" I bellowed, not caring if I woke any late rising neighbors. This time, I thought I heard Angel "answer." I twirled around, trying to get a bearing on the ethereal song, but just then my cell phone rang, drowning out the sound. My phone said the call was from Dave who had just left the house.

"What?" I said.

"Open the gate and walk out by the road," Dave said.

About halfway down our property Angel's head was sticking out through a row of tightly planted evergreens.

"Woo-ooh-ooh-ooh!" Angel called.

Angel had pushed all the way through the hedge and poked her head out between the slats in the fence, and the feathery evergreen branches had closed around her, creating the optical illusion of a disembodied dog head floating in space. I tried to push Angel's head back through the fence, but as hard as I pushed, Angel pushed back harder. I realized that since she couldn't back up, she figured she would just push her way through. I sprinted back through the gate and pushed through the hedge. Lifting the dog off the ground, I disengaged her forward gear. Then I balanced her seventy pounds against one knee and guided her head back through the fence.

So much for my schedule. It had quickly turned into a two-shower morning!

~Wendy Greenley

72

Bologna and Cheese

Never trust a dog to watch your food.
~Unknown

Jabba lay listlessly on the couch, his head resting on his shaved paw. His thick black fur was conspicuously absent from both front paws, exposing rings of sickly gray skin. Usually alert and watchful, his eyes today were dull and half-closed. The days following chemotherapy were often like this. Jabba would spend the day on his favorite couch, uninterested in food or walks or Frisbees. In spite of coaxing him with a homemade meal, Jabba just couldn't be bothered with life. Every three weeks, Jabba went through another round of chemo and his larger-than-life alpha personality went on hiatus. For close to a week, he would shirk his guard dog duties and abandon his German Shepherd attitude. His big black body would give up on life until he could gather enough strength to continue the fight.

This was one of those weeks that he lay on the couch recovering from chemo. His normally attentive eyes barely registered my presence. As I made my lunch of bologna and cheese, I cooked him chicken, rice and green beans—anything to get him to eat. But that day, not even his favorite meal could entice him. Looking at him, I knew that the end was probably near.

Ten years of memories filled my mind. I pictured the most adorable black puppy happily chewing up every shoe in the house, one ear flopping down and one ear sticking straight up. I remembered the adolescent Jabba, who once rearranged the living room furniture, dragging it into the dining room because I left him home alone. I had visions of a young black Shepherd chasing the Frisbee at the speed of light, and visions of a strong adult Shepherd guarding me relentlessly.

The sound of the doorbell brought me back to reality. Leaving my sandwich untouched on the counter, I walked into the living room to answer the door, Jabba's eyes following my movement with little interest. A minute later, I returned to the kitchen, passing Jabba on the way. I reached for my sandwich only to find it missing. After looking all over the kitchen, I retraced my steps, looking for my missing sandwich. Just as I reached the living room, I looked up to see Jabba gulping down the last bite. He slowly climbed back up to his favorite spot, plopped down, and gave me a satisfied sigh. For just a second, his beautiful brown eyes twinkled with his usual love of life and I knew he would be able to fight just a little longer.

~Stephanie Smithken

73

Twenty-Five Pounds of Strength

I am joy in a wooly coat, come to dance into your life, to make you laugh!
~Julie Church

I was surprised how captivated I was by his blond curls and deep brown eyes. I'm not one who is stuck on good looks. I really do believe what's inside is more important. But I have to admit: those eyes, curls, and that stubby tail wagging his entire body completely captured my heart. It really was love at first sight. My mom wasn't a pet person, so we never really had pets growing up. My husband, however, grew up with a menagerie—dogs, bunnies, snakes, even a chinchilla. When he and I married, we always knew we'd get dogs, and sure enough, a couple of years into our marriage, he called me to tell me about a three-year-old Cocker Spaniel that needed a home. While I'd never owned a Cocker, and in fact, had never really spent time with one, Cockers were my favorite dogs. They were just so cute. We went to visit this blond, twenty-five-pound fur-ball of joy, and I was hooked. We had Todd for almost eleven years, and I learned about strength through adversity during those years.

He lived every moment to its fullest. He loved without limit, expressed joy with abandon, relished each mouthful of favorite foods, and stood up to others when appropriate. But mostly, he showed me how to age gracefully, to handle adversity without complaint, and to die with dignity. As he grew older, he had all kinds of health issues, cataracts, deafness, and skin problems. But even without most of his senses, his nose worked, and he, without fail, sniffed me out and sat on my feet.

"I found you," he seemed to say. "Now don't move again."

In his last months, his joy never dimmed. He still loved being held and loved on. He still ate with exuberance. He never whined. He never lost his puppy-like happiness. He just accepted each new hardship with his usual *joie de vivre*. Oh, that I would do the same. I've had my share of health issues, and unlike sweet Toddy, I don't always handle my pain with anywhere near the same acceptance he did, let alone with joy. But when I think of him, running his body along walls to get around the house, sniffing the air to find me, enjoying the feel of the sun on his body, I can't help but want to be more like that.

Then the day came that no pet lover wants to face. I came home from work and went to greet my four-legged kid. With body wagging, he showed his love for me as always. As I guided him back to the house, he collapsed. The emergency vet said he was in congestive heart failure. It was time to put my sweet boy out of his misery. They took him to the back to give him some oxygen, and when he returned and smelled me, he found just enough energy—just enough strength—to wag that body just one more time. It was if he wanted me to know that it was okay. He still loved me with that limitless love. I held him as he fell asleep, and as I cried, I thanked him for all he'd taught me, for being more than a dog, more than a pet. For being my friend. And each time I see blond curls, big brown eyes, and a wagging body, I remember him. How he found joy in the moment. How he showed love to the very end.

~Sauni Rinehart

My Purpose

The purpose of life is a life of purpose.
~Robert Byrne

For years, I considered Tyson to be my husband's dog. Even though it was my idea to adopt this hyper canine, he decided that Craig would be the primary recipient of his gratitude. It's not that he didn't like me. He did. He just liked Craig better. He dropped his toys in Craig's lap when he wanted to play. He sought Craig's help when he ripped his dewclaw at the dog park. Craig. Craig. Craig. Just the sound of my husband's voice over the phone or the hum of his car engine in the driveway sent him into a wriggling frenzy that nearly propelled him off the ground.

I tried to bond with Tyson whenever it was just the two of us in the house. If Craig was working in the yard, I waved Tyson's rope toy and encouraged him to play. But Tyson didn't want to play with me. He wanted to sit by the window and watch Craig work in the yard. If Craig went down the road to the car wash, I took the opportunity to throw Tyson's tennis ball for him to fetch. Tyson eyed the tennis ball as it rolled down the hallway and then walked over to the window. He sat and waited for twenty minutes for Craig to return. Craig tried to make me feel better by rationalizing Tyson's preference.

"He was raised with a bunch of guys," he said, matter-of-factly. "That's who he feels most comfortable around."

I wanted to tell Tyson that it was that "bunch of guys" that wanted to surrender him to an animal shelter and it was his new mommy who intervened and gave him a luxurious life, one where he never had to sleep outdoors or eat anything less than premium dog food. But what was the point? He would never understand any of that.

Over the years, Tyson and I grew a bit closer. He occasionally brought me his toys and he did wriggle when I came home from work, but when it came to choosing between the two voices calling out to him from either side of the living room, he always ran in Craig's direction. He definitely loved my husband more.

Last year, at Tyson's checkup, our vet pointed out some suspicious bumps on Tyson's body.

"Those don't look good," she said. "They need to be taken off."

We scheduled an appointment for Tyson to have seven tumors removed. Since Tyson's vet is on my way to work, I dropped him off that morning and picked him up that afternoon.

When I arrived at the vet's office that day, he looked much worse than I had expected. He had seven, large, shaved patches on his body and he was standing motionless in the front lobby. Tyson stared right past me, completely unaware of who I was or where we were going. I had to scoop up his fifty-five-pound body and tote him to the car where I had already spread his favorite comforter across the back seat.

Once we got home, he was still too sedated to stand. Again I had to carry him up the steps and into the house. It was not an easy task. I curled up on the floor with him while he slept and I was there when he started to come around. He whimpered and panted from the pain and I ran back and forth to get his medicine and extra treats. I caressed his head and body until he was able to fall back asleep but it was hard to pet him without my hand bumping into an incision.

I slept on the floor with Tyson for three weeks. Craig took turns with me and helped as much as he could. But I was the one who took Tyson to medical daycare each morning, dabbed ointment on his incisions each afternoon, and drifted off while cradling him each night. Something changed in those weeks of providing Tyson round-the-clock care. He sat beside me more when we watched TV on the couch. He followed me around the house, as I was getting ready for work. He came to me when he was hurt or not feeling well. Tyson and I developed a bond.

Tyson is a few months away from turning nine. He still has a lot of playful puppy in him and he still loves to race through the house, but he is starting to slow down. He becomes winded quicker and he seems to sleep deeper and more frequently. It's only natural. Tyson is a senior. When he feels like playing fetch or rope toy, Tyson usually still chooses Craig as his partner. But when he wants to cuddle and take a nap, I am his choice. The other day, Tyson climbed onto the couch, circled around a few times before finally lying down and resting his head on my lap. I stroked his graying muzzle and hugged him tightly, grateful to be blessed by this dog's life and grateful that he has finally found a purpose for mine.

~Melissa Face

My Dog's Life

A Walk Down Memory Lane

75

A Man and His Dog

If there is a heaven, it's certain our animals are to be there.
Their lives become so interwoven with our own,
it would take more than an archangel to detangle them.
~Pam Brown

I woke up somewhere over the patchwork quilt of Kansas. From 35,000 feet Kansas looks like an earthen blanket of brown and green hues, stitched together like the quilts that my Grandma used to sew. Seeing the patterns of squares and circles with no apparent rhyme or reason, I sleepily recalled my first glimpse of the landscape below. It had been a happy trip to Colorado that time so many years ago, but not so today. I was going to say goodbye.

Scout had been a good friend and a great companion to my son, Nicholas. The twelve-year-old Coonhound was sick and both Nicholas and his dog needed some comfort. So I made the trip to do what fathers do best when they are at their best. I hoped I was up to the task. Nicholas had planned to spend a weekend in the mountains with Scout, away from the sights and sounds of their normal everyday life, away from the interruptions of work and the stresses that accompany it. He invited me to join them.

Life moves a little slower at 10,000 feet above sea level. It has to, I guess, based on the limitations of oxygen infused into the human bloodstream, but it seemed just the opposite for Scout. As we climbed higher and higher into the Sawatch Range of the Rocky Mountains, he gained energy. He stood tethered in the back seat and sniffed the air coming through the open windows. His nostrils flared slightly, and with his head back and mouth open he howled with enough force to likely shatter a nearby eardrum.

Over the weekend I watched Scout. I watched him lay his head next to my son's arm. I watched him look at Nicholas every time he spoke, watched him follow his movements. And I saw that bond, that bond between my boy and his dog, a bond so special that if you've never experienced it you'll never know you've missed something extraordinary.

When I petted Scout he hardly noticed. He was truly my boy's dog, not mine. They had lived together, and worked together, for nearly five years. Never apart, where you found one you found the other... NickandScout. We said their names in the same breath. Nick found him up for adoption in Vermont. Blind in one eye from a round of buckshot surely meant to kill him, Scout carried the scars, and some lead pellets, as evidence of his early West Virginia life.

Using the same techniques he learned while working with guide dogs for the blind, Nick taught Scout to be a companion and a trainer. Together they worked teaching pet obedience, and made the rounds of schools to educate children about service dogs. Scout relished the role. When Nick would place the service dog cape over his back and snap it beneath his trim belly, Scout seemed to stand a little straighter, hold his head a little higher, and realize that for now, no howling was allowed. And as they walked together, Nicholas seemed to stand a little straighter, and hold his head a little a higher, too. But now it was ending. The few weeks since the discovery of cancer in Scout's organs had been a miasma of emotion. The disease had made a sneak attack, and it would win the battle. They both knew it.

For the weekend, though, Scout was young again, and in his glory. He waded in the cold mountain stream, he sniffed and howled at the scent of the horses outside our cabin windows, and he mercilessly begged snacks as Nick and I sat and played cards in the fading daylight. When he was tired, he would curl up on his bed with a new blanket made by his grandma, and close his eyes and dream, perhaps, of chasing the coyotes that were crying in the bright mountain moonlight. I'd look at Nick, my son, my boy, and feel his pain, unable to help.

We said goodbye at the airport. With Scout in his cape and harness, I knelt and hugged him and kissed his head, and told him what a special dog he was. He paid little attention for he was focused on my boy, his partner, his companion. Scout died a week later on Father's Day. He took my boy with him, and left behind my son, for now a sad and lonesome man.

~Gary B. Xavier

76

Chicken Soup for the Soul

Doggone Wake

The one best place to bury a good dog is in the heart of his master.
~Ben Hur Lampman

Anyone who has ever owned a dog knows that actions speak louder than words. This is especially true when a beloved pet passes—it is only then that one truly understands the sounds of silence. No more tinkling of tags, no more tail swishing to welcome you home, no more sad puppy-dog eyes watching as you eat. When our dog Maile died, my husband Barret suggested having a wake.

"A wake? Like having people over to talk about Maile?" I asked.

"Well, she was an Irish Setter," he replied. "I think a wake would be appropriate."

"But she had a Hawaiian name," I said, ready to argue.

"Doesn't matter," our son John interjected from across the room. "I think it's a great idea!"

John had taken Maile's death to heart. Growing up, the two were inseparable. My mother thought it was because she'd put peanut butter on John's toes when I brought him home from the hospital.

"Dad's right," John stated matter-of-factly. "Let's have a doggone wake." And much to our amazement, we laughed.

So at Barret's suggestion we invited family and friends over to celebrate Maile's life.

Holding up her canine college degree, I began: "Although Maile graduated last in her class, she always obeyed. She was never a dog to think 'no' only applied to the last negative command."

"Here, here! A toast to higher education!" my brother said, causing a few chuckles around the room.

"But, being born in May, Maile was a bull-headed Taurus and was doggedly determined to have her own way," I continued.

"Like going for car rides," John added. "The UPS driver wised-up early on. He'd give her a treat after he got out of his truck and closed the door. That way, she couldn't jump in."

"Maile was so cute," a neighbor said, wistfully. "I had to coax her out of my Mustang more than a few times."

"She wasn't so cute when she wouldn't get out of the Roto-Rooter truck," I said.

"You called it Maile's 'sit-in,' Mom. I thought you thought it was funny," John teased.

"Funny? The guy charged by the hour. That demonstration cost me a small fortune!" I retorted.

"I don't remember you telling me about that," Barret said.

"I'm sure I did," I said, changing the subject. "A toast to Maile's persistence!"

"Well, she sure provided comic relief when your grandmother died," Barret said.

He was right. After the service, family and friends came over for lunch. Perhaps because she was angry for being left behind, Maile slipped into our car when we got home and refused to budge. All afternoon, people tried to lure her out of the back seat to no avail. After everyone left, I had to drive her around the block, not once but twice, before she agreed to get out.

"I remember she didn't touch her dinner because she'd eaten all the bribes," said John.

"Almost unheard of because that dog loved food," I laughed.

"I remember when she consumed the casserole you'd made for a dinner party," my friend Nancy said.

"Maile ate an entire taco casserole without batting an eye," I explained. "Its ingredients included three pounds of ground chuck, a block of sharp cheddar cheese, a bag of Fritos, a can of kidney beans, and a cup of sour cream."

"And remember the bag of Hershey's Chocolate Kisses she ate?" Nancy asked. "It was gift wrapped on the floor under your Christmas tree."

"Do I?" I answered. "What's amazing is that she ate every scrap, foil and all."

"Isn't chocolate bad for dogs?" my neighbor asked.

"Miraculously, Maile didn't even get sick," I said.

"No, but she had trouble passing the tin foil and we had to take her to the vet in the midst of that snowstorm," Nancy said.

"Oh yeah," I groaned. "And one of your old boyfriends drove us… in his Fiat convertible with the top down!"

"I thought it was snowing," someone said.

"It was, but he'd put the top down the night before and it got stuck," Nancy explained.

"A toast to Maile and her iron insides," Barret said, lifting his glass.

"And to Nancy's old beau, wherever he may be," I teased.

"Seeing everyone smile, I remember Maile's smile," John said.

"I've never known a dog to smile like she did," my brother added.

"Like the Cheshire Cat. All teeth," I said.

I paused to think about the overarching span of life, for all species. When death comes, it roughs up life's waters, and the result is a strong wake behind us.

But the ripple is wide and the memories are many. When your pet passes, you might think no one could possibly understand your grief, but anyone who has ever loved and lost an animal of their own has experienced a similar sorrow.

"Maile's grin was as wide and beautiful as a rainbow," my friend Nancy chimed in, sighing.

"And now she's come to the end of that rainbow," I said. "And may she rest in peace."

"Amen," someone said.

"Amen."

~Laurie Birnsteel

77

Two Bills

Sometimes I feel like a fire hydrant looking at a pack of dogs.
~Bill Clinton

Our pooch Sophie could barely move from her bed to the rug. When she messed herself, I cried out her name in despair. Embarrassed, she staggered to the back door, slid painfully down the four steps, onto her butt on the lawn. Her systems were breaking down. She was thirteen and the end was near.

She waddled under our deck, toward an open hatch to the crawl space beneath the house. I was afraid she would slip through and die. I lay down in the mud, grabbed her rear legs, and pulled our ninety-pound mutt out from under the deck as gently as I could. I replaced the hatch cover, and Sophie ran to the other end of the mucky world under the deck, far from my reach. She stayed there for hours.

The next day, I had a funny feeling and went to check on her. She lay unmoving on her bed, the light gone from her eyes. The grandfather clock in the living room struck noon, reminding me of my dad, who had built it for us ten years before. Now Pop was immobilized in a Phoenix hospital after a massive stroke, and Sophie was dead.

A few weeks later I called my mom on my cell phone.

"Mom, I'm sitting at Bill Clinton's desk in New York, in his chair!" I said. "We're interviewing him today for *The West Wing Documentary Special*. Tell Pop I'll be there tomorrow. And tell him where I called you from."

Clinton told us that he ended his tenure in the White House more idealistic than when he started. Asked about future plans, he mentioned casually that both he and strategist James Carville are apparently eligible to run for President of France. Because Carville and Clinton were born in Louisiana and Arkansas, respectively, both parts of the formerly French Louisiana Purchase, they could hypothetically move to France, establish residency, and run for office.

"I don't think I will," said Clinton, with a broad smile. "I'm sure I would soon start to take flak for my French accent."

Our talk was his first major television interview since leaving office, and he stuck around for pictures and a chat afterward. His dog had died recently and I wanted to bring that up, but the woman who catered our shoot had a lot to say to him about Bush, and I was too starstruck to break in.

The day after meeting Clinton in New York, I visited Pop in a rehab facility in Scottsdale, Arizona. My dad had always been a Renaissance man—a musician, teacher, and author of over thirty books on crafts, hobbies, and the outdoors, a tough old bird who could build or do anything. I've always been different, more one-sided, focused on my career as a cameraman.

Nearly ninety, about the same dog age as Sophie, the man who once could do everything now lay helpless in bed at a nursing home, fed by a tube, his eyesight and hearing impaired, paralyzed on one side and incontinent. During our visit, I described shooting the documentary.

"We interviewed Bill Clinton yesterday in New York," I told him, "and tomorrow we'll meet Gerald Ford in Palm Springs."

"They named a theater after him," he replied, with a twinkle.

"You mean Ford's Theatre, where Lincoln was shot?" I said and laughed.

He grinned, happy that I'd gotten his corny joke. He'd always been a force of nature, and somehow, we still fully expected him to recover.

As time passed, I realized that I regretted never speaking to Clinton about Sophie, and I decided to write him a letter:

Dear President Clinton:

What was in my heart the day we transformed your lovely office into a little studio was wishing to offer my condolences on the death of your dog Buddy. My family recently went through the same kind of loss. Our pooch Sophie died in March at age thirteen, and life has changed since then. The house feels very empty without her. She was big and black, a Boxer-Lab mix, scary-looking but meek as a lamb, and great with kids.

My wife and I always walked Sophie to school with our son and daughter. For years, children we didn't know would come up to us on the street, greet Sophie by name, and exchange a scratch behind the ears for a wetdown. She had a prodigious tongue and a thick whip-like tail. Together they made for an intense licking and wagging experience, especially when she was happy, which was most of the time.

After she died, we scattered Sophie's ashes one evening at sunset at the dog park on San Francisco Bay where she spent many happy hours. Then we spent the evening digging through old photos and movies of our family growing up with her. Laughing and spending time together helped us heal the hurt of losing her.

That's what I wish I had told you at the time we met, but being busy and tongue-tied prevented my saying all that. In any case, I hope you are able to have some peace about losing Buddy. Remember the good times and the wonderful, unconditional love that only dogs and precious few humans practice regularly.

If you do run for President of France, I wish you the best of luck. You can always work on your French accent.

With best wishes,
Bill Zarchy

I didn't expect Clinton to respond, but writing to him about Sophie was cathartic.

Two days before *The West Wing Documentary* aired on NBC, Pop passed away. I watched the show with my family and close friends. Shooting this network primetime special had been a great opportunity for me, and I burst into tears during the opening music as I saw my credit over an aerial shot of the White House. Pop didn't get to see my show, but at least I got to tell him about it. Four months later, I received a reply from President Clinton:

Dear Bill:

> *Thank you for the kind letter you sent to me after the filming of* The West Wing Documentary. *I was so touched by it and regret that I was unable to respond sooner.*
>
> *I was sorry to learn about the loss of your dog Sophie. While our family has a new puppy now, I still miss Buddy very much. He will always hold a special place in my heart, which, as a fellow dog lover, I know you will understand.*
>
> *It was a great pleasure for me to participate in* The West Wing *special episode, and I'm grateful for all you did to make it such a success. I'm glad you took the time to write and send you my best wishes.*

Sincerely,
Bill Clinton

Like the Clintons, we've gotten a new puppy, a cute, rescued mutt named Montana. Abused or abandoned at an early age, she is timid and a bit neurotic, the opposite of her predecessor. But we lavish her with unconditional love. That's how we keep Sophie in our hearts.

~Bill Zarchy

Meme

They motivate us to play, be affectionate, seek adventure and be loyal.
~Tom Hayden

Our heads bopped to the music like teenage schoolgirls. We were the same age, in our thirties, but our lives couldn't have been any more different. I was married, a stay-at-home mother. Rachel, my best friend from high school was single, ambitious and driving a new red convertible. As we steered down an old country road, out of nowhere, Rachel slammed on the brakes, causing my seatbelt to tighten up against my chest as we swerved in the middle of the road.

"Are you okay?" I asked, while my hands visibly shook.

"I think so. My heart is about to beat out of my chest! Did you see that dog? It ran out in front of me!" Rachel said in a frantic voice.

I hadn't seen anything except the palms of my hands that were covering my face. The mother in me was coming out, "Rachel, do you know you could have gotten us killed? How fast were you going?"

I was suddenly longing to be back in my tan minivan with a safe, hard top above my head. But my words were falling on deaf ears because Rachel was already out of the car and heading toward the woods just yards from where we were.

"Come here," I heard her say in a singsong voice. "It's alright." I watched her reach down and pick up a little black ball of matted fur. We couldn't see its eyes but it seemed to be wincing in pain.

"Oh, it's shaking. I think it's cold," Rachel whispered.

"That makes two of us," I mumbled. She placed it gently in her back seat, and even with the top down, the dog smelled like it had spent the better part of its life inside a trashcan. Rachel didn't seem to notice though because she gently wrapped it up tightly in her long plaid Burberry coat. Within twenty-four hours, Rachel named the little Poodle mix Meme, interviewed three veterinarians and had the filth washed, combed and polished out of her new furry companion. Meme's nails were painted bright red with a satin bow at the top of her head to match.

Meme quickly became Rachel's baby. The single, career-driven, mortgage banker took a week off from work to introduce Meme to her new surroundings. The two set out to play at local dog parks, visit an array of pet bakeries and walk side by side throughout her neighborhood. I couldn't help but laugh when I received Rachel's Christmas card. She and Meme were on a friend's boat, both sporting sunglasses. Rachel had always loved life, but she had spent the last decade successfully climbing the corporate ladder. Meme had given her a reason to slow down a bit and enjoy all that surrounded her.

Those months were priceless since next Christmas there would be less to smile about, as Rachel was diagnosed with lung cancer in the fall. She had never smoked a day in her life. We rallied around our energetic friend, hoping to keep her spirits high. When we visited Rachel after her exhausting rounds of chemo, we were always greeted by Meme. She jumped on us for a moment, panting as if to ask for a good scratch behind the ear, before leading us to Rachel, who was usually covered in a blanket. Meme would hop up beside her and maneuver into her lap, with her head on her chest. It made Rachel smile as she petted the little black dog.

Rachel made countless trips to the hospital. Through it all, the persistent coughing and shortness of breath, she remained optimistic. On more than one occasion, she'd ask her friends to smuggle in Meme. We did, of course, and the little black dog would burrow her head into Rachel's side and lick her hand where the IV dug into her skin. Despite the prayers of many, Rachel's cancer spread into her bloodstream. She was sent home with a heartbreaking prognosis.

Family and close friends were by her side around the clock. The nights I would visit, it was painful to leave her. I was going home to a husband and children. Rachel must have sensed my reluctance because each time I left, she'd say, "Go on, I have Meme. I'm fine."

But she wouldn't be fine. At Rachel's funeral, her family shared pictures of her life that flashed on a screen at the front of the church: pictures of her as a child, a cheerleader in high school, graduating college and of her first home. Tears flowed throughout the building. But within seconds, a few giggles were heard. Snapshots of Rachel and Meme appeared on the screen. The pictures revealed Meme and Rachel in matching scarves, the duo in her convertible and the two sitting out by a pool—Rachel enjoying life alongside her pampered pup.

We never knew how old Meme was. The veterinarian guessed between five and seven when she was rescued. After Rachel's death, Meme stayed at a friend's home. She was spoiled and given lots of attention. However, less than six months later, she passed away. Much like Rachel, it was peaceful. She was discovered in her bed when our friend came home from work. I've never been much of a dog person. I rolled my eyes a few times when Rachel showed up with Meme dressed in pink, prancing around in a new outfit. I've since changed my tune. Recently I found myself at a local pound, alongside my three excited children, picking out a new family pet. We stopped at the cage of a frightened little dog hovering in the corner. I'm not sure what kind of breed we brought home that day, but it resembled a black, little matted fur ball I once met alongside a country road with my best friend.

~Amanda Dodson

79

Tiny Dude

If you are a dog and your owner suggests that you wear a sweater... suggest that he wear a tail.
~Fran Lebowitz

Tiny Dude was my dad's dog. He had a long, fancy name—the kind of name dogs are required to have when they have papers and pedigrees, but we always just called him Tiny Dude. He was a miniature, shorthaired Dachshund, black as a licorice stick, and he was, indeed, tiny. And he was a dude, of sorts, since he was a boy dog—at least till Daddy took him to the vet school and got him fixed.

Calling Tiny Dude a dog was like calling the Venus de Milo kind of cute—a great understatement. He was more than a dog—he was my dad's best friend, another sibling, a seven-pound wonder capable of superhuman feats, and full of love.

He lived the most spoiled life of any dog I ever knew. Long before the Hollywood "it" girls began carrying their Chihuahuas around in pink Louis Vuitton cases, Tiny Dude set the standard for pampered pets.

Daddy always made sure that the "Dude" had the finest—food, clothing, whatever he wanted, and not necessarily what was best for him. Sometimes Daddy would buy frozen yogurt on the way home from work and bring the Dude a small cup of vanilla as a treat. Also, I remember many times sitting at the kitchen table, slicing bananas and peeling grapes for him to eat. Tiny Dude did love his bananas, but of course, he simply could not digest or chew grapes with the skins on. I often wondered if my sister or I would have to fan him with palm fronds while we fed him, but I didn't dare suggest it, even in jest, for fear Daddy would think it was a good idea.

Tiny Dude went everywhere with Daddy. If we dared leave him at home, and didn't take him out, he would leave a big "surprise" for Daddy in front of his big-screen TV. He would ride in his own special seat between Daddy and Joe Bob, the man who drove Daddy around to different construction jobs. Daddy owned a construction business, and Joe Bob was one of his workers. Since Daddy didn't like to drive, and was usually on his phone or two-way radio, Joe Bob was his chauffer, and also helped take care of the Dude. I used to smile at the sight of two 250-pound, six-foot-plus men riding around in a big pickup truck, with Tiny Dude riding shotgun in his little bed, like the king of the world.

I wasn't ever jealous of Tiny Dude, even though he had a better wardrobe than me or my sister ever dreamed of. I wondered if any of Daddy's girlfriends were jealous of the time and attention paid to Tiny Dude, rather than to them, and I often remarked that Daddy might have more luck with the ladies if he treated them as well as he treated his dog. Daddy wasn't real appreciative of those comments. I guess he did all right in that department anyway and didn't need any relationship advice from me. It was fun dressing up Tiny Dude though, putting on his orange-and-blue sweater for Auburn football games, a tuxedo for Mardi Gras balls, and even a little grass skirt and coconut bra whenever we had a luau celebrating Daddy's birthday. Tiny Dude was very patient and didn't seem to mind the get-ups we put on him, or the numerous photos we took of him in his different outfits.

After a while, and a few thousand cups of frozen yogurt later, Tiny Dude wasn't so tiny anymore. We tried to get him to lose weight by feeding him a healthier diet. My sister would walk Tiny Dude around the neighborhood as best she could, although he got tired real easy, with his poor little belly dragging the ground, and his little legs going as fast as they could carry him. He did lose some weight, which was good, because we all loved the little fellow and wanted him to live a long, long time.

Daddy let Tiny Dude sleep in his bed. I have heard that pets begin to resemble their owners, and this was the case with the two of them. I went in one night to tell Daddy good night, and both he and the Dude were tucked under the covers, their bellies poking out, lying in exactly the same position. Tiny Dude had become the dog version of my daddy.

Daddy kept Tiny Dude's little doggie toothbrush and toothpaste beside his own, and they even showered together. Matter of fact, Daddy broke his shoulder one time when he fell getting out of the shower, with Tiny Dude in hand. Daddy didn't want him to get hurt of course, so he held Tiny Dude up with one hand, and landed on his shoulder. Daddy was bruised all over but Tiny Dude was just fine.

We always thought Tiny Dude was invincible, but he began to show his age. It got to where he could barely walk, and Daddy continued to shower him with the same love and affection he always had, picking him up and putting him near his food and water to eat, then taking him to his papers to do his "business," and making sure he was comfortable in his bed. I dreaded the day when Tiny Dude would be gone, because I knew how badly Daddy would miss him, and did not know if any other dog, or person, for that matter, could ever fill the void his death would place in Daddy's life. When Tiny Dude finally passed away, I didn't think any of us, especially my dad, could bear it. We grieved, cried, and were very sad, but we started to remember all the wonderful things that had made him a great little dog with a big, big heart.

After Tiny Dude died I found out that he had once saved my daddy from being robbed, and maybe even saved his life. Daddy and a friend had stopped at a rest area one night, and Tiny Dude began barking up a storm, growling, and acting very un-Dude-like—he was usually the friendliest dog in the world to everyone. Two men approached my daddy and asked for some money. They said they had run out of gas. As Daddy talked to them, he noticed one of them had a gun under his coat. The men asked Daddy if he was going to let

Tiny Dude off his leash after them, and Daddy, laughing, said, "Yeah, I'm going to sic him on ya'll, all seven ferocious pounds of him." The two men were scared to death and left. Daddy, his friend, and Tiny Dude, got in their car and hauled it out of there. Daddy said it was like Tiny Dude knew those men were up to no good, and he was going do everything he could to protect Daddy.

Come to think of it, Tiny Dude was more than a dog. He was my daddy's best friend, protector, and confidant. Daddy always told me if people acted like dogs, the world would sure be a friendlier place. I do know if folks acted like Tiny Dude, the world would be a wonderful place indeed. We would all be a lot better off if we spent more time lolling in the sun, playing, giving wet, wonderful kisses, and simply enjoying every day to the fullest. And of course, eating a peeled grape. Or two.

~Melanie Adams Hardy

"You don't see me going around
saying 'Hey dude' all the time."

80

My Sunshine Boy

Wherever you go, no matter what the weather,
always bring your own sunshine.
~Anthony J. D'Angelo

My husband and I decided to adopt a puppy for our son's thirteenth birthday. Those teenage years can come with a great deal of angst and we thought what better way to help him through that difficult period than a dog that would provide unconditional love. My husband had grown up with English Setters so he found a kennel and picked out a spunky boy. We named him Kelty and over the years he became the brother that our son, Colin, never had.

From the moment he arrived, we were challenged by his mischievous ways. We kept waiting for him to grow out of his "puppy stage," but it never happened. A perfect example of his impish behavior was an incident that occurred when he was being watched by the neighbors. It was a cold winter day and when our neighbor came to let out Kelty, he escaped and ran up the road. We live in a close-knit neighborhood with lots of houses nearby, so usually Kelty was easy to locate. This time the neighbor had a difficult time and was starting to get nervous because of his delayed return. Just as he was getting ready to hunt him down by car, he spotted Kelty heading down the sidewalk carrying something in his mouth. When he got close, the neighbor couldn't believe his eyes. Somewhere in his travels, Kelty had stolen a five-gallon bucket of ice cream from one of the neighbors and was excited to be bringing the treat home. We never did figure out where he had found the ice cream, but often think about the people who were most likely very puzzled at the loss of their dessert.

As naughty and undisciplined as Kelty was, he possessed an even bigger heart. He was one of those dogs who just couldn't sit close enough to you. He greeted me with such enthusiasm it just warmed my soul, and he had one of those intuitive spirits that turned a challenging day into a joyful one. He made me so happy that I began to call him my "sunshine boy." I sang "You Are My Sunshine" to him from the time he was a puppy all the way through his life. When I sang the song, he would thump his tail, give me kisses, and smile. If I sang other songs to him, he listened but didn't respond. It was only with the sunshine song that we shared a special connection.

Kelty lived for twelve and a half years. We walked twenty-five miles a week and he loved running errands with me in the car. When our children left for college, he was the one who soothed my heart and reminded me that I was not alone. I still had my sunshine boy. So when he became ill, it was heartbreaking. I hadn't realized how much he had infiltrated every aspect of my life. It broke my heart that the time was coming when I would have to say goodbye. Kelty taught me so many lessons, most of all what it meant to give unconditional love. He truly made me a better person.

One of the saddest days of my life was when we took Kelty to the veterinarian's office to say goodbye. Although it was very difficult to stay with him for his last breath, I wouldn't have had it any other way. The last words I spoke to him were to remind him that he was my sunshine boy.

The house was so incredibly empty and my husband and I were really struggling with our loss. We decided to travel to New York City and we put together a busy itinerary that included a trip to the Statue of Liberty and Ellis Island. We had to wait in line for an hour and a half and toward the front of the line there was a street performer who was entertaining the crowd. He was asking the tourists where they were from and then singing a song about their hometown. He was very funny and I was enjoying his witty songs.

When I got toward the front, I was munching peanuts, as was a young man behind me. The street performer picked on the two of us about being peanut lovers and challenged the young man to sing a song to me, his fellow peanut enthusiast. The young man was quite embarrassed and graciously declined. The street performer told him that was okay and that he would sing me a song. And what song, out of all of the songs in the world did he choose? Yes, he sang, "You Are My Sunshine." I stood totally overwhelmed with tears running down my face for he was singing the song that had brought such joy to Kelty and me.

I do not believe in coincidences. I believe it was a message to me, from my loving dog to remind me that he may not be physically alive, but that his spirit would forever live within my heart. I believe it was his way of letting me know that he was just fine and that special relationships have the ability to transcend death.

He will always be "my sunshine boy."

~Laurie Whitermore

81

The Last Gift

A dog has one purpose in life. To bestow his heart.
~J.B. Aukerly

I met her at a stable of all places. I had gone there to see a friend's new horse even though I've never been a horse person. The barn dogs knew it and took charge of me. I, a dog person, was a rarity in this place. The Australian Shepherd assigned to the owner kept busy with the main man's movements. It quickly dispatched me to another dog. The dog that undertook my care was the obvious hostess, a Golden Retriever, that made me feel at home as graciously as a southern lady would do.

It was only later, as I was leaving, that I saw the one I would come to think of as Brown Lucy. No one knew her name, they said, but that was what I called her. Abandoned, a stable hand told me. They awoke one morning months earlier to find her there, dropped off. She was a chocolate Labrador. There was something in the way that she sprawled on the ground that got my attention. I tried to look away after I'd realized what I had done, but it was too late. She'd felt my lingering attention, and just as if I had called her, she struggled to her feet. As she made her way toward me, I realized what had struck me about her. She had been busy dying there on the straw.

But she tried to take a break from death as she limped down the long walk past several stalls. I reached out my hand, hovering it over her head in the still of the barn. Her tail was paralyzed, and the odor of the urine that had run down her hindquarters stung my nose.

Her fur was matted and sticky looking. Flies surrounded her back end. But none of those was the reason I was afraid to touch her. At first it was an automatic reaction. There were no welcoming signals from her, no expression. But I finally realized she was too paralyzed or too sick for expression. The very fact that she had dragged herself all that way to greet me said it all. It's with shame that I admit I was afraid of what I would feel if I began to pet her, as if all the pain of dying could somehow come up through her stiff-as-a-whisk-broom fur. But I caught the selfishness of it, remembering the trouble she'd gone through to interrupt what must be the incredible absorption of dying just to see me, a dog person.

I tentatively lowered my hand onto her head and was shocked at how quickly we began to bond. She had an indescribable sense of peace about her. It was clear that this dog knew what love was—knew it enough to put aside the dying for it. As I stroked her gently, my hand became coated with barn filth, but I didn't want to release the feeling I got from this exquisite creature. There was such a beauty about her.

Dogs accept death much more easily than we do. They don't think about what was or what might have been or what may come. They just live and accept dying as part of it. Her calm, easy embrace of life—along with its end—was joyously complete. I needed to feel it as much, if not more, than she needed to remember what love was. I wondered if she had been loved by an older person who couldn't take care of her when her bladder started to go. Maybe a grown child had struck a compromise and dropped her here to finish. The horse people were kind. They had taken her to a vet, but the dog was clearly very old. She would live her last days treated with dignity. She lay down at my feet, almost collapsing, exhausted from the journey of perhaps twenty feet. I knelt down and tried to give her the honor she deserved. I waved away the flies and stroked her enough, I hoped, to last all of her remaining time.

I later learned that Brown Lucy died peacefully the next day. I thought of all she had gone through just so that she could spend her last minutes with a dog person. I felt proud that she had derived her last moments of love from me. I was glad I could give her that one last gift. But no, I was told. The stable owner had fallen in love with her, too. Everyone doted on her. That was when I realized it. It wasn't for her sake that she had dragged her dying self to collapse at my feet. It was for mine. That, after all, is what a dog's heart is… a gift. A generosity of spirit that reaches out to the last breath, into the deepest beginnings of the soul. It is genuine, selfless, a sacrifice sometimes. And isn't that what love itself ultimately is? I will forever be honored at Brown Lucy's gift — the gift of a few minutes, the gift of an invaluable lesson. The gift of a lifetime.

~T'Mara Goodsell

A Boy and His Dog

A dog teaches a boy fidelity, perseverance,
and to turn around three times before lying down.
~Robert Benchley

Every boy in America should grow up with a dog. I grew up with Queeny, a mixed-breed mutt that my family rescued from the local dog pound. Obtained as a one-year-old puppy, Queeny and I were about the same age. She was seven in dog years and I was nine in people years.

It was a match made in heaven. Having just moved to a new home in rural, southern Ohio, Queeny and I enjoyed the perfect place for a boy and his dog to grow up together. This bucolic, five-acre lot possessed a peaceful pond, a small woodland, and a meandering creek, all meant to be played in. And play we did. Queeny ran the bases with me when my brothers and I played baseball. She jogged along beside me during bicycle rides. She revealed my hiding spots when we boys played hide-and-seek. She was my scout dog when we played Army.

However, over those two years of playing, Queeny matured faster than I did. She became a frisky female of twenty-one in dog years, while I was an ignorant boy of eleven in people years. Consequently, Queeny taught me about "the birds and the bees" in a way that no tongue-tied parent ever could. My dad, God bless him, tried to explain to me how Queeny was "in heat," but the words went right over my head. All I knew was that suddenly every male dog in the neighborhood was frequenting our backyard. For some reason, they all tried to climb upon Queeny's back, and it looked like they were hurting her. Thus, I remember chasing them all away with my Daisy BB gun. Evidently, I missed one, because Queeny began to change. First she became antisocial. A normally affectionate and loving dog, Queeny preferred to be left alone. Second she became a ravenous eater. I wondered why.

Six weeks after the beginning of these changes I was playing with a very sluggish Queeny. I rolled her onto her back because she loved to have her belly scratched, and I noticed eight tiny protuberances beginning to show through her fur. What was going on? But it didn't really matter because Queeny didn't like playing anymore either. She was easily tired after having gained so much weight, and all she wanted to do was sleep.

Nine weeks after the start of those changes, Queeny surprised us all. Up until then Queeny never slept in the doghouse that we had built for her. Instead, she always slept on the back deck where she could survey the domain that she had been charged with protecting. But for some reason on that April night, she chose to crawl into the doghouse and curl up on those old, musty blankets. Leave it to Queeny to educate a clueless, eleven-year-old boy on the miracle of birth, maternal instincts, and mother-offspring bond. Mouth agape and eyes wide open, I trained a flashlight upon the slimy fur balls crawling around her belly. In my pre-teen awkwardness, I stared at Queeny nursing those same slimy fur balls. She actually nipped at my hand when I tried to pick up one of the puppies.

Life marched on. With the removal of the "FREE PUPPIES" sign from the end of our country lane, Queeny and I entered a more responsible, working stage of our lives. Queeny sat at the bottom of the ladder as I painted the barn. She slept with me in the garden to prevent raccoons from ravaging our sweet corn. She walked along beside me as I mowed the backyard. Over the next two years of toiling, Queeny matured faster than I did again. At thirty-five in dog years, she was at the peak of her femininity. Meanwhile, I was a dorky boy struggling through life at thirteen in people years.

Then one summer night, a tragedy occurred, and thank God I slept through it. Queeny's incessant barking woke Mom and Dad and they went outside to investigate. At the end of the house, they saw a marauding raccoon scurry into the pond to escape Queeny's wrath. Naturally, she dove into the pond in hot pursuit. In the ensuing chase, the raccoon pulled a rapid reversal of direction and pounced upon Queeny, shoving her head under water.

The next morning, being the oldest boy, I was assigned the obvious task. As I waded into our pond to retrieve Queeny's body my bottom lip quivered. I found her floating head down, with rigor mortis having already set in. I grabbed her tail with both hands and pulled her stiff, dripping body from the water.

My brothers and I buried Queeny on "Cemetery Hill" overlooking the pond. We laid her to rest next to King, a male dog that had been hit by a car, and an unnamed duckling, an Easter gift that had died. With a tear in my eye, I placed the last shovel load of dirt upon the grave. Even in death, Queeny was still teaching me lessons. That life is a precious gift, and it can quickly be snatched away, far earlier than expected.

I suppose that Queeny's story would be more worthy of "Lassie status" if she had performed a heroic deed during her lifetime. Unfortunately, Queeny never barked in the middle of the night to awaken us to a burning house. And she never drove off a burglar, intent on ravaging our humble home. She never pulled my injured body from the railroad tracks as a train approached. No, Queeny was just a country dog. But she was my dog—like the one that every boy in America should grow up with.

~John Scanlan

Her Unforgettable Smile

Faithful friends are gifts from heaven:
Whoever finds one has found a treasure.
~Author Unknown

I didn't plan on finding her. And I most certainly didn't plan on keeping the thin, smelly, slightly mangy stray. But there she was, having just been rescued from a chilly rain, dripping wet and shivering on my kitchen floor. As I mused about her future—attempting to dry her with an old towel—she smiled at me. And I mean smiled. This wasn't an ordinary smile. This was a lip-curling, nose-wrinkling, eye-squinting, smile with a mangy tail beating *allegretto vivace*. At thirty-three years old, I had never experienced anything like it. I'd witnessed contented canine expressions from friends' dogs, an excited beaming from family pets, and even glimpsed mischievous smirks on proverbial dog calendars, but this was an exchange of high-voltage joy that leapt from her heart into mine and instantly guaranteed her rescue.

It wasn't until much later that I realized it was she who rescued me. Frannie taught me to fully embrace life. Throughout our thirteen-year journey together across two states, three cities and two suburbs, Frannie taught me how to be authentic and find joy every day. Her unbridled love of water taught me how to jump right in. Her tireless delight in playing tug of war modeled how to grab hold and not let go. Each time she disemboweled a stuffed toy, I was reminded to look for what's inside. Watching her prance on a walk, or run through the field, I learned how to move forward and how to finish first. Every tilt of her head at the sound of my voice instructed me in how to question, every prod of my hand to pet her reminded me how to ask for what you need. Her insatiable delight at getting treats taught me grace in accepting gifts.

I learned how to always find the light as I watched her seek out the warmest spot of sunlight on the floor every morning after break-fast. I learned just when to be small and when to be grand, watching her nap sprawled across the bed or curled into a crescent. I even discovered the intense courage it takes to own fear and vulnerability, sitting alongside her on the floor of my closet as she trembled during thunderstorms. But most of all I learned the magic of a smile.

She smiled valiantly at everyone. Friends, family, the vet, deliv-ery boys and pedestrians all experienced her generosity. Even the frequent wide-eyed responses, "Oh, isn't that a Pit Bull? Mister, hold her back, she's showing her teeth!" didn't daunt Frannie. She would simply continue to smile, until they got it. Until they felt it. Time after time, I witnessed Frannie's smile work its magic as human apprehen-sion melted into grins, erupted into smiles and rose to laughter. Old or young, male or female, every race, religion and culture responded with widespread glee to the universal joy of her unforgettable smile.

As weeks became months and months turned into years, the exuberant, loving presence of this sweet dog worked more and more of its magic on me. I began to find myself thinking less about my own life's direction and more about our collective passage. From Hudson County, New Jersey to Columbia County, New York, down to my hometown in central Jersey and then to Manhattan, we were a team. I rejected dozens of apartments in unsavory neighborhoods or with pet restrictions in New York City until we settled in upper Manhattan. I planned a vacation based solely on my desire to take Frannie someplace she could swim every day. While exhilarated by the idea of a cross-country change of life in California together, I secretly rejected the plan wondering whether that much upheaval might be too challenging for her at her elderly age.

In the summer of 2007, our journey took us on yet another adventure, from a fourth-floor studio walk-up in Manhattan to a Bronx one-bedroom apartment with an elevator. On the interminably hot August night Frannie and I drove to the new apartment I excitedly prepared her, "Wait until we get home Frannie! It's a brand new place… quieter, with more space, and no more stairs!"

I was ecstatic. I had succeeded in finding her a home without stairs to irritate her fourteen-year-old joints. Even better, it was near a huge park with a large pond blocks away. At last, her senior years would be spent in greater comfort. Ironically, as our new life was expanding, so was an undetected cancerous tumor inside her. Returning from a two-day out-of-town job one late November night, I found Frannie breathing laboriously and without her usual energy. That night, four days before Thanksgiving, she was hospitalized and diagnosed with an inoperable mass in her left lung and suffering from fluid building in her chest cavity every twenty-four hours.

True to form, she left the hospital smiling at all her caregivers, with a bleak prognosis and difficulty breathing. At that moment we became inseparable. For the next three days, we rested on the bed together listening to music, looking at pictures of our shared life, having friends visit. I read her poetry and told her how deeply I loved her. After days of praying, crying, and bargaining with the universe, I awoke at four o'clock on Thanksgiving morning to her coughing. As I watched her straining to breathe, I made the heartbreaking decision I'd been avoiding. I began cooking. The turkey, stuffing, gravy, potatoes and cranberry sauce I made were not to grace my table, but simply for her. A friend joined us as I fed her, played with her, and cried when she smiled once again in my arms while her doctor sent her to rest in the living room of our new home.

It will be three years without Frannie in November. My heart remains filled with light in all the places she touched, and somehow still broken as well. My now not-so-new home is much quieter. The world around me seems at once more solitary and more beautiful, and every day I remember her lessons. Amidst life's stresses and trials, I'm both challenged and inspired to ask for what I need, to look for what's inside, to jump right in and to always find the light. But most importantly when I see the stars shining or feel the sun on my face, I remember the transformational power of Frannie's spirit as I forever carry with me her unforgettable smile.

~Victor Barbella

My Dog's Life

Over the Rainbow

84

Unexpected Blessing

Dogs have a way of finding the people who need them,
Filling an emptiness we don't even know we have.
~Thom Jones

My brother, Chris, swung open our door with a very cheery "Merry Christmas!" This greeting was swiftly followed with a "Surprise!" as a big dirty Siberian Husky named Ghost came in behind him. He handed the dog's lead to my sixteen-year-old daughter, Aubrey.

"Wow!" she squealed with delight, as she ran up and grasped the dog by his neck in an embrace, her long blond hair dangling over the dog's head. The dog's piercing blue eyes showed little concern.

I was not happy about this. My dog, Fremont, was ill. She was a Shiba Inu, a smaller stocky dog, which I had owned for sixteen years. I didn't want another dog in the house to take care of. All I wanted was my dog to get better. However, I also knew that my daughter was dealing with teenage pressures and needed and wanted her own friend, so I didn't say no to Ghost entering our little family.

"Get him cleaned up. He's filthy," I complained.

Ghost had been living outside on my brother's farm. Chris decided to give him to Aubrey because Ghost liked to kill chickens, and he was afraid another farmer would shoot the dog. It was better for Ghost to live in a house with two women and a sick dog than to get shot. Even I couldn't argue with that.

Chris and Aubrey pulled the unwilling dog into the bathroom.

He didn't whine, but he didn't do anything to help them either. I could hear the laughter and splashing of water. When the door opened the wet dog walked into the middle of the room and shook. Water and hair went everywhere.

"Get him dried off and keep him away from Fremont," I snapped.

"If you give him a chance you'll like him," Aubrey whined.

"We don't need another dog and I am not going to be the one stuck with taking care of him," I said. I paused and added, "We are on a week trial. If it doesn't work out, we will need to find him another home."

Fremont wandered into the living room. Her frail body showed signs of advanced age, with ribs protruding through thin hair. Her hearing was almost gone as was her eyesight. The cancer had progressed, but she was still able to get around. The vet's words echoed in my head, "If she seems to be in pain for more than three days, we will know it's time." We all knew these were her last days, but I cleaned up her messes and took care of her without complaint. I knew that it wouldn't be long before I would be without her.

Ghost, being a young dog, was big and playful. With his tail wagging, he lunged at Fremont. On wobbly legs, Fremont bared her teeth and growled, the brown hair on her neck standing.

"Aubrey, get that dog out of here!" I yelled, pulling Ghost back by the scruff of his neck. "Fremont comes first; keep that dog away from her!"

"I will, I will," she promised. But by the end of the week I was at my wit's end.

There were clumps of white fur everywhere. Ghost bothered Fremont, acting like her boss. I resented Ghost more than anything else because he was healthy. That night I spoke with Aubrey at the dinner table.

"The week is up and Ghost needs to go," I said. "We can find him a home or take him to the shelter." Aubrey's blue eyes filled with tears.

"No, I love him! He's my best friend. You can't do this," she pleaded.

"He is just too much work. He sheds everywhere and he is so big. He is always in the way," I said.

"If you get rid of him, I'm leaving too," she said, her little body shaking as she cried.

There wasn't much else I could do. Ghost would have to stay and I would just have to get used to it, whether I liked it or not. I decided that I could put up with him, but that's all I would do.

If he whined to go on a walk, I wouldn't take him. If he asked for a treat, I wouldn't give him one. If his water bowl was empty, I wouldn't fill it. When he laid his head in my lap, his eyes looking sad, ears back, I wouldn't pet him. Anything he needed would just have to wait until Aubrey could do it for him. He wasn't my dog and I wasn't dealing with him.

I called the vet on a rainy Monday morning. Fremont was up all night, in pain. She tried to go up the stairs and fell. She couldn't eat or drink. It was time to relieve her suffering. The vet came to the house and put her to sleep, quietly, peacefully. We buried her under a green leafy tree in the woods where she liked to run. I thought she would like that.

The first few weeks after her death were the hardest. For sixteen years, she went to bed with me, sleeping on a blanket next to my bed. That night I went to bed and faced the dark by myself. I felt completely alone. She wasn't there to greet me when I returned home from work, her tail wagging with joy. She wasn't there to eat the left over tuna fish when I made a sandwich. She wasn't there to make sure I got my exercise because she had to go for a walk. The pain and loneliness were almost unbearable.

It is strange how animals sense things. Ghost knew something was wrong. He was quiet and reserved, like he was trying to keep a low profile and not get in the way. His bouncy attitude was gone. It was like he was sad too. So, when he came to me and laid his head in my lap, I petted him. He was actually a lot softer than I thought he would be. His white coat felt like down pillows, his light blue eyes seemed kind, and his ears perked up at my touch. Suddenly all the things that annoyed me about him disappeared. I smiled.

I started going on walks with Aubrey and Ghost, and it felt comforting. Ghost's happy, spunky personality seemed to bring out some happiness in me. Watching him wag his tail and run around, or get so excited about the snow that he tripped going out the door, made me laugh. And although I still missed Fremont, letting myself love Ghost added great joy to my life and was a blessing.

Now when someone compliments me on what a great dog I have, I smile and say, "Yes he is." Until Aubrey retaliates, "Just remember... he's my dog."

~Robin Sokol

The Bus Stop

The bond with a true dog is as lasting as the ties of this earth will ever be.
~Konrad Lorenz

At a time in my life when nothing was clear and I was feeling overwhelmed, it was the love and consistent behavior of my dog that allowed me to endure. Some people have a baby as a mechanism to save their marriage, but I chose to rescue a dog in the hopes that the dog would rescue my marriage. This half-Labrador, half-Newfoundland was the runt of the litter and could not have been more odd looking. With his small chiseled Labrador face that gave way to a pear-shaped Newfoundland body, he seemed to represent just how divergent my marriage was, and I fell in love with him immediately.

During the first few days of our life together, I was feeling particularly vulnerable and uncertain about myself. He seemed to sense this and stayed by my side constantly. When I went to bed, he would sleep on the floor by my side of the bed. I would lean over and pet him as we were falling asleep, as much to comfort myself as to comfort him.

"You are a beautiful boy and I am a wonderful person," I said. "So you be you, and I'll be me, and we will be fine." And that is how he was given his name, UBU.

For years we enjoyed an incredible relationship that was not understood by anyone but envied by many. I would speak in a normal tone of voice and Ubu would respond to my directions without hesitation. It would drive my mother crazy that the dog would obey a soft-spoken word from me, but could not be bribed to listen to her.

The first time I had to travel for business, I took Ubu to my mother's house along with three pages of written instructions for his care. My mother, having raised four children and nurtured countless cats and dogs, disregarded the instructions. The next day when I called to check in, my mother sounded exhausted and frustrated.

"That dog of yours would not lie down for one minute last night. He kept pacing around the house, looking out the windows, and whining at the door," she said.

"Did you follow my instructions for his bedtime?" I asked. She was supposed to say, "Ubu honey, Mama is not coming home tonight, but she loves you, and she will be home soon."

Declaring that that was the most ridiculous thing that she ever heard, I was expecting my mother to again endure a sleepless night. However, when I called the next day, my mother started the conversation with, "I would have never imagined…" and proceeded to tell me that after speaking those magic words, Ubu slept soundly on the side of the bed all night.

Ubu's dedication to me never faltered even after I gave birth to my daughter. For the first several nights, Ubu would parade back and forth between my side of the bed and my daughter's crib, until I finally told him, "You know your mama loves you and she knows that you love her, but it is time for you to take care of your sissy, so you stay with her." From that moment on, Ubu would come into my bedroom once during the evening and then spend the rest of the night in my daughter's room.

Ubu endured so much from us, an infant that used him as a sleeping bag, a divorce that left him wondering why his other master was not coming home, a toddler learning to walk by using him to pull herself up, and finally a move to a new home. Regardless of the changes in his life, Ubu was constant in his love and devotion to me, so I was devastated when the veterinarian told me that he had cancer and would live only six more months. I was not ready to live my life without Ubu, so every day, I said, "You are a healthy boy today. Your mama loves you."

For six more years, no one would believe that Ubu had cancer. He ate well, played with his sissy, walked her to the bus stop each morning for school, and continued to enjoy the daily loving attention from his mama. The only indication that something was not right was that Ubu no longer slept next to Sissy or my bed in the night. Instead, he started to sleep on a blanket near the back door. At first, I would go out and ask him if he wanted to join me in the bedroom, but he would just gently thump his tail and put his head on his paws. We altered our bedtime routine so that I could lie next to him for several minutes and give him loving attention.

One night, Ubu's breathing became labored. I spent the night with him on his bed. It was the first time that I could see he was struggling. I assured him that I would call the vet in the morning and that I was strong enough not to have him suffer. I would stay with him and love him and allow him to leave. The next morning, I called the vet and he agreed to see us as soon as my daughter left for school. My daughter wondered why Ubu was not walking her to the bus stop but I just told her that he wasn't feeling well, so she had better give him some extra hugs and kisses.

As we walked out the back door, I looked back at him with love in my eyes and a smile on my face. After putting my daughter on the bus, I thought I would never be able to make the walk up the driveway to bring Ubu to the vet. I was so afraid that I could not endure to watch the vet put him down. I was trembling, sobbing, and could barely breathe, but before I got to the back door, I knew that I had to show Ubu the same love and support that he had shown me all those years. I straightened my shoulders, lifted my head, wiped my eyes, and swallowed the lump in my throat. When I opened the back door, I saw that Ubu had passed while we were at the bus stop. Knowing that I would have suffered considerably if I had to take him to the vet, even in his death, Ubu took care of me.

~Judith Fitzsimmons

86

The Last Hunt

There is no faith which has never yet been broken,
except that of a truly faithful dog.
~Konrad Lorenz

That November was not like any November that I can remember. The weather had been unusually warm with clear skies, calm winds, and temperatures in the fifties. It was as if we were in an Indian Summer after Indian Summer. Not the best weather for hunting ducks but we had a few in the area. Another difference was that I was a year older, and so was my beloved black Lab, Boo. Boo was eighteen and in two months he would be nineteen. The old man had chronic hip problems, cataracts in both eyes, and was almost deaf, but the drive and love of the hunt was still in him.

My father called and wanted to hit the water the next day. I told him I would see him at 4:00 a.m. After I hung up the phone I began to prepare for the next day's adventure. After years of witnessing this routine Boo knew exactly what I was doing and anxiously followed me around the house. As I piled my loot by the back door Boo inspected it all. Seemingly satisfied that I had not forgotten anything, Boo went to his bed. Uttering the sounds made by old men with ailments, Boo grunted, then settled into his nest. I massaged his legs and back which always seemed to help him sleep. Once he appeared to be counting sheep I retired to bed.

Three a.m. came early and I was surprised to find that Boo was not in his bed. Groggy-eyed, I stumbled into the other room and found him sleeping near the stuff I had piled by the back door. Apparently I wasn't the only one looking forward to a day in the field. The phone rang and it was my dad.

"Have you looked outside this morning?" he asked.

Phone in hand, I went to the back door and noticed that it was a bone-chilling eighteen degrees. I went outside to find the wind blowing the snow sideways. The frozen water felt like razor blades as it bit into my cheeks.

"Looks like duck weather to me, Dad," I said.

"Maybe to you, but I'm staying home," he replied. I laughed and teased him about getting old, and told him I would call when I got home. After loading the truck I found Boo waiting for his courtesy lift into the flat bed. The old man could no longer jump up there by himself. Once Boo was in we hit the road. I parked in the edge of the trees about a quarter mile from my favorite quacker hole. I helped Boo from the truck, grabbed a bag of decoys, and my gun, and we were off.

Unlike past years Boo no longer bounced from bush to bush with his nose to the ground, searching in every crevice that a bird might hide. With age and wisdom came the realization that if he just walked patiently beside me I would eventually drop a feathery treat from the skies for him. We reached the water's edge and the old, rundown plywood blind I had constructed many seasons prior. Boo felt right at home, adjourning to his spot under the bench while I tossed decoys into the pond. When I was done I joined the old man inside the comfort of the blind, out of the wind and the bad weather. Together we patiently waited for the first rays of light, the wind still howling and the icy snow still traveling on its horizontal trip.

As dawn began to break I could hear the faint whistling of wings in the distance but the weather prohibited me from seeing my quarry. The first birds to come in, two hens and a drake, were traveling with the wind at mach 4. I raised my shotgun and fired at the greenhead which subsequently fell from the sky.

Boo bolted from the blind to the edge of the water and froze. He twisted his head left and right while pawing at the water's surface. I had seen this several times over the last few seasons; the bird had come down outside of Boo's failing vision. I put my gun down and stepped out of the blind. Boo was whining with excitement, so desperately wanting that downed greeny. As I have done many times, I dragged the old rickety canoe from its hiding place in the cattails and pushed its nose into the water. The boat crunched through the thin skiff of ice that had formed at the water's edge. Boo gently stepped into the boat and took his place in the bow. I took up a paddle and silently moved us across the choppy surface, Boo watching intently with his ears perked up.

As we neared the downed bird Boo saw him and locked in. I paddled up beside the drake and the old man reached over and plucked him from the water. With the grace and ease that only comes with years of practice Boo walked the length of the canoe without so much as a wobble and deposited the dead fowl in my hand. Fully expecting and thus receiving the ear scrubs and head pats for a job well done, Boo laid down between my feet for the ride back to the reeds.

After settling back into the blind, the wind and weather started to break and the warm rays of a fall sun began to warm us up. Out of nowhere a single hen came screaming into the decoys. It took three shots to bring her down. Boo saw this one and in no time I had her in hand.

The rest of the morning was slow, no birds to speak of, no more shots fired. I sat waiting for just one more bird. Boo was unusually restless. He would sleep for a while and then sit up and put his head in my lap. I would give him pats and love and he would lie back down, only to repeat the process a short time later. After a while, Boo stood up and stretched, and I knew what that meant, nap time. Boo couldn't hunt all day like he used to and it was normal for him to take a nap in the late morning sun.

Boo got up and I watched over my shoulder as he stepped behind the blind into the full rays of the sun. The old man did his three circles and lay on the ground. I continued to wait for "just one more duck" but that bird never came. It was almost noon and the sun was high, the weather once again warm. The birds were done flying for the day and I figured it was time to head in. I exited my shoot house to wake the old man. As I stepped to the back of the blind and placed my hand on Boo's head my heart broke. I knew in an instant that this had been Boo's last hunt. My dear old friend was gone.

In a daze I sat down beside him and pulled his head into my lap. I sat there in the warm sun and petted my dog. I have no idea how long I sat with him. I finally noticed the sun was getting lower. I had been expected home hours ago. I pulled myself to my feet and picked up my friend. Cradling him in my arms I left everything else behind and walked the quarter mile back to my truck. I placed my companion in the back seat and made the never-ending drive home.

I dug a grave for him under a weeping willow tree where he used to lie in the shade. I placed his bed in the bottom, gave him one last hug, and moved him into his eternal home. The sun was almost gone, and the sky was on fire with shades of red, orange, and gold glowing on the horizon. As I knelt beside a pile of earth that held within it one of my dearest friends I heard a single, hollow honk of a goose. I looked up to see the distinctive "V" of a flock of geese flying low over the pasture. The air was still and the only noise was the wind in their wings as they flew closer. As they approached I stood up and the birds broke, flaring in all directions as they passed overhead. A short distance later, like a squadron of well trained fighter jets, they were once again traveling in formation. As they drifted out of sight one bird sounded off with a single "honk." I know it was just birds doing what birds do but with all my heart I would like to believe that they did it for Boo.

~D.V.C.

87

Letting Go

A dog will teach you unconditional love. If you can have that in your life,
things won't be too bad.
~Robert Wagner

He was the kids' dog, really. Even though my husband, David, and I had Blaze for years before the kids came along, from the moment we stepped from the car with that first little bundle in our arms, he was theirs and they were his. David gave Blaze a lecture, that day, about watching over the baby, a lecture he seemed to take seriously. Anytime I strolled any one of our three infants, Blaze managed to walk alongside the stroller with his head tucked inside resting on the baby, stopping from time to time to give the neighborhood dogs a don't-even-think-about-it look.

When our second daughter was born, Blaze found a spot under a tree equidistant between the two girls' bedroom windows and that's where he slept each night, ready to protect his girls from anything that might threaten them. As toddlers they learned their body parts by poking Blaze in the eye and proclaiming "eeeeye," yanking on his ear and announcing "eeeeear," lifting up his floppy gums to reveal "teeeeeeth." They learned to walk by steadying themselves with a hunk of his hair and took many a nap curled up against him.

When they started school, Blaze perfected an internal clock that told him the exact moment the school bus would appear each day and his kids would be home. If I got caught up in a project and lost track of time, it was Blaze who reminded me it was time to take a walk to the end of the driveway and wait for them. Yes, he was their dog and they were his kids.

That's why I began to worry when I noticed him slowing down. For a year before Blaze died, whenever the opportunity presented itself, I pointed out to the kids that Blaze was getting older and that dogs don't live as long as people, hoping to prepare them for the inevitable. But at sixteen he looked so hearty that none of us were prepared for the day we took a walk and, for the first time, Blaze didn't join us. I laughed "What do you suppose that old rascal's up to?" But I privately offered a prayer, "Oh, please, God. Not yet."

We kidded ourselves, when he refused to eat, that he must have been double dipping at one of the neighbor's houses and just wasn't hungry. But within a few weeks the kids were coming into the house with reports of "Mom, Blaze won't play with me" and "Blaze just lies there looking sad, Mom," and finally "MOM! Blaze is acting like he can't breathe!"

The next thing I knew, we were standing at the vet's office deciding whether to take him home to die or have him put to sleep. I looked at the kids, Haley who was eight, Molly, six, and Hewson, three, who were searching my eyes to try to understand what was happening. I thought about my own childhood dog, Sarge. When Sarge was killed by a car, my parents told us he'd gone off to live on a farm where he'd have lots of room to run and play.

It was a lie I believed until I was grown and figured out the truth. I couldn't do that to my kids. This was their dog and a member of our family. But I wanted desperately to spare them the pain I felt welling up inside me. I thought about rushing out, today—this second—and buying them a puppy. They'd fall in love with it, forget Blaze, and their hurt would disappear, and with it my pain at watching their pain. I looked at the vet for help. She gave me a look which told me what I already knew. He was their dog. They were a big part of his life. I couldn't deprive them of being part of his death, too.

I sat down on the floor next to Blaze, who was struggling to breathe. "You all have taken such good care of our Blaze. Every single day of your lives, he knew he was loved. You always made sure he had food and water. You played with him, shared your ice cream with him—even when I told you not to. How many millions of peanut butter and jelly crusts do you think he ate?" We laughed and Blaze dropped his old head in my lap. I could feel the tears coming and didn't try to stop them. "Blaze is in a lot of pain, now, guys. We don't want to let him keep hurting. Do we?" The vet said she that she would leave the room and give us time to say "Goodbye."

The next ten minutes were hard. I explained to them what the vet would do and tried to help them understand that it was the only decision we could make. We said our last goodbye a dozen times but just couldn't bring ourselves to get up and walk out the door. Finally, we decided to give him a family hug, count to ten, and leave without looking back. When we got home, we held a ceremony in his sleeping spot between the kids' bedroom windows. We hung a hand-painted sign with his name on it. Molly read a poem she'd written about him. Haley presented a piece of artwork she'd made from a photo of him and her together. "All he ever wanted was to love us and make us happy," she said. I had underestimated my kids. They understood—maybe better than I did. They loved Blaze and wanted what was best for him. I'm sure I'll be answering questions and drying tears, for months to come. But I'm glad I decided to let them be a part of the end of Blaze's life. He was, after all, their dog.

~Mimi Greenwood Knight

Saving Grace

Here, Gentlemen, a dog teaches us a lesson in humanity.
~Napoleon Bonaparte

A dog named Grace died in my minivan on date night. That's not what we planned for our evening out. My husband and I had escaped from Chaos Central, aka home, and were returning home after dinner. We were on a busy five-lane road when a bleeding Spaniel slowly limped over and lay down in the middle of the road.

"Oh God," I said, upon closer look. "Someone just hit him."

My husband, who is in law enforcement, slowed down the car. Should we just drive by? Call for help? Who should we call? We pulled over into the turning lane to block anyone else from hitting it. Traffic whizzed past us. It was dangerous in the middle of the road, but I looked into the dog's pleading eyes. We had to help.

We had given up our Beagle several years before when my dad was diagnosed with brain tumors stemming from melanoma. Our adorable but needy dog had required constant attention, the kind of attention you can't provide when your dad is suddenly dying, your spouse is out of town for three months, one baby is toddling, and the other is potty-training. We made the difficult choice to place her with a family who had a farm and another Beagle. We kissed our cutie-pie goodbye... and never forgave ourselves.

Was this some kind of dog karma?

My husband ran to the nearby fire station to get help. I stood with the van's headlights and hazard lights on, and reassured the dog that it was going to be okay. I realized, as semis barreled by, that a chunk of the dog's body was missing. As the dog whimpered, I wondered what were we doing. This was supposed to be date night. My husband ran back, and said that the fire station had refused to help. Luckily, the dog's collar had a number and name. Her name was Grace.

We called Grace's owner. He lived nearby and he sprinted down the highway to where we were. We were shaken by his audible cry. He scooped up Grace and cradled her. We told him to get into our van and we'd drive to an animal hospital.

The ride was intense. The dog murmured and breathed quietly. The man's anguish was palpable. Grace was laying on him in our middle row, next to our daughter's booster seat and pink blanket. The man called his wife, and somewhere in our race against red lights, the sounds from the dog stopped.

We sprinted into the animal ER with the man and his lifeless dog. He was yelling, "Grace, hang in there, c'mon Grace!" His wife soon came running in. I will never forget her loud cries of despair. It was a scene that mimicked my heavy grief-stricken sobs when I'd lost my father: deep, guttural. We turned and walked out.

Grace died that night. Grace's owner told my husband the next day when he called to check on her. He thanked us, but either in grief or shock, he was surprised we called. Did he think we hit her? Did he wonder why we would stop for a random animal on the road?

I don't know why we were at that scene. Were we being punished for giving up Avery? Was it to comfort the dog or the owner? Realize the frailty of life? Or was it just luck I had a pastel blanket that could wrap his four-legged companion with love? And if we were going to risk our lives darting into five-lane traffic, why couldn't Grace have lived? Couldn't there have been a happy ending? What good did stopping do? Maybe we stopped because it was the right thing to do. Maybe we stopped because of the guilt over our Beagle. It was primal, but it was like we intruded on another family in crisis.

The pet smell was in my minivan for a while, yet I didn't rush to clean it out. I wanted to remember what it was like when I needed help, with my toddlers, my out-of-town spouse, and my dying dad who I loved more than anything. People reached out: neighbors offered hugs; coworkers' families made casseroles. We connected, if only for a moment. It was time to give that comfort back. We had been like that family—hearts heavy, gaping wounds, minds adrift. It was then when grace covered us. We are given the grace to bury dogs... or bury people. Grace is also reaching out to others in their sorrow—even if it's date night. But often grace comes when we least expect it, and sometimes it is just a dog.

~Kristine Meldrum Denholm

Double Love

I guess you don't really own a dog, you rent them,
and you have to be thankful that you had a long lease.
~Joe Garagiola

"It's a moving van," Joel, my six-year-old, announced one summer morning as he ran from the breakfast table to the front window. I joined him and we watched the truck move warily past us toward the only other house on our narrow, gravel road.

"Let's give them a country welcome," I suggested. Tami, my twelve-year-old, helped me make chocolate chip cookies and our family headed to meet our new neighbors. Rex, the Golden Retriever we'd recently rescued, bounded beside us. A Japanese woman answered the door. Within moments a man and a boy about Joel's age stepped up beside her.

"Hello," she said with a little bow, her eyes glowing with pleasure as I handed her the cookies. "I am Machiko Tomita. This is Mas, and our son Ken."

I introduced my family. Her eyes settled on Rex.

"He is so big," she said, her eyes sparkling. "And so beautiful. We have no dogs like this in Japan."

"He is very handsome." Mas nodded.

Rex was handsome, ninety pounds of gleaming, feathered coat, doleful brown eyes in a broad face, and a gentle disposition.

"How old is he?" Machiko asked as Ken tentatively ran his hand along Rex's long back.

"About two and a half. A teenager in dog years," I replied.

"A teenager. He wants to be busy and always meeting people," she said laughing. "Please come in. Excuse the boxes. Our boys can play."

We accepted a cup of tea and chatted for a few minutes about the neighborhood and about Mas's work.

"Where did you get Rex?" Machiko asked.

"His first owners didn't want him. They hardly fed him," I answered.

"How could anyone not want him?" Machiko asked in wonder, kneeling beside him and petting him. We visited a few more minutes, then my husband Hal, Tami and I headed home, leaving the boys to play. Rex trotted at our side. An hour passed before I realized Rex wasn't underfoot, as usual.

"Rex," I called out.

He didn't come. I went outside and called again. If he wandered down our road to the street it intersected, where the occasional car sped by, he'd be in danger. My heart lifted when I looked toward the Tomitas and he galloped into view, long ears flying.

"You're grounded for a week," I told him as he skidded to a stop and I gave him a hug. "You really worried me." But I couldn't be very angry with him. As a puppy, he probably hadn't felt wanted. Now he had new friends.

Within a week Rex was making daily trips to visit the Tomitas, like a teenager hanging out with his buddies.

"It's wonderful," Machiko assured me. "I never had a dog before."

At first I felt a stab of jealousy, but the feeling quickly evaporated. How could I deny Rex the added love and attention?

Rex courted Machiko the way a high school sophomore courts his first big crush. He often took her gifts, a slightly damp apple or orange from the fruit platter, cookies from a tray left on the counter, or a bag of chips intended for a child's lunch. Heading into the kitchen one afternoon, I saw him nose open a deep kitchen drawer, take a bag of corn flakes in his mouth, and carry it to the front door. Standing on his long hind legs, he put a front paw on the curved door handle and pressed down. One click and he was off to the Tomitas. In return, Machiko always had a dog treat for him.

With the awkwardness and exuberance of youth, he knocked flowerpots off the Tomitas' deck, stole sushi off their counter, and splashed water from a proffered water bowl all across their tiled kitchen floor. She forgave him everything.

It was a halcyon summer. The boys ran through a sprinkler on Machiko's front lawn, Rex pushing the sprinkler head around with his nose, spraying everyone from surprise angles. They gathered materials from our house-cum-construction site and built forts in the woods of fir, maple, and scrub oak that covered the hillside between our houses, Rex darting about, acting as foreman. Boys and dog splashed in the shallow creek that ran along the edge of the Tomitas' pasture, happy shouts filling the crisp country air. Then Rex put the Tomitas' generous hospitality at risk in true teenage style.

Machiko had been cleaning and cooking for days so she and Mas could entertain all the dignitaries connected with his job. I made sure Rex was at my side as the chatter of guests reached us, followed by the aroma of steaks on the grill. I was making a simpler meal of turkey tacos for my family and turned to offer Rex a bite of browning ground turkey, but he wasn't in the kitchen.

"Have you seen Rex?" I called to the kids, panic tightening my chest. I needn't have asked. I knew where he'd gone. I grabbed a leash and car keys. A big, salivating dog was surely the last thing the Tomitas would want on this important occasion. It took me minutes to drive up the hill, but Rex had already crashed the party and was circulating among the guests, feathered tail wagging. Machiko had filled a lovely, lacquered wooden bowl with water for him. Mas had given him a steak.

"He can stay. He is very welcome," Machiko assured me as I hurried to the deck, leash in hand, gushing apologies and feeling as out of place as my dog. I couldn't believe they weren't cross. Then

I looked at Rex's big Golden Retriever smile and understood. They truly loved him.

Over the next four years, our families shared every snow day, every outing to the park, every holiday. Rex was always with us. Then one day he grew desperately ill and I rushed him to the vet. An hour later I called Machiko, sobbing. "He has congestive heart failure. The vet can't do anything to save him."

"I want to say goodbye," Machiko said, her voice breaking.

We got Tami and the boys out of school and gathered around Rex in the waiting room of the veterinary hospital, tears streaming down our faces. I cradled his head in my lap, Machiko stroked his back, and the kids patted him and told him what a great dog he was. Machiko and I were both with him when he was euthanized and the two families gathered to bury him in the woods between our homes.

"It's so sad," Machiko said dabbing her eyes with a handkerchief. "Just six years old." I put my arm around her shoulders.

"But he had four wonderful years. Not many dogs have two families."

Machiko smiled wistfully. "That's right. We all really loved him. He went from no love to double love."

~Samantha Ducloux Waltz

No More Pain

When you are sorrowful look again in your heart, and you shall see that in truth you are weeping for that which has been your delight.
~Kahlil Gibran

I sat at the kitchen table reading the paper, working on my first cup of coffee when I heard the faint sounds of a dog's nails clicking on the hardwood floors. "Hey Spiker," I called out. The sound stopped so I got up from my chair, coffee cup in hand, and peeked down the hallway.

Spike had stopped in the middle of the hallway. Her hind legs had given out and were unable to carry her aging body further. Her tail began wagging as I walked toward her.

"Oh, Spiker, what's wrong?" I said as I bent over and gently picked her up. Her bones were stiff from arthritis and I could tell by the slobber under her chin that she recently had another seizure.

Spike was nearing the age of fifteen, which in people years I guess qualified her as a "centurion." Her once thick black hair was now gray and thinned. Spike's eyes were cloudy which I diagnosed as possible cataracts. Her hearing had failed, along with her eyesight. Her body, due to age and arthritis, no longer moved at speeds that once kept our backyard squirrels and birds on constant alert.

Tears welled up in my eyes.

"Oh, Spikerdog," I whispered, my voice cracking from emotion. "Is it time?" I continued, while tears poured from my eyes. "I don't know if I can do this." My heart ached.

"You know Spiker, you and I have been though a lot of stuff together," I said. Spike, who had been licking the tears from my face, stopped for a few seconds and started up again.

"Hey Mom, what's up?" interrupted my daughter.

"Good morning, Hannah. Spike's not doing so well," I replied.

"Are you crying?" she continued.

"Yes," I managed to whisper. I cleared my throat and continued talking, hoping my voice sounded stronger. "Spike's body is failing her. She can't use her back legs anymore."

"Oh Spikerdog," Hannah sobbed. "You are such a good friend."

Yes, Spike was a good friend. In the fifteen years that Spike had been a part of my life, we had lived in Washington, DC, Montana, Virginia, and Minnesota. Our family had grown and changed, too. Spike adapted to every change and welcomed the new smells, whether they resulted from a new house or new baby.

Of the towns we called home, Spike most enjoyed Montana, where she developed a taste for rolling in cow and horse droppings. Fortunately for Spike, we lived near the local rodeo grounds that were home to many cows and horses.

The local dog catcher nicknamed Spike "Houdini" due to her ability to wiggle out of even the most secure areas. Spike often escaped from our fenced-in yard or the dog catcher's truck and sniffed her way to her favorite spot in town, the rodeo grounds. After a couple of hours of fun, Spike returned home with evidence of her visit mashed into her coat.

My thoughts were interrupted by my son, Daniel.

"Mom," he said. "Is Spiker sick?"

Daniel walked over and rubbed Spiker's face. She licked his nose and then cleaned the sleep from his eyes. No matter how much pain this dog felt, no matter how little energy she had left in her body, she still felt that it was her job to care for us. Yes, she was a wonderful dog. But it was now time to say our goodbyes.

I drove up to our vet. Neither Hannah nor Daniel chose to accompany me. I was glad they had come to that decision on their own. I opened the front door and the receptionist immediately greeted me by first name. She told me she was so sorry to hear that Spike was not doing well but that she supported my decision.

"It generally works best if you pay up front," she said. "That way, we get the paperwork stuff out of the way."

"Oh, good idea," I said. Obviously, she had experienced this situation before.

I can't remember when spending fifty dollars hurt so much. My heart ached. I was shaking visibly and I found breathing difficult.

We sat in the waiting room. I wanted so badly to turn back the clock to when Spike was a puppy. I wanted her to run around her backyard or her "Queendom" as we often called it. I wanted her to chase the birds and the squirrels with the energy and enthusiasm of a puppy one last time.

"Sue," I looked up. It was our vet. In a quiet voice he told me that he was ready for us. I carried Spike into the examination room.

"I want to be here with her," I said.

By now my throat felt ten times its normal size and I could no longer control my tears.

"That's fine," he said. "You stay with Spike as long as you need to. You can hold her, too. I will give her a shot. Almost immediately, her eyes will close. It's painless. After a few seconds, I'll check her heart. It doesn't take too long. There will be no more pain."

No more pain. That's all I wanted now for this dog who had given me so much over the last fifteen years. No more pain for Spike. The vet injected the medicine and Spike's eyes closed. After a few seconds, the vet placed his stethoscope over her chest. He looked at me, nodded his head, laid his hand gently on Spike's side and whispered, "No more pain."

The vet left the room and I was now alone with my dog. I knew Spike was gone but I needed to stay with her. I laid my head on her body and cried. I thanked her for being such a good dog. I thanked her for loving us more than we ever expected. I thanked her for giving me so many memories and for the funny stories about cows and horses.

As I was getting ready to leave the examination room, I removed

Spike's collar. It was worn and tattered just like her body. I laughed as I held her collar and remembered how many times it went through our washer and dryer because of her adventures at the rodeo grounds.

It's been nearly six years now but I still have Spike's old collar. I keep it in a drawer in my nightstand. Every so often I inventory the items in that drawer. And every so often I toss a few things out but never the old collar. No, along with the pictures of Spike, that collar is full of memories and will always remind me of a wonderful dog. A dog I am grateful has no more pain.

~Sue Thompson

91

Going Home

Until one has loved an animal, a part of one's soul remains unawakened.
~Anatole France

When Dad surprised us with a visit he would ring the ship's bell by the entrance door of the garage until someone opened it. Then he would grin, revert back to his Navy days and salute before walking inside the house. A farmer in a small community and a career Navy man, Dad was small in stature but larger than life. He had bright, sky-blue eyes and was known for being a jokester, a rascal, and full of energy. His nickname was "Stubby" and he was a treat for all who knew him, especially his children and grandchildren. Dad was the glue that held the family together.

One Christmas Dad received a black Lab as a gift and he officially named him Bo. He took Bo to meet each of his children and grandchildren that day, his pride obvious. Bo was a smart dog and well behaved, even as a pup. After receiving that unique Christmas gift there wasn't a day that Bo wasn't with Dad everywhere he went.

The following spring, when Bo was only five months old, Dad was shocked to discover that he had cancer. For the next four weeks Dad and Bo were at our house every day, and he and I spent most evenings in the backyard, watching Bo play with the kids.

I will never forget the morning Dad rang the bell and came into the garage without waiting for someone to answer the call. My husband, Keith, and I went out to greet him, and we immediately knew the visit wasn't for pleasure.

"What's up Dad?" Keith asked his father.

"I'm having surgery tomorrow," Dad said. He reached over and patted Bo's head, the smile that followed sad but determined. "I need you to take care of Bo for me… just for a while."

I stood beside Keith and felt his hand clutch mine. We knew his father was asking us to keep his best friend and companion forever, because Dad was dying.

"Sure Dad," Keith answered, his voice momentarily catching. "We'll take care of Bo as long as you need us to."

Dad nodded and looked away, his once bright, sky-blue eyes now faded due to the cancer.

"Winter will be here soon," Dad said, closing the door on the subject of his sickness. "How's that garden gate coming, son?" He leaned down and patted Bo's head, "Stay Bo." He patted him again and quickly turned away.

Keith let go of my hand and walked out of the garage with his father. Bo whined and walked over to lean against my leg. I was to learn that the lean was a practice Bo had when picking up on someone's stress or sadness. As I stood barefoot on the cold, cement floor it became obvious to me that Bo knew Dad was sick and soon to leave us.

The day before Dad died the nurses let us sneak Bo into the hospital to see him. Keith picked Bo up and put him on the hospital bed beside Dad. Dad smiled, the comfort Bo brought him obvious, and Bo lay calm and still, once in a while gently licking Dad's hand. When Dad passed, the only thing that got us, and Bo, through that sad, holiday season was our kids.

We raised Bo with enjoyment, love and amazement. He was so intelligent and loyal. He insisted on sleeping in front of the door every night, as though determined to protect the family. I believed that until I got up in the middle of the night to find him sleeping on the couch, the blanket pulled over him, just as he used to do when taking naps with Dad. I couldn't get mad at Bo for being on the couch, the memory of seeing him faithfully napping with Dad, the two of them snuggling under an afghan, bringing tears to my eyes.

Bo watched over our toddler, Megan, as though he were her guardian angel. Where she went, he was right beside her. If Megan left the sandbox, Bo would block her from any direction other than straight to the house. He was attentive to the boys as well, better than any older sibling. If the boys argued, Bo would get between them, lay his head on one lap and look at the other with his soulful, dark eyes, and softly whine. The boys would fall quiet, the argument over. Bo was the best companion our family could have asked for.

Fifteen years passed with Bo faithfully watching over us. It was in that fifteenth year that we noticed he would cough once in a while, but we figured he had a cold. One morning I got up to find Bo's paws and chest swollen, and he could barely stand. The vet said he had congestive heart failure.

A few days later we had to put Bo to sleep and, for Keith and me, it was like losing a child. For the children, it was like losing a sibling. As Keith and our boys buried Bo under the dogwood tree, tears falling from our eyes, my daughter and I clutched hands. A soft rain began to fall, and I swear the angels were mourning with us.

Bo was missed so much. The house wasn't the same without his presence, and it left a void. A few weeks passed, the family quieter than usual in mourning, and one night the soft summer wind blew through the windows as the family slept soundly. For no obvious reason I woke and immediately sat up.

"Bo!"

I heard Dad yell for Bo in the backyard, then whistle for him to follow as he always did when leaving. I jumped to my knees just as Keith's feet hit the floor.

"Come on Bo!"

"Tena, did you hear that?" Keith asked as I turned to the window and pushed aside the curtain. I held my breath and peered into the night, listening intently while Keith looked out the other window. Quiet, peaceful night was all there was to see.

"Tena?"

"I heard him Keith," I said softly. Tears fell from my eyes as I silently looked across the quiet yard where Bo had played with our kids, Dad looking on with his sky-blue eyes twinkling. I whispered, "Thank you God," certain Bo was fine now. Dad had come to take him home.

~Tena Green

92

The Cycle of Life

If you have a dog, you will most likely outlive it; to get a dog is to open
yourself to profound joy and, prospectively, to equally profound sadness.
~Marjorie Garber

Our daughter Nicole has always been a very independent child. That was a good thing except when it butted against our wishes when she became a teenager. My husband and I would let out enough rope for her to safely try her wings, but her idea of "slack" was different than ours, and she would yank when she wanted more. To add to our worry, she had a steady boyfriend, and he was nice, but he was still a teenage boy.

"Patrice's dog had nine puppies. Please can I have one?" she begged one spring day, bursting into the kitchen with her friend from a neighboring farm. Their female had just surprised them with a big litter and they were desperate to find homes for the puppies.

"Absolutely not," my husband said with his usual end-of-story voice. "We're too close to the highway. It'll get run over."

Later that night, I laid the facts before him. "The way things are going around here, there's going to be a puppy in this house or a baby. You choose."

Sure enough, a fat golden ball of exuberance with large paws careened into our house. The movie *Steel Magnolias* was in all the cinemas. The heroine's name was Shelby so our pup was named Shelby. It meant "sheltered," an appropriate name as it would turn out. Most farm dogs don't come with distinguished pedigrees. Although

Shelby had the beautiful coloring, build and good nature of a Golden Labrador, somewhere in her obscure past, a German Shepherd had lurked. Consequently, one of her ears stood at attention while the other flopped down tiredly. She would never win ribbons or trophies at a dog show, but her lopsided, perpetually puzzled look endeared her to us that much more.

Nicole took her responsibilities as a dog owner seriously as she always did when she committed to something. From my kitchen window, I watched as she patiently trained her pup. After months of persistence, the loose marbles that rolled around in Shelby's puppy brain aligned, and the goofy girl morphed into a decorous, mindful lady who guarded our house and was trained to the yard. When life as a teenager got too hard, I would find Nicole in the garage, her arms wrapped around Shelby's neck, leaning into the big dog for comfort. The love of her faithful dog calmed our daughter and brought peace to our house. I knew that we had made the right decision.

However, I had not thought of the consequences of a high school student acquiring a pet. At the close of her graduating year, Nicole announced her intention to study in France.

"Who's going to look after your dog?" I asked uneasily, hoping it wouldn't be me, the confirmed cat-lover. The leash was firmly transferred to my hand as our beautiful daughter flew away. Our hard struggle had produced a fearless and confident woman. With a dog to exercise, I stepped into a new regimen of physical activity encouraged by my eager and enthusiastic partner. With Shelby at my side, we logged a lot of healthy miles—two addicts addicted to "walkies." My love of animals broadened. I converted and became a dog-lover too.

Nicole had also grown up in the intervening years. When she returned from Europe, she turned to her studies with a vengeance, graduated from university with honours and became an award-winning teacher. She had also married a good man and was happy except for the baby that didn't come.

Time passed. Shelby was getting older; her body thickened and her shiny coat grew dull and matted. She had been with us for twelve years, a good age for bigger breeds. She had a hard time dragging herself upright with arthritis in her hips, and cheeky magpies stole chunks of dog food from her dish without fear, since she was too old and slow to be any real danger. I knew what I should do but it was too painful and I put it off, hoping that I would find her in eternal sleep stretched out in my flowerbed, her favourite forbidden place. One blistering hot day in July, she went missing. Then the guilt and remorse set in.

"Why didn't I put her down responsibly?" I berated myself, imagining coyotes taunting and circling her for the kill. Thankfully I was spared that grief. Shelby staggered home, disoriented and covered in yellow canola flowers from a nearby field and fell at my feet.

"Thank you, Lord," I whispered as I cradled her in my arms. I was ready.

Later that day, I cried into the phone, "Nicole, I can't put Shelby down by myself. You have to come home and help me."

I made the fatal appointment. Ill and confused, Shelby followed us slowly into the veterinary's office. We lifted her big body onto the cold aluminum table. Fixing her trusting eyes on my face, Shelby quietly allowed the vet to insert the needle that would stop her heart. The rise and fall of her chest slowed while Nicole and I stroked her head and fingered her soft floppy ears. With one last lingering breath, she slipped away.

My daughter had been receiving unsuccessful treatment at a fertility clinic in Calgary. That same afternoon, she and her husband had their last scheduled appointment.

"Mom, I'm pregnant!" Nicole announced joyfully a few weeks later. "In the spring!"

The day Shelby died, Nicole had conceived. Something precious would replace our beloved dog. And we would be further blessed. Nicole would give birth to two healthy babies, girls, just like Shelby.

~Jeannette S. Richter

My
Dog's Life

I'll Always Love You

93

Never Too Soon

The best way to get over a dog's death is to get another soon.
~Ronald Reagan

We allowed ourselves less than twenty-four hours of bereavement. Some folks would view it as impetuous and insensitive to replace a beloved friend so soon. But as a pair of dog lovers in our seventies, we dared not let too much time pass. Losing any number of precious animals had been a part of living and dying on our ranch, but none had struck us harder than the most recent. The older we were, the harder we fell. While holding our girl close at the veterinarian's, we were two old fogies choking back mournful tears, then letting them spill.

Our beloved Keeshond had brought years of uncompromising joy as a herder and steady companion. Long ago at the shelter her dark liquid eyes had pitifully begged, "Please folks, take me home with you," and we were smitten. No other would do, this Dutch barge dog, this silver and black treasure who asked nothing but unconditional love. She guarded us and our critters for fourteen years, and never left my husband Ken's side when he fell seriously ill.

We left our veterinarian that morning with instructions to cremate her, and drove five hours to take care of essential business. As the miles rolled by we recalled happy Keeshond moments, recalling our smart and devoted girl in between helpless and woeful bouts of weeping.

Red-faced and hankies handy, we stopped at noon for a sandwich and a city newspaper. Finding too many depressing headlines, I glanced at the want ads under "Pets." Finding the rare Keeshond was a silly notion, but in fierce loneliness and desperation one grasps at straws.

There before my eyes was an ad by a veterinarian dog breeder another three hours south with one male Keeshond left in their current semiannual whelp. Could it be? I picked up my cell phone and asked if the pup was still available. He was, the man said, but we needed to arrive before 8 p.m. Excited, waterworks overwhelmed me this time.

All but dragging Ken in and out of previously scheduled appointments, we made it to the vet's country kennel with a half hour to spare. We began a search up and down the immaculate cages, but there were no Keeshonds in sight. Holding back disappointment, a blast of heat rose from my pounding heart, washing red-hot over my face.

"Someone must have taken the pup, Ken," I moaned like a spoiled child.

"The Keeshonds are out for their evening stroll, ma'am," offered the doctor. "You must be the folks interested in our last Keesh pup," he said. I nearly kissed the poor man while shoving a half dozen pictures of our late girl at him.

"I too have a wonderful lady Keeshond over at the house. In fact we've worn out three of them in our family," he said smiling.

"Don't be so fidgety," whispered Ken while I paced and gazed impatiently at the outer door. Suddenly, the baby flew through the back door, his curly tail doing a jig atop his back. The doctor made the three of us comfortable in a private room to get acquainted. Even though I feared his reaction to the steep price, Ken came through, for this was one beautiful little fellow.

While driving the 200 miles home listening to our favorite western tunes on the XM, we sang "A Boy Named Sue" together, and stopped a few times for father-son piddles in the darkness of nightfall. "Sue," I mused as our baby slept soundly against my hip, but Ken suggested "Corky" after a great dog in our past. I leaned back contentedly and somehow felt assured that our beloved lady had forgiven our haste in finding another Dutch ancestor.

~Kathe Campbell

Bearing Loss

Things that were hard to bear are sweet to remember.
~Seneca

My fifteen-year-old Miniature Schnauzer died last month. Her name was Stephanie. I held her in my arms when she was put to sleep and I tried to convince myself that I was only doing for her what I would want done for myself.

I had taken her to the vet the night before, and he told me she could no longer fill her lungs with air. I am ashamed to say that I couldn't bear to part with her. I took her home and prayed for a miracle that never came. All through that night I heard my tiny Schnauzer gasping for air, her rib cage heaving with the immense effort it took for her to breathe. The next morning I drove her back to the doctor. I sat with her in my arms and tried to come to terms with saying goodbye to my beloved friend. She breathed her last labored breath next to my heart and I still haven't stopped my tears.

Stephanie belonged to an elderly couple who had moved to a place that didn't allow pets. A wonderful mutual friend called and asked if I would take her. I can still remember the couple coming to my house to give her a bath for the last time. I watched them groom this little dog with more love than I had ever seen lavished on any living thing. After I got to know Stephanie I understood why. Throughout fifteen years together, I never had to raise my voice to her, and I never had to clean up after her. She gave me nothing but joy and endless affection.

Stephanie had a wiggle in her walk that would make a stripper blush. She was so provocative that I have heard people call out "Cute dog!" or "What a HONEY!" Small children have abandoned their tricycles and galloped toward Stephanie to pet her.

Every time I thought of losing her, I added another dog to my family. Then, if she died, I would be too busy caring for the others to grieve. First there was Esther, then Harold, then Jake, then Charles, then Amy. The list seems endless, and many of the new additions went to doggy heaven many years ago. Only Stephie endured.

Oh, I knew I loved her too much. And I knew she understood. I could almost see her shake her head in wonder as I ushered in her new brothers and sisters. I could almost hear her say, "Another one! Where on earth will he sleep?"

I am a woman who lives alone. I have no children although I love children with all my heart. I have no family although my neighbors have opened their arms to me. But everyone needs a little living thing to love who loves you back. Stephanie gave that kind of love to me and I returned it.

She is a memory now and a beautiful one. The affection she lavished on me can never be diluted by time. It was too dear. I console myself as my tears drop on the keys of my computer; I remind myself that Stephanie has gone to a better place where she can breathe heavenly air with ease. And that picture of my happy little puppy with a wiggle in her walk and devotion to spare will never die as long as I am alive. It warms my memory like a brilliant flame. Her goodness and her charm will always be with me.

~Lynn Ruth Miller

95

The Miracle of Return

Every action in our lives touches on some chord that will vibrate in eternity.
~Edwin Hubbel Chapin

As a professional animal communicator, I have been blessed with the gift to hear messages from animals, both alive and in spirit. This communication happens telepathically. Telepathy is the basis for all communication and it is something that everyone does naturally. It is a matter of training ourselves to listen to these intuitive communications to be able to readily communicate with animals. I have talked with more than 35,000 animals in the past twenty-three years.

Almost twenty years ago, on October 31, my life changed instantly. In just thirty minutes, a rapid-burning fire took the lives of twenty-four animals on a farm and animal sanctuary that I cofounded. After the fire, I shut down a piece of my heart. Fortunately, twenty-five horses, two dogs, and one cat managed to get out of the burning building. Although I spent the next ten months caring for them, a part of me stayed distant for fear of losing them too.

Ten months later, my beloved horse, Deeteza, an Arab mare and spiritual teacher, died unexpectedly. Deeteza was the animal teacher who opened my heart and helped make me aware of my telepathic communication skills. She was the animal closest to my heart and soul. After the fire and her death, my grief was so great that I decided not to let another soul into my heart.

However, a year later, the following October, Deeteza, from spirit, informed me that she was sending me a birthday present. I had no idea what that could possibly be, or how it would happen. But Deeteza told me that it would be something that I could cuddle with and that it would soothe my heart. I was very skeptical that I would receive her gift. However, three weeks later, a friend called to tell me that her Labrador had just had a litter of puppies. For some reason that she couldn't explain, every time she looked at one of the yellow puppies, she kept thinking of me. She offered to give him to me as a gift.

As soon as she said that, I heard Deeteza say, "Happy Birthday Dawn, my gift has now arrived. I've sent you someone to warm your heart and teach you about trust." My friend then told me the date the puppy was born. It was my birthday.

I named the puppy Jason. I could write a whole book on the fourteen years I spent with that amazing dog. He was so full of life and unconditional love that he, indeed, opened my heart again. Sadly, fourteen years later, I watched as dementia overtook him in the last year of his life and he could no longer function. During that time, I felt my heart wanting to close again, yet I was so grateful for this amazing being.

One day, months before Jason died, he communicated to me about the journey he was soon to take into Spirit. I did not want to hear what he was saying. I just wanted to focus on him in his present aging body and not worry about the next one. But he wouldn't let it go. He explained that he would leave his body and come back to me. Jason explained that he was going to return as a Golden Retriever puppy. And he said specifically that my friend Lillie Goodrich, who runs a Border Collie rescue, would find him. A Golden Retriever through a Border Collie rescue? I asked. Trust me, he said. He told me to name him Tucker in his new form. He told me exactly when he'd be back, by mid-July, at the start of a camp for dogs where I would be teaching.

After he passed on, Jason remained in contact with me periodically with updates on what things were like for him in spirit. One time, he told me that when he came back he would bring a friend with him. His friend would need help and he thought it would be perfect to bring this friend to us so we could help him. Again Jason reiterated that he would return as a Golden Retriever—not necessarily a pure breed, but that he would look like a Golden Retriever to be named Tucker.

It was hard to trust that all of this was true. But then... it happened. My friend Lillie received an e-mail about a litter of Border Collie/Golden Retriever mix puppies that needed to be rescued. It turned out that in the litter only one looked like a Golden, and it was a male.

I didn't expect that finding Tucker would be so clear and feel so strong, but as soon as the woman handed me the golden puppy and I held him, I knew instantly that it was Tucker. The feeling of what it was like to be with Jason filled every cell of my body. I felt his unconditional love and his essence. I just knew that it was him. It felt too good to be true.

I set little Tucker down to nurse, but instead of going directly to his mother, he took himself off, away from his mom and his littermates. He sat down, threw his head back, and howled, just like a little wolf. One of his siblings waddled over, sat down beside him, threw her head back, and howled with him. As they howled in unison it was clear. She was the friend Jason brought with him. A week and a half later the puppies were ready to come home. It was July 18. Just when Jason said it would be.

As I drove to pick up Tucker, it was staggering to me that I could have found him. The puppies were several hours away from where I lived, in a different state. It also turned out that the listing for the puppies had only been on the Internet for a couple of hours before it was removed. Yet in that narrow timeframe, someone saw it and forwarded it to my friend Lillie. Lillie then contacted me.

We named Tucker's sister Grace, and the day after we brought her home, we realized that she had something very wrong with her. It turned out she was born with a defect in her brain which causes her neurological problems. Again, Jason was right. He brought with him a friend who needed help.

Each day I look at my golden boy and consider the journey he has been on to get back to me. It brings tears to my eyes just to look at him. It warms my heart to feel his wonderful soul energy back in my life. Even now I have a hard time believing Jason could get back to me the way he did, and that he knew about his path before he left. His message is clear. Love transcends time. Relationships transcend time.

~Dawn E. Hayman

96

I Just Knew

We never really own a dog as much as he owns us.
~Gene Hill

"I don't think you are ready to let go of her yet," the vet said to me. I held my dog and couldn't put her down on the examination table. My husband and I had moved from Virginia to Ohio and our new vet had only seen my dog twice as of that day.

"We don't have to do this to today. She could wait a while, but you need to consider her quality of life," the vet said.

He handed me a bottle of pain medicine and left the room for me to decide what to do. When he came back, I asked him how I would know when the right time was. He smiled and said I would know. I took Pogo home. Although we weren't sure of her age, since we had adopted her, we thought she was fifteen or sixteen now. Making the decision to let her go was the hardest thing I could imagine doing. Even though I knew she was ready, I needed more time.

Pogo, who in her younger days was twenty pounds, was thirteen pounds now. She had survived two strokes, an ulcer in each eye and a back injury. She couldn't hear me when I got home from work or see to go outside. Her arthritis was so bad that she could hardly walk. However, I had had her since I was eight years old and we had grown up together. At twenty-two, I couldn't bring myself to make the decision to put her down. I kept hoping someone else would make it for me. How was I supposed to know when the right time was?

During a trip to visit family back in Virginia, I realized it was time. Rather, Pogo decided. Not one to get carsick, Pogo started throwing up in the car. Then she lost control of her bodily fluids. I cradled her in my arms, not caring that she was covered in vomit. She was breathing heavily and slowly. The car ride was silent. And I knew.

"I think I may take her to the vet in the morning," I said to my husband, keeping my eyes straight ahead.

"You are?" said my husband, looking over to see if I was crying.

"Yes, it makes sense. I didn't want her to die in Ohio. It's not her home. Virginia is her home."

We arrived at my in-laws and they knew it was time too. They helped us clean the car, bathe Pogo and attempt to give her water to drink. She refused water and slept. I didn't sleep well for fear that she wouldn't wake up in the morning. The next morning I called the vet as soon as they opened.

"How can I help you?" the cheerful receptionist asked.

"I need to put my dog to sleep, today," I said, emotionless. I had cried enough. I just said it. I just knew.

"Okay," the receptionist said, her voice not so cheerful anymore. "Well, the doctors all have appointments. I'm sorry, but you won't be able to stay with her."

I let those words sit for a moment. I knew I had to do this today. She had suffered long enough.

"That will be fine," I told her and hung up. My husband didn't want to go with me. I called my brother.

While I drove to the vet my brother cradled Pogo infant style. I parked the car in the usual spot. This time Pogo didn't sniff every leaf and every tree leading up the front door, and she couldn't greet the other dogs and wag her tail. My brother carried her in and sat down while I talked to the receptionist. Signing a form to end Pogo's life was the hardest part of the day.

The receptionist told us to take a seat while she got a room ready. I looked around the waiting room as I sat next to my brother. The others avoided our eyes and looked sorrowfully at my poor little dog. They all knew. We sat in the same seats my brother and I had sat in so many times before. I was so thankful my brother had come with me. We three had all grown up together.

"You can bring her back now," the receptionist said.

"Does that mean we can stay?" I asked.

"Yes, if you like," she answered.

We went back into one of the small rooms that we had been in so many times before. My brother passed Pogo to me. I held her in my arms as the vet talked to us about her favorite things to do when she was younger. The only time I thought that maybe I had done the wrong thing was when the vet checked her heartbeat and said she was gone. With friends and family by my side for the rest of the day, I got through it. My mother took me shopping, and I watched movies and went to dinner with friends.

A month later, at a friend's house, I was sitting next to my husband on a sofa that faced a sliding glass door leading to the backyard. As we were talking and catching up, out of the corner of my eye I saw a puppy walk by the door. I kept watching and another puppy came into view. I gasped. I poked my husband so he would look outside too. He sighed.

We had talked about getting another dog in the fall after we moved into a new apartment. Neither of us felt we had given ourselves enough time to heal since losing Pogo. My eyes kept watching the puppies until I heard my friend say, "Do you want one? Go pick one out and take him home."

I looked at my husband with the eager eyes of a child.

I walked out and scooped up a particularly energetic one. Having that wiggling bundle of joy lick my face with puppy breath and scratching my arms with puppy claws, I just knew that it was the right time.

~Rebecca Vaughan

Teacher's Pet

Acquiring a dog may be the only time a person gets to choose a relative.
~Author Unknown

My students knew something was wrong the minute they entered my classroom. I had printed a reading assignment on the board, and a worksheet awaited them as soon as they finished the reading.

"Okay, class, your assignment's on the board. Let's get started."

"Mrs. Foster, aren't you going to introduce the story to us?"

"Not this time, Elisa. I don't think it needs an introduction," I said.

"Can't we read it aloud as a class?"

My jaws tightened. "Just do the assignment, please."

I turned my back to the class. How was I going to get through the day? I had driven into town debating whether I could control my emotions in front of six classes of seventh graders.

I sat down at my desk and noticed the students looking at one another with questioning glances. My head began to pound with unshed tears that were forced to stay where they were—at least for now. I blinked back tears, forcing myself to open the text and pretend to read. It's just a dog, I told myself.

I remembered the day my husband, David, had brought Charlie, our Australian Shepherd, home. He was just a fuzzy, gray ball of fur. My daughter, Farrah, had been just a few weeks old. One evening when Grandma lifted Farrah out of her baby swing, protective Charlie snarled at her. We had to reassure him that Grandma was okay. From then on, Charlie was suspicious of strangers, barking and baring his teeth when he saw someone for the first time. After receiving our reassurance, he'd return to his friendly self, rolling over for someone to scratch his belly.

Over the years our family grew. When Farrah was three, we brought Jill home from the hospital. Charlie had sniffed at her bassinet, licking her tiny fists through the wooden bars on each side, his way of saying "I approve." Then came Jackie and, fifteen months later, Ben. Even though each additional child demanded more of our attention, Charlie accepted each one as he had the first. Charlie was both a playmate and protector. He possessed a gentle sixth sense when playing with the children. But little by little, thirteen-year-old Charlie began slowing down.

Yesterday when I came home from school, Charlie wasn't in his customary place beside the door.

"Hi, kids, I'm home," I said.

"Hey, Mom, we can't find Charlie," said Ben. "Dad said he hasn't seen him all day, either."

When there was still no sign of him at bedtime, I became worried. After calling futilely for him, I trudged back inside to tuck the kids in bed. Then, just as the ten o'clock news came on, I saw the familiar form on the patio. I opened the door to let him in but knew instantly that something was wrong. Barely able to move, Charlie staggered into the house and dropped to the floor, hardly acknowledging us. Despite coaxing, he wouldn't eat or drink anything.

We went to bed and I eventually drifted off to sleep, but I was awakened around five o'clock by the sound of his labored breathing. Sometime during the night he had managed to move from the family room into our bedroom where he had collapsed at the foot of the bed and now lay, barely breathing.

"I think Charlie's dying," I managed to choke out as I shook David awake. He knelt by Charlie, untangling the back leg that was bent abnormally under him.

"Yes," he said, "he's already getting stiff." He cradled Charlie in his arms and gently carried him where he'd be out of sight of the children when they awoke.

I had hoped to wait until after school to break the news to the kids, but they knew something was wrong when they saw my puffy eyes and tear-streaked face. How could I tell them that the dog they had grown up with, who had played with them, protected them, and had eaten all the cooking disasters they refused to, was gone? The tears began again.

"Charlie died this morning," I blurted.

We all cried. Ben recovered sooner than any of us.

"It'll be okay, Mom; we'll get another dog," he said.

As I walked Ben to preschool, he said, "Mom, don't tell Miss Marcie about Charlie. It'll be embarrassing." I laughed. Then I cried.

I looked up from my desk to realize the students were staring at me. I wiped a tear and walked to the chalkboard, replacing the customary "thought for the day" with these words:

"My thirteen-year-old dog died at the foot of my bed this morning. Please understand my inability to talk about it."

"Mrs. Foster, can we write in our journals?" someone asked.

Unable to respond, I nodded. A common thread was woven throughout the journal entries: A pet is the one member of the family who exhibits unconditional love. You can scold him and he'll tuck his tail between his legs but return to lick your face ten minutes later. You can miss feeding him once in a while, and he'll still jump with elation when you go out to play with him. You can be in the bluest of moods, and a pet has the knack for making you smile.

~Sandra Frazer Foster

98

Maggie and Jake

Death leaves a heartache no one can heal,
love leaves a memory no one can steal.
~From a headstone in Ireland

Maggie was our first. We wrapped our new bundle of golden fur in a fuzzy blanket as we drove home that blustery fall evening. She was followed two years later by Jake, another Golden Retriever. I held him in my arms as my husband drove us, with Maggie in the back, from the kennel to our home in the foothills of Colorado.

It was obvious from the start that Jake loved Maggie. As a young puppy, he found much comfort when snuggled up to her. Her habit of washing his fur with her warm tongue continued far into adulthood. Jake, now weighing at least twenty pounds more than she, would sit patiently while Maggie gently licked his face and ears before retreating to her own bed each evening.

For years, in the spring, our lawn required new sod to repair worn and tattered spots injured by the romping of two big Goldens. Ten years passed, and my husband and I enjoyed the escapades that only a true dog lover would understand. That December, we took them in for their holiday grooming. They came back sleek and shiny, smelling of shampoo, with ribbons in their fur, Maggie's pink and Jake's blue. As soon as they returned home, Maggie, as usual, rubbed her head on the carpet until the bow was removed. Jake, always the show-off, pranced proudly around the house showing off his pretty new adornment.

The day before Christmas it began to snow. I let both dogs out for their morning run in the yard. After a while, I whistled for them to come in, but they were nowhere in sight. I grabbed my jacket and went to see what was wrong. Behind the garage, Maggie was lying in the snow barely breathing, with Jake by her side. I called to my husband, and we were at the vet's door in less than thirty minutes.

After a brief exam, our veterinarian suggested he run some tests. He reappeared an hour later to tell us that she had a mass that had ruptured in her spleen. It was cancer, and the kindest thing we could do for our beloved Maggie was to put her down. We asked to be alone with her to say goodbye. We held her and cried into her soft golden fur. When it was over, we asked to have her cremated.

We returned that evening to a puzzled Jake. He paced through the house that night, and spent the next several days looking for his buddy. At the end of the week, I received a call from the vet. Maggie's ashes were ready. Upon our arrival, we were given a small box that held the ashes and her collar with tags.

We came through the back door holding Maggie's worn collar. Upon hearing the sound of her tags jingling, Jake came bounding and barking down the hall expecting to see Maggie. With tears streaming down our checks, we knelt and held him in our arms. I do not know how much dogs understand about death. But that day our beautiful boy knew something.

Less than four weeks later we returned to our vet worried about Jake's loss of appetite and lack of interest in his daily walk. We were asked to wait while some tests were run. Finally our trusted vet asked us to join him in his office. As gently as he could, knowing our pain was still fresh from the loss of Maggie, he told us that Jake also had cancer and that it had spread throughout his lungs. Once again we had to say goodbye.

That spring, in a place where Jake and Maggie used to dig holes, we spread their ashes and planted a maple tree in their memory. Later that fall as I gazed out the porch window, my eye glimpsed something in the crisp morning sunlight. I called my husband to join me. The maple tree's leaves had turned gold overnight. We went out and tied a pink ribbon and a blue ribbon on one of the branches to remember.

~Catherine Kopp

99

Never Say Never

One's first love is always perfect until one meets one's second love.
~Elizabeth Aston

I t was supposed to be a routine Saturday annual checkup and visit to the vet for Indy's shots. Since Indy had been lethargic lately, I wanted to see if perhaps some new vitamins were in order. At twelve years old she was now a "senior citizen."

"I can run some routine labs, if it makes you feel better," Dr. Oliver said. "A chest X-ray might be good too."

"Well, I would like to know what is causing her to lie around all the time," I said.

The attendant came in and took Indy to the back for her tests while I waited.

Soon Dr. Oliver was back with Indy in tow. I could tell by the look on the doctor's face that something was wrong. Without a word she put an X-ray on the wall and flipped the light-box switch.

"The picture tells the story," she said pointing.

All I saw were two black blobs on what were Indy's lungs. I was dumbstruck and then an overwhelming sadness hit me.

"How long does she have?" I whispered.

"A week, maybe two," Dr. Oliver said, putting her hand on my shoulder.

I left the office and took Indy home to await the inevitable. My husband and I spent a horrible weekend watching Indy deteriorate until she could hardly breathe.

First thing Monday morning my husband and I were back at Dr. Oliver's office. We said our goodbyes and stayed with Indy until her last breath. My husband cried for the first time in a long time. Together we walked out of the animal hospital clutching each other for solace. I vowed I would never give my heart to another dog again.

The house seemed so empty and I quickly disposed of Indy's dish and collar. I kept her tags and put them in my memorabilia treasure box. The days went by and I missed the little fur ball on my feet at night. I expected Indy to come running into the room to announce the arrival of the mailman. Other dogs out for a stroll quickly made me look the other way. I threw myself into my job but there were no warm doggie kisses when I arrived home after work. The next six months were very hard. Just when I thought I might be over Indy, memories would come flooding back. One day I found a picture of her in her puppy days and I cried for an hour.

As summer turned to fall, I encountered some health challenges which would push me into early retirement. I had my days free and all the time in the world. I was alone all day and wasn't coping well with this new routine.

One night at six o'clock I heard the garage door open and knew it wouldn't be long before my husband Paul would come through the door. How I dreaded his arrival. I loved him dearly, but recently he was really getting on my nerves.

"Hi babe, I'm home," came his booming voice. "Where are you?"

"In here," I replied. I was lying on our bed watching the five o'clock news in my PJs.

"You're still in your pajamas, again? You would feel better if you got dressed."

"Why? I'm not going anywhere," I replied testily.

He just sighed and walked out of the room shaking his head. I don't think he knew what to do with me.

I had tried to pull myself out of this funk. I tried shopping as a diversion, but without my income this was a bad idea. One of my friends asked me why I was avoiding her, but truthfully, getting dressed up and doing lunch was just too tiring. I tried reading. I had an entire bookshelf waiting to be devoured, but how much can one read? Working in my craft room also took up part of my day. Somehow these activities didn't hold my interest for very long and I would find myself wanting to sleep. Some days I would be as tired when I woke up as when I fell asleep.

I had envisioned retirement with trips to the doggie park, long walks, and time for leisurely drives along the beach with Indy. But my friend was gone and I was alone.

Everyone kept telling me it took time to adjust, that I would be very busy if I gave myself a chance. But I didn't want to be just busy. I wanted my life to be carefree and happy again like it was when Indy was alive.

My husband suggested we get a new dog. I was adamant. I never wanted to experience that heartache again. But Paul was relentless. The next Wednesday morning he said, "Hey, get dressed. Today we're going to the shelter."

"Oh, no... I can't."

"Why not? You going somewhere?" he asked.

"Well, um, I'm just not ready. It takes time. Dogs are a huge commitment," I replied.

"What? I've never known you to shy away from dogs. You're the most committed animal lover I know."

"I don't think I can do it again... give my heart away just to have it crushed," I said with tears in my eyes.

"Sallie, honey, Indy was your baby, but there is another dog out there that is just waiting for you."

"Okay, I'll go but I'm not promising anything," I replied.

All the way to the shelter I kept thinking of the day we put Indy down and how much it hurt.

We combed the runs that housed the dogs. We were about to leave when a little black Beagle poked her nose through the bars. There she was—a small female stray. I let her lick my fingers and she looked up with big brown eyes. The fact she was in stall 220, my birthday, didn't hurt either.

"I think she was meant to be mine," I told Paul.

"Well by the looks of her tail, she feels the same about you," he replied.

Mollie came to live with us. It's been a year now and I have my long walks, and drives along the beach with Mollie. I adore her. We are inseparable and I am no longer depressed. I have learned that she will never replace my love for Indy, but they are different and I have enough love in my heart to go around.

~Sallie A. Rodman

Too Happy to Die

Dogs' lives are too short. Their only fault, really.
~Agnes Sligh Turnbull

After our German Shepherd died, we couldn't bear the thought of ever getting another dog, and for four long years we didn't. During those years, we moved from the small town where my children grew up, to a small horse farm, farther north, the farm of our dreams. My son Eric stayed in touch with the young, new local vet, named C.J., who, as Eric grew older, became one of his best friends.

One day, I heard Eric's truck pull up outside, and seconds later, C.J.'s voice. A moment later, the door opened to reveal not two, but three, figures, Eric, C.J., and a white German Shepherd peering around Eric's knees with huge, frightened eyes. I stared at the German Shepherd, who was shivering uncontrollably and clinging to Eric.

"You have to help her, Mom," said Eric. "She was supposed to be euthanized, but C.J. didn't want to do it. There's nothing wrong with her except that her owner said she wasn't mean enough, and he's got himself a Pit Bull. He said if we found her a home, she could live."

"What's her name?" I asked, with resignation.

"Duchess."

I'd never seen such a forlorn and timid specimen in my life.

"She's not a Duchess," I protested. "She's just a pooky!"

The moment I said this, Duchess aka Pooky detached herself from Eric's knees and scuttled over to reattach herself to mine. I started speaking to her in caressing tones, calling her my "pooky-puppy." She brightened visibly, wagging the tip of her timid tail and licking my hand.

"We are not calling her Pooky," said Eric, with all the firmness of an eighteen-year-old. "I'm not having all the girls laughing at me because I'm walking down the road shouting 'Pooky! Pooky!'"

I am a fair-minded woman. I could see his point.

"Very well, then. How about we officially call her 'Spooky'—how's that? After all, she is white," I asked.

We all agreed that Spooky was less humiliating than Pooky. But in private, I always called her my pooky-puppy.

Spooky settled in gratefully. She never left my side for long. She was my shadow. She liked to guard the horses, and almost visibly threw out her chest with pride if praised for doing a good job. Her favorite song on the radio was "Spooky," and we always laughed at how excited she got when listening to the singer's voice repeating her name. She was kind, gentle, loving, the very antithesis of an aggressive dog. I could only imagine the hell she had endured with the macho, aggressive owner who wanted a "mean" dog. It was easy to see the scars of her former life. She was absolutely terrified of every man except Eric. We continued along very happily until a heat wave the next summer. Spooky seemed unusually lethargic, and so hot, water actually dripped from her tongue. I worried about it.

"That's how dogs sweat," my husband reassured me. "It's just because of the heat."

The next morning, I woke to find the morning pleasantly cool, but Spooky still lay on the floor beside me with water dripping from her tongue and nose. Alarmed, I called C.J. When he examined her, he seemed worried.

"I hate to tell you this, but I think she's got a problem. She needs X-rays and tests, stat," he said. He recommended that we take her to another veterinary clinic, telling us the equipment they had was more specialized than he could provide. I worried aloud about Spooky's fear of men.

"That won't be a problem," said C.J. "Every single staff member there is female."

We loaded Spooky into the car, and drove her to the clinic. The staff was wonderful, very gentle and kind. Spooky went with the Nice Ladies happily. But the news couldn't have been worse.

"She has congestive heart failure," the vet told us sympathetically. "We can drain her chest of the fluids that have accumulated for now, but you should know she may have as little as six weeks to live."

I was devastated. She was only six years old. Our former German Shepherd, Lisa, had lived to be fourteen. I had been looking forward to a few more good years with my pooky-puppy. The fact that she felt so at home with the Nice Ladies proved to be a good thing, because over the remainder of her life, Spooky had several visits and stays there. We monitored and medicated her carefully. Her six weeks passed, and then six months, with Spooky still very much alive.

"She's got no intention of dying," laughed the vet one year later. "She's just too happy."

I was granted two more precious years with Spooky. It wasn't nearly long enough, but Spooky and I packed a lifetime of love into that period. I remember sitting with her on the back patio one morning early in June, my coffee untouched. Spooky lay pressed against my ankles, blissfully happy, as always. It was a perfect morning, perfumed with the scent of lilacs, but my heart was breaking. I knew what Spooky didn't. Our time together was at an end. The great Canadian recession had hit, and we had been forced to sell the farm and our horses—the dream that my husband and I worked so hard for twenty years to achieve—for little more than the amount still owing on the mortgage. We would be moving to an apartment in the city and starting all over again, and there would be no more perfect mornings looking out over the fields. And Spooky was dying. There was no denying it this time. Yet there she lay, the happiest dog in the world on that perfect June morning, just weeks before we would have to leave the patio she loved so much, where she and I always quietly enjoyed our special morning time together. I wished Spooky and I had many more days like that to come. I wished I could stay on my dream farm, but life just doesn't allow perfect endings, it seems.

Spooky died just days after that. I was glad she didn't have to undergo the stress of packing up and moving. I was glad she didn't have to deal with my sadness. I never did get another dog, but not out of grief. You see, I still feel Spooky all around me, as alive as when she was here. I'm not claiming it's supernatural. It's just that, whenever I think of her, and that is surprisingly often, I am instantly back inside that perfect June morning again, with Spooky beside me. Only this time, I don't feel sadness. All I feel is gratitude and joy. I never got to experience Spooky's puppyhood—four precious years was all the time granted us—but the love I received from the dog who was too happy to die was so big, it will last me a lifetime.

~Marya Miller

Inherited Love

*The little furry buggers are just deep, deep wells
you throw all your emotions into.*
~Bruce Schimmel

We've all heard the saying "Mother knows best." Well, my mom always seemed to know what was best for me. Even before her passing she knew what it was that I needed in my life, and my mother, God rest her soul, left me her dogs. It may sound like a funny thing to be left, but she knew what she was doing and how they would change my life.

I had come to stay with her for her last few months. We had not had any contact for a long time due to an abusive marriage that lead to my substance abuse, incarceration, and living on the streets. I had no one in my life and God was still working on me from the inside, healing the guilt, the pain, and the disappointment that I had created. But my return was a wonderful time for both of us. She got to see her little girl again, clean and sober, happy and carefree—just like she had raised me to be: a beautiful woman.

One of the many things that Mom knew about me was that I had always had an attachment to animals. When I was growing up I surrounded myself with animals in any way that I could. They would follow me home, or did I really *invite* them to come with me? I thought I would save them from the harsh world, and they would save me from the hurt and the pain that I felt inside. Why? Because animals love unconditionally and in the world I grew up in there were conditions placed on love.

My life was changed the minute I walked through the door into her home and met all four of her dogs. They greeted me with barks, growls, and snarls. I was a stranger to them and she was dying of cancer. They were protecting her and I loved them immediately. It took them a while, but they finally accept me, seeing me as not a threat but as some part of her. Over time she told me how she came to have these little dogs.

Sergi, an American Eskimo, was brought to her at a time when she was in great need of someone or something to love. She had lost her fiancé to cancer. She was one month from becoming his wife when he died. She was stricken with depression and my aunt, her sister, brought her the dog to take care of. Then she went looking for a friend for Sergi and found Nevada, a female American Eskimo. These two dogs are as white as snow, one rambunctious and the other docile, yet much attached to each other. They grew up together and relied on each other for companionship.

Mom's two black Pomeranians, Prince and Princess, brother and sister, had been neglected before she took them in. They had been kept in small cat cages and relied on each other so much for companionship that they are inseparable. They are more serious. Prince, the male Pomeranian, never left my mom's side. We would have to force him to go outside to use the bathroom or he would just go where he was. When he was done he went right back to her side. Mom worried about him and how he was going to be once she was gone. Bless her heart, she was in pain from having cancer and she was concerned about her little guy. Princess was active and happy-go-lucky, and she would lick you all over. She loved my mom and would wait until all the other dogs were out of the room before secretly jumping up on Mom's bed to snuggle.

On the day that Mom died, I saw the animals shift their caring to me. They seemed to know that I was her daughter, that she was gone and that I was there. They adopted me as their new person to love.

My mom left me what she had been given… love… in a four-legged fashion. My mom always knew what I needed because I was her little girl, and what she left me changed my life forever. These animals are more than just animals to me. Now, I know and feel her love, unconditionally, through the dogs that I inherited from her.

~Lady Harrison

Meet Our
Contributors

Cynthia Culp Allen, an award-winning writer and mother of five, has published more than 1,000 articles in newspapers, magazines and books. The author of several books, Allen is a popular speaker and media guest who can be reached at www.cynthiaculpallen.com.

Pamela Altendorf lives in the Midwest with her husband. She is currently a volunteer tutor in English as a Second Language, and enjoys traveling throughout the U.S. and abroad. Her stories have appeared in the *Chicken Soup for the Soul* series as well as several newspapers and magazines.

Kathy Baker resides in Plano, TX, with her husband Jerry, and two precious pups, Hank and Samantha. She enjoys writing, needlework, and fishing. She has contributed to newspapers, anthologies, magazines, online e-zines, *Chicken Soup for the Soul* and writes a weekly column entitled "The Heart of Texas." Visit her website www.txyellowrose.com or e-mail her at Lnstrlady@aol.com.

Nancy Baker resides in College Station, TX, with her husband and Golden Retriever. Upon retiring, she pursued her lifelong love of writing and has been published in numerous national magazines and anthologies. She has three children, eight grandchildren and nine great-grandchildren, all a source of inspiration for her.

Carol Band is an award-winning humor writer who reports on life from the trenches of suburbia. In addition to parenting three almost-adult kids and one almost-human canine, she also raises champion dustbunnies. Visit her website www.carolband.com or e-mail her at carol@carolband.com.

Victor Barbella is a professional actor and educator from New York City who earns a living as an executive coach-trainer and a teaching artist. He was educated at West Chester University and the London Academy of Performing Arts. His passions are travel, writing and... dogs. E-mail him at vicbarb06@verizon.net.

Laurie Birnsteel is the author of *Sunspot: The Best Ever Astrological Guide to Your Dog* (Turner Publishing) and *Kahala: Growing Up in Hawaii*, (McKenna Publishing Group). E-mail Laurie at LBirns99@gmail.com.

Jan Bono taught school for thirty years on the Long Beach peninsula in Southwest Washington State. She now works as a life coach, writing coach, Law of Attraction presenter, and freelance writer, with numerous articles and several books to her credit. Check out her blog at www.daybreak-solutions.com/blog.

Sheri Bull lives in rural Illinois and operates a family fruit farm with her husband Vince. She enjoys freelance writing and plans to publish her own book of non-fiction short stories. She has three grown daughters and one grandson. Sheri enjoys her family, gardening, singing, baking and playing with her dog. E-mail her at sheribull5@gmail.com.

Barbara Ann Burris lives in a log cabin in rural Wisconsin with her husband, Bruce and her Belgian Tervuren pup, Alex. Barbara began writing as a student of Ann Linquist and polished her skills in "Coach" Marshall Cook's creative writing classes at UW Madison. Her interests include photography and painting.

D.V.C. is an avid hunter and fisherman from the mountains of Colorado. He works as a police officer and spend all of his off time exploring the wilds of his state.

Kathe Campbell lives on a Montana mountain with her mammoth donkeys, a Keeshond, and a few kitties. She is a prolific writer on Alzheimer's, and her stories are found on many e-zines. Kathe is a contributing author to numerous anthologies, *RX for Writers*, and medical journals. E-mail her at kathe@wildblue.net.

Lisa Ricard Claro is a freelance writer whose columns and stories have been published online, in the *Atlanta Journal-Constitution*, and in multiple anthologies. For more of Lisa's writing please visit her blog, "Writing in the Buff!" at www.writinginthebuff.net or e-mail Lisa at lisaricardclaro@bellsouth.net.

Shirley Corder is a registered nurse, cancer survivor and multi-published freelance writer. She writes mainly inspirational material from her home near the sea in the beautiful city of Port Elizabeth, South Africa, where she lives with her husband. Learn more at www.shirleycorder.com.

Kristine Meldrum Denholm is a freelance journalist and essayist, published in anthologies, magazines, newspapers and trade publications. She holds a Journalism degree, magna cum laude, from Duquesne University, and is currently being lobbied by her kids for a hypoallergenic dog. Learn more at www.KristineMeldrumDenholm.com.

Charlene Dickinson is a retired Master's degree social worker who likes entertaining. She has traveled internationally with her husband for years. Using this experience she writes travel articles for her local newspaper, *Herald-Citizen*, searching for the human side of the topic. She has won several writing prizes.

Toni Louise Diol, married forty-five years, grandmother of ten, a former preschool director and pediatric office manager, writes poetry, short stories and has published the book *Roses & Lollipops*. She motivates and teaches how to journal and record information for future generations. E-mail her at mylollipops@comcast.net.

Amanda Dodson is a wife and mother to three. She homeschools her children and is a contributing writer for her local newspaper. She has also contributed to other *Chicken Soup for the Soul* books.

Janice R. Edwards received her BAT, with honors, from Sam Houston State University in 1974. She taught English and Journalism before working for Texaco, retiring in 2004. Now she writes for local non-profit organizations and is a regular contributor to *Image Magazine*, which showcases Brazoria County.

Melissa Face lives, teaches, and writes in Virginia. She and her husband, Craig, spend their free time with Tyson, a nine-year-old Boxer. Tyson has been a true friend and a teacher of many valuable life lessons. E-mail Melissa at writermsface@yahoo.com.

Jane Marie Allen Farmer works for the National Park Service, teaching people about the awesomeness of nature. In her spare time, she makes visits to people who are hurting with her two registered therapy dogs, Leala and Tim Russell. She is also a passionate equestrienne, artist and a homeschool mom. Learn more at www.agapehands.com.

Judith Fitzsimmons is a freelance writer who lives in middle Tennessee with her daughter Chelsea and their dog Rusty. It is with love that she remembers Ubu.

Jennifer Flaten is a freelance writer who lives with her family in

Wisconsin. When she is not writing she enjoys jewelry making, gardening, baking and, of course, walks with the dog. E-mail her at flaten5@sbcglobal.net.

Sandy Foster teaches language arts to middle school students in south central Kansas and is a participant in the National Writing Project. She enjoys reading, writing poetry and short stories, and spending time with her children and grandchildren. She plans to write a collection of splice-of-life stories. E-mail her at sandy_foster@live.com.

Linda Frankel lives in Long Beach, CA, with her husband and rescued Labrador, Cassie. Since becoming a therapy dog in 2009, Cassie (who allows Linda to tag along) volunteers weekly in the BARK literacy program, in which elementary school children read to dogs while being tutored by an adult.

Beth Fredericksen lives in St. Louis with her three beautiful children and one three-legged Boxer. She is a marketing professional by trade, a writer by choice, a devout reader and semi-fanatic editor who will occasionally sneak a red Sharpie into restaurants to correct glaring grammatical errors on the menu.

Peggy Frezon is a freelance writer specializing in pets, with a twice-monthly column "5 Things About Pets" and stories in *The Ultimate Dog Lover, Miracles and Animals*, and others. She is a contributing writer for *Guideposts* magazine. Her first book is *Dieting with my Dog* (Hubble & Hattie) available August 2011. Learn more at her blog www.peggyfrezon.blogspot.com or on Twitter @peggyfrezon.

Ronni (Pollack) Geist is the owner of GeistWriters, a firm specializing in writing, editing, and document design. Her husband Harry is a PC technical consultant. Formerly, she served as a technical writer and managed the documentation department at a computer firm; these days, she focuses on more creative projects.

Nancy Lowell George is a freelance writer in Dallas.

Josh Gloer is a professional writer living with his wife and dog in Los Angeles. Lily is a rescue dog saved by the good hearts at Camp Cocker in Sherman Oaks, CA. Please support animal rescue at www. campcocker.com. Learn more about Josh at www.joshgloer.com.

T'Mara Goodsell has been published in several *Chicken Soup for the Soul* books as well as other anthologies, newspapers, and publications. She has a degree in Education from University of Nebraska and lives with her two children and beloved mixed breed dog near St. Louis.

Tena Green has written *The Catalyst* (2003), *A Woman's Touch* (2006), and *X-30* (2007), a collaboration with Richard Dean. Published works include magazine articles, *Your First Year as a Principal* (Atlantic Publishing 2009) and *How to Be Successful in Your First Year of Teaching Elementary School* (Atlantic Publishing 2010).

Maria Greenfield is a retired over-the-road truck driver now residing in Florida. She is married and lives with her husband and stepson, who has autism, and a menagerie of "therapy" animals. E-mail her at ladyW900Ldriver@yahoo.com.

Wendy Greenley is a graduate of the University of Delaware and the Villanova University School of Law. When she isn't chasing dogs, she is writing. This is her fourth story published by Chicken Soup for the Soul. She is currently working on several picture books and a middle grade novel. E-mail Wendy at wgreenley@comcast.net.

Connie Greenshields lives in Okotoks, Alberta. She is a part-time pharmacist, but prefers to volunteer in different arenas to keep things interesting. She continues to volunteer with Alberta Guide Dogs, and wrote this story to help fellow puppy-raisers see the importance of their efforts.

Melanie Adams Hardy received her BS with honors from Spring Hill College, and JD from Concord University School of Law. She is an attorney and writer. She enjoys cooking, Pilates, volunteer work, and spending time with her family. She write stories about her wonderful and wacky Southern family. E-mail her at rhardy212@charter.net.

Lady Harrison is working on her Masters in Social Services. She is a full-time college student in Tennessee, and volunteers at a non-profit organization. She plans to work with women who have been lost to the streets. This is her very first story. E-mail her at ladyharrison@comcast.net.

Janet Hartman's articles about coastal towns, exceptional people, boating, and writing have appeared in national magazines and online. Her work is in several anthologies, including *This Path, Making Notes: Music of the Carolinas,* and *From the Porch Swing.* She is the Long Ridge Writers Group 2010 guest columnist. Learn more at www.JanetHartman.net.

Lynn Hartz has a PhD from the Union Institute & University in Cincinnati, OH. She was a psychotherapist for many years and now writes full-time. She has written four books titled *Club Fed Living Inside a Women's Prison, Praise Him in Prison, Time Stood Still* and Discoveries of Eve's Daughters, as well as many stories in anthologies. E-mail her at lynnhartz@juno.com.

Dawn E. Hayman is co-founder of Spring Farm CARES, animal sanctuary and center for interspecies communication, in upstate New York. She has been a professional animal communicator since 1987. The focus of her teaching is predominantly on the death/dying process and the connection between the physical and spiritual realms. Learn more at www.springfarmcares.org.

Dawn Hesse lives in the exceptionally scenic and beautiful state of Michigan where she celebrates the natural splendor of the four seasons. She enjoys sailing the Great Lakes, sand volleyball on the endless beaches, meditative yoga, reading and spending time with her furry companions and remarkable friends.

Camille Hill, an Animal Intuitive, works with animals in many capacities. She's talked with animals since she was a child. She writes a pet column for a local paper and is currently writing a book about her animal adventures. She and Ed live with their two dogs and two cats. E-mail her at chill@hilladvisory.com.

Renee Hixson received her BA from the school of hard knocks. One husband, a dog, two goldfish and four kids later she graduated with a Master's in the field of common sense and hope. She's currently editing her journey for publication. E-mail her at rhixson@telus.net.

Colleen Ferris Holz lives in Wisconsin with her family. Her writing has been published in Health Communications, Inc. books and various magazines. She graduated from the University of Wisconsin Oshkosh with a BS in Human Services and works as a volunteer coordinator for a non-profit organization.

Carol Huff enjoys spending time with her horses and donkeys on her farm in Georgia. She enjoys inspirational writing, and her work has been published in several national magazines. E-mail her at herbiemakow@gmail.com.

An award-winning author—most recently, *The Complete Idiot's Guide to Wine and Food Pairing*—**Jeanette Hurt** still cooks for her rescue dog, Olivia, but today she's more apt to cook for people. She lives in Milwaukee with her husband and son. Visit her at www.jeanettehurt. com or follow her on Twitter.

Robbie Iobst is a writer and speaker living in Centennial, CO, with her husband John, son Noah and dog Scooby. Her stories have been featured in four other *Chicken Soup for the Soul* titles. E-mail her at robbieiobst@hotmail.com or read her blog at www.robbieiobst.blogspot.com.

Stacy S. Jensen received her Journalism degree from the University of Georgia in 1993. Stacy enjoys spending time with her family and traveling. E-mail her at stacysjensen@gmail.com.

Kara Johnson is a freelance writer living in Boise, ID, with her husband Jim, and dog, Barkley. She is a mentor for high school and college girls, and enjoys reading, traveling, and all sorts of outdoor adventures.

J.J. Kay writes novels for children and memoirs and sailing stories for adults. She and Schooner live in Florida where they enjoy boating and beaches. J.J. Kay is a mediator in the courts and ombudsman for nursing homes. E-mail her at janice@posners.net.

Mimi Greenwood Knight lives in South Louisiana with her husband, David, and four magnificent children, Haley O'Hara, Molly, Hewson and Jonah. The Knights are blessed to share their lives with McFly, Tootsie, Opie, Belle and Molly-the-Dog.

Catherine Kopp received her BS from Framingham State College and Master of Education from Lesley University. She has been teaching elementary school since 1973. Catherine teaches fifth grade in Denver, CO, where she lives with her husband, Jim. She enjoys writing, literature, yoga, and gardening.

Joyce Laird is a freelance writer living in Southern California with her menagerie of animal companions. Her features have been published in many magazines including, *Cat Fancy*, *Grit*, *Mature Living*, *I Love Cats* and *Vibrant Life*. She contributes regularly to *Woman's World* and *Chicken Soup for the Soul* books.

Cathi LaMarche is the author of the novel *While the Daffodils Danced* and has contributed to various anthologies. She currently teaches high school English and is working on her second novel. She resides in St. Louis with her husband, two children, and three spoiled dogs.

Jamie Lee received a BS in Broadcasting/Journalism. Her creative talents extend to video production, photography, and writing for pleasure and business. Jamie's passion has always been animals. She operates an animal wellness business and studies aromatherapy and holistic animal healing. E-mail her at jlee.lee274@gmail.com.

Brendalyn Crudup Martin began writing as a child. Her first love was poetry, and she currently holds the title of Poet Laureate of the Arizona Supreme Court. She later began writing devotional and personal experience stories. Inspired by her grandchildren, she is now working on a series of children's stories.

David Martin's humor and political satire have appeared in many publications, including *The New York Times*, the *Chicago Tribune* and *Smithsonian Magazine*. His latest humor collection, *Dare to be Average*, was published in 2010 by Lulu.com. David lives in Ottawa, Canada with his wife Cheryl, his daughter Sarah and their dog Oreo.

Kim Kluxen Meredith received her BA in Spanish from Washington College in 1974. In addition to teaching high school Spanish, Kim just published her first book, *Listen for the Whispers: Coping with Grief and Learning to Live Again* with Cable Publishing in July 2010. E-mail her at kimkmeredith@verizon.net.

Lynn Ruth Miller's writings have appeared in more than 200 publications. She compiled her essays into two books: *Thoughts While Walking the Dog* (2001) and *More Thoughts While Walking the Dog* (2003). She published two novels: *Starving Hearts* (2000) and *The Late Bloomer* (2006). E-mail her at lynnruth@pacbell.net.

Marya Miller first started writing at age eight when she produced a gripping melodrama about her teddy bear. A busy sales copywriter by day, she relaxes in her free time by working on *The Secret of Night-Must-Fall Farm*, a young adult equestrian mystery. E-mail her at marya@knottwood.com.

In 1990, **Lisa Morris** received her BA and Master's of Education from LaGrange College. She currently teaches fourth grade Language Arts in Niceville, FL. Lisa enjoys writing, spending time with her Labs and children, and reading. E-mail her at lovealab@aol.com.

Rachel Neumeier began writing fantasy novels to relax while in graduate school—the same time she got Lotka, her first dog. Her writing skills have since improved, but she doubts she will ever have a dog who improves on Lotka! She can be contacted via www.rachelneumeier.com or www.anaracavaliers.com.

Marc Tyler Nobleman is the author of more than seventy books including *Boys of Steel: The Creators of Superman* and one due out in 2012 about the "secret" co-creator of Batman. His cartoons have appeared in more than 100 international publications. At noblemania.blogspot.com, he reveals the behind-the-scenes stories of his work.

Andrea Peebles lives with her two dogs and her husband of thirty-three years in Rockmart, GA. She currently works full-time in the insurance industry and owns and operates a part-time garden wedding facility at her home. Andrea enjoys nature, travel, photography and writing. E-mail her at aanddpeebles@aol.com.

Ava Pennington is a writer, speaker, and Bible teacher. She has published numerous magazine articles and contributed to twenty anthologies, including fourteen *Chicken Soup for the Soul* books. She has also authored *One Year Alone with God: 366 Devotions on the Names of God* (Revell, 2010). Learn more at www.AvaWrites.com.

Saralee Perel is an award-winning columnist/novelist and a multiple contributor to Chicken Soup for the Soul. Her newest book, *The Dog Who Walked Me*, is about her dog who became her caregiver after Saralee suffered a spinal cord injury and her cat who kept her sane. E-mail her at sperel@saraleeperel.com or visit her website at www.saraleeperel.com.

Mimi Pollack, whose native tongue is French, has always had a great love of dogs and of the English language. She lives in Florida where she raises her five children and trains her Coton de Tulear, Trixie. This is her first published work. E-mail her at mimi@pollackhome.com.

Marsha Porter is an author of numerous short stories, articles and a teacher's handbook. She holds a Master's in Educational Administration and currently teaches English. She co-authored an annual DVD and Video Guide. Ms. Porter has written a monthly column and does freelance writing and editing.

Tim Ramsey is a school administrator in Arizona. He has been an educator since 1983. He lives with his wife, daughter and seven cats. Tim shares his joy of writing with students and teachers alike in a variety of settings. E-mail him at tramsey@q.com.

Rhonda Richards-Cohen is a graduate of Greenville College and Stanford University. She resides in Dallas with her stepchildren Ashley and Garrett, her husband Todd, and her dog Hanger. She is writing a memoir about her time as a caregiver for an elderly aunt who was a hoarder.

Jeannette Richter farms with her husband John in Alberta, Canada. She is currently working on a novel about the struggle of French-Canadians to maintain their language and culture after the Louis Riel Uprising in Manitoba in 1870.

Sauni Rinehart speaks and sings at women's events and retreats. She has self-published four books, and her stories have appeared in several anthologies, national magazines, and on www.christiandevotions.us. Sauni has been happily married to Russ since 1988 and resides in Eastvale, CA. Learn more at www.saunirinehart.com.

Sallie A. Rodman lives with Paul and Mollie in Los Alamitos, CA. Her work has appeared in numerous *Chicken Soup for the Soul* anthologies. When Mollie and Sallie aren't out playing, she mentors other writers, is working on a book and does mixed media art projects. E-mail her at sa.rodman@verizon.net.

John Scanlan is a native of Circleville, OH. He is a 1983 graduate of the United States Naval Academy, and retired from the Marine Corps as a Lieutenant Colonel. John resides on Hilton Head Island, SC, and is pursuing a second career as a writer. E-mail John at ping1@hargray.com.

Elaine Ernst Schneider is a teacher, artist/illustrator, and freelance writer. An accomplished writer for many audiences, including children, Elaine is a freelance curriculum writer and is the managing editor of *Lesson Tutor*, a lesson plan site found at lessontutor.com. Her book, *Taking Hearing Impairment to School*, is published by JayJo Books, a Guidance Channel Company.

Loretta Schoen grew up in Brazil, New York, and Rome, Italy. She currently lives in Boca Raton, FL, with her husband, two cats and two dogs. She enjoys traveling and has a passion for working with abused animals. She is currently writing medical stories to inspire and empower patients.

Michelle Sedas is author of *Welcome The Rain* and *Live Inspired* and co-author of *The Power of 10%*. She is host of the Inspired Living Café and cofounder of Running Moms Rock. Michelle graduated from Texas A&M University and lives in Texas with her husband and children. Visit Michelle at www.michellesedas.com.

Mary Z. Smith is a regular contributor to *Chicken Soup for the Soul* as well as *Guideposts* and *Angels on Earth* magazines. When she's not penning praises to God, she can be found tending her flower garden or walking her Rat Terrier Frankie. Mary and husband Barry live in Richmond, VA, enjoying visits from their children and grandchildren.

Stephanie Smithken is a freelance writer and online copywriter with degrees in both English and Psychology. Since 2006, she's written about lifestyle, health, small business and marketing topics for a variety of sites and businesses. Other creative projects for Stephanie include two children's picture books in the works.

Robin Sokol recieved her BA in English and Masters in Communication from the University of Dubuque. She works as an IT administrator and she volunteers for the Humane Society. Robin enjoys traveling, reading, writing, trap shooting, and spending time with her three children. E-mail her at epfan09@yahoo.com.

Laurie Sontag is a California newspaper columnist and author of the popular blog, Manic Motherhood. Her work regularly appears in books, magazines and on the Yahoo Shine Network for Women. You can see more of her work at www.lauriesontag.com.

Joyce Stark lives in Northeast Scotland. Retired from local government, she is now a freelance writer. She has travel and children's books in the process of publication. She and her husband have travelled forty-five of the U.S. states as their hobby. E-mail her at joric.stark@virgin.net.

Meg Stragier graduated from Pomona College in 1953, taught school, raised four children, worked in the family business, and started writing. She lives in Arizona with her husband Marc and their German Shepherd and Newfoundland dogs. She treasures time with her family, gardening, hiking, and boating. E-mail her at mmstragier@gmail.com.

Joyce Sudbeck is happily retired. Writing has opened the door to challenge and excitement with modest publishing successes including two *Chicken Soup for the Soul* books, *Liguorian* magazine, *Thin Threads*, *Good Old Days* magazine and prize winning poetry in 2009/2010.

Writer, speech therapist, memoir teacher, wife and mother, **Tsgoyna Tanzman** credits writing as the supreme "therapy" for raising an adolescent daughter. Published in numerous *Chicken Soup for the Soul* books, her humorous essays and poems can be read on www. more.com, www.motheringmagazine.com and in *The Orange County Register*. E-mail her at tnzmn@cox.net.

Linda Elmore Teeple writes passionately about her personal foibles and flubs—and God's gracious response. Family and friends also provide a wealth of object lessons for her writing. Linda loves being a wife, mother, and grandmother. She is a family therapist and enjoys mission trips and fostering service dog puppies.

Sue Thompson lives in Northwest Minnesota with her husband, children and dogs. She is working toward her PhD at the University of North Dakota. Sue enjoys golfing, gardening, and spending time with family and friends. She writes a column for the *Crookston Times*. E-mail her at sthom4@hotmail.com.

Rebecca Vaughan received her BA in English and Creative Writing from Hollins University in Roanoke, VA. She now resides in North Carolina with her husband and two dogs. She enjoys working with animals (especially dogs), taking photographs, beach trips, and hiking.

Suzanne Vaughan has a BS in Education, is the author of the book *Potholes and Parachutes*, and is a motivational speaker who has delivered personal growth programs to corporations and associations for more than twenty-five years. She is past-president of the Colorado

Speakers Association. E-mail her at Suzspeaks@comcast.net or visit her website www.suzannevaughan.com.

Sharon Dunski Vermont is a full-time wife and mother, part-time pediatrician and freelance writer. She received her MD degree from the University of Missouri-Kanasas City School of Medicine in 1993. Her daughers, Hannah and Jordyn, and husband, Laird, are the inspiration for everything she does. E-mail her at svermont1987@yahoo.com.

Samantha Ducloux Waltz, an award-winning freelance writer in Portland, OR, currently has numerous stories anthologized. Her dog, cat and horse are her favorite muses. She also teaches the Tell 'Em and Sell 'Em workshops and has written fiction and non-fiction under the name Samellyn Wood. Learn more about Samantha at www.pathsofthought.com.

Laurie Whitermore has always enjoyed writing, a special gift she shared with her mom. She serves as a School Counselor for the Dunkirk School District and loves the challenges and wonder that come from working with young people. Her family—Greg, Colin and Allison—is her greatest joy.

Paul Winick, MD lives in Hollywood, FL, with his wife Dorothy. He practiced there for thirty years and is currently Professor of Clinical Pediatrics at Miami Medical School. He's the proud father of two and grandfather of five. This is his sixth *Chicken Soup for the Soul* contribution. He has published a memoir, *Finding Ruth*. E-mail him at paulwinick@pol.net.

Susan Winslow is a therapeutic horseback riding instructor and lifelong animal lover. She lives on a small farm in Boxford, MA, with her husband Scott, three children—Lexie, Sam and Keelie, and an assortment of horses, donkeys, cats, dogs and birds. She writes for three national equine magazines and is working on a novel.

Linda C. Wright left the hustle and bustle of the business world to pursue her passion for writing. She lives on the Florida Space Coast and enjoys traveling, photography and reading. She's working on her second novel. E-mail her at lindacwright@ymail.com.

Gary B. Xavier is an author, lecturer, and newspaper columnist. He has enjoyed four decades with his wife Linda, and they have two sons and a marvelous granddaughter. They have enjoyed the company and comfort of eleven dogs. This is his third *Chicken Soup for the Soul* story. E-mail him at gary_xavier@yahoo.com.

D. B. Zane is a writer, teacher, and mother of three. In her free time, she enjoys reading, walking the dog, and taking her for the occasional trip to the beach. E-mail her at dbzanewriter@gmail.com.

Bill Zarchy is a writer, teacher, and director of photography. Film credits include *West Wing Documentary*, *Conceiving Ada*, and *Read You Like A Book*. Published writings include a story in *Chicken Soup for the Soul: Empty Nesters* and two dozen essays and technical articles. He teaches cinematography at San Francisco State. Learn more at www.billzarchy.com.

Meet Our Authors

Jack Canfield is the co-creator of the *Chicken Soup for the Soul* series, which *Time* magazine has called "the publishing phenomenon of the decade." Jack is also the co-author of many other bestselling books.

Jack is the CEO of the Canfield Training Group in Santa Barbara, California, and founder of the Foundation for Self-Esteem in Culver City, California. He has conducted intensive personal and professional development seminars on the principles of success for more than a million people in twenty-three countries, has spoken to hundreds of thousands of people at more than 1,000 corporations, universities, professional conferences and conventions, and has been seen by millions more on national television shows.

Jack has received many awards and honors, including three honorary doctorates and a Guinness World Records Certificate for having seven books from the *Chicken Soup for the Soul* series appearing on the New York Times bestseller list on May 24, 1998.

You can reach Jack at www.jackcanfield.com.

Mark Victor Hansen is the co-founder of Chicken Soup for the Soul, along with Jack Canfield. He is a sought-after keynote speaker, bestselling author, and marketing maven. Mark's powerful messages of possibility, opportunity, and action have created powerful change in thousands of organizations and millions of individuals worldwide.

Mark is a prolific writer with many bestselling books in addition to the *Chicken Soup for the Soul* series. Mark has had a profound influence in the field of human potential through his library of audios, videos, and articles in the areas of big thinking, sales achievement, wealth building, publishing success, and personal and professional development. He is also the founder of the MEGA Seminar Series.

Mark has received numerous awards that honor his entrepreneurial spirit, philanthropic heart, and business acumen. He is a lifetime member of the Horatio Alger Association of Distinguished Americans.

You can reach Mark at www.markvictorhansen.com.

Jennifer Quasha is an award-winning writer and editor. She is a published author of more than 40 books, including three dog books: *Don't Pet a Pooch... While He's Pooping: Etiquette for Dogs and their People*, *The Dog Lover's Book of Crafts: 50 Home Decorations that Celebrate Man's Best Friend*, and *Sew Dog: Easy-Sew Dogwear and Custom Gear for Home and Travel*.

She graduated from Boston University with a BS in Communication and has been writing ever since. Jennifer has been a contributing editor at *Dog Fancy* and *Dogs for Kids* magazines, and has written monthly columns on rescue dogs, etiquette, and travel. Jennifer has also been published in Chicken Soup for the Soul books and is thrilled to be a co-author of *My Dog's Life* and *My Cat's Life*.

In her free time Jennifer loves to read, travel and eat anything anyone else prepares for her. She lives with her husband, kids, and two dogs, Sugar and Scout. You can reach her by visiting her website at www.jenniferquasha.com.

About
Wendy Diamond

Since adopting her Maltese, Lucky, along with a rescued Russian Blue cat named Pasha, **Wendy Diamond** has dedicated herself to animal rescue and welfare. She launched Animal Fair—a lifestyle media company in support of fairness to endangered animals and animal rescue—in 1999.

When Animal Fair launched, 12 million animals were euthanized in shelters. Since then, that number has decreased to 6 million. Animal Fair is dedicated to highlighting non-profit animal organizations, giving them the opportunity to tell their inspirational stories and to provide information so the community may be involved.

Wendy is a frequent pet lifestyle contributor to NBC's *Today Show* and has starred in television shows on CBS, NBC, Style Network, FOX, and Animal Planet. Wendy and Lucky Diamond were judges on CBS' primetime hit *Greatest American Dog*! Wendy has also contributed and has appeared on CBS' *The Early Show*, *The View*, Fox News, CNN, *Extra*, *Good Morning America*, E!, VH1, MTV among many others. She has been featured in numerous publications including *The New York Times*, *Forbes*, *Time*, *People*, *The New Yorker* and *Vogue*.

She also has written three books—*How to Understand Men Through Their Dogs*, *How to Understand Women Through Their Cats*, and *It's a Dog's World*, a lifestyle guide to living with your dog.

For the last decade Wendy and her team have created and

executed numerous original events with Animal Fair including Toys for Dogs, Paws for Style (the first-ever pet charity fashion show), Mutt Makeover, White House Pet Correspondents Benefit, Halloween Pet Costume Benefit, and Yappy Hour®, raising hundreds of thousands of dollars for local animal rescue.

Currently, Wendy serves on the board of advisors for the United Nations Millennium Development Goal Achievers and World Entrepreneurship Day. She continues to extend her wealth of animal knowledge serving as a keynote speaker on numerous pet lifestyle topics at seminars across the world from Harvard University to the United Nations.

You can find more information about pet lifestyle, animal rescue, and Wendy's work at www.animalfair.com.

Thank You

T hank you dog lovers! I owe huge thanks to every one of you who shared your stories about beloved dogs that have touched your lives. You have made me laugh, cry and nod my head. My heart soared when you got a new puppy; I chuckled at your teenage dog's shenanigans; I even found myself mellowing when I read about your adult dogs settling into who they were; and I promise that I cried with you when old age or sickness took your best friend from you. I know that you poured your hearts and souls into the thousands of stories and poems, and many times bravely opened yourselves up. Thank you. All of us at Chicken Soup for the Soul appreciate your willingness to share your lives with us.

We could only publish a small percentage of the stories that were submitted, but at least two of us read every single submission—and there were thousands! Even the stories that do not appear in the book influenced us and affected the final manuscript.

A special thank you goes to long-time Chicken Soup for the Soul editor and Assistant Publisher D'ette Corona, who read all the stories and poems with me. This book could not have been made without her expertise, input, and innate knowledge of what makes a great Chicken Soup for the Soul story. Amy Newmark, Chicken Soup for the Soul's whip-smart publisher had my back during every stage of creating this book and guided me gracefully and with quick replies. I also want to thank Chicken Soup for the Soul editor Kristiana Glavin for her assistance with every detail. Nothing is too big or too small for

Kristi to handle. I also want to thank editors Barbara LoMonaco and Madeline Clapps for proofreading assistance.

Thank you to cartoonist Marc Tyler Nobleman for giving us twelve reasons to giggle throughout the book. Lastly, I owe a very special thanks to our creative director and book producer, Brian Taylor at Pneuma Books, for his brilliant vision for our covers and interiors. Finally, none of this would be possible without the business and creative leadership of Chicken Soup for the Soul's CEO, Bill Rouhana, and president, Bob Jacobs.

Keep writing, friends. I can't wait to hear from you again!

~Jennifer Quasha

Improving Your Life Every Day

R eal people sharing real stories—for seventeen years. Now, Chicken Soup for the Soul has gone beyond the bookstore to become a world leader in life improvement. Through books, movies, DVDs, online resources and other partnerships, we bring hope, courage, inspiration and love to hundreds of millions of people around the world. Chicken Soup for the Soul's writers and readers belong to a one-of-a-kind global community, sharing advice, support, guidance, comfort, and knowledge.

Chicken Soup for the Soul stories have been translated into more than forty languages and can be found in more than one hundred countries. Every day, millions of people experience a Chicken Soup for the Soul story in a book, magazine, newspaper or online. As we share our life experiences through these stories, we offer hope, comfort and inspiration to one another. The stories travel from person to person, and from country to country, helping to improve lives everywhere.

Share with Us

We all have had Chicken Soup for the Soul moments in our lives. If you would like to share your story or poem with millions of people around the world, go to chickensoup.com and click on "Submit Your Story." You may be able to help another reader, and become a published author at the same time. Some of our past contributors have launched writing and speaking careers from the publication of their stories in our books!

Our submission volume has been increasing steadily—the quality and quantity of your submissions has been fabulous. We only accept story submissions via our website. They are no longer accepted via mail or fax.

To contact us regarding other matters, please send us an e-mail through webmaster@chickensoupforthesoul.com, or fax or write us at:

Chicken Soup for the Soul
P.O. Box 700
Cos Cob, CT 06807-0700
Fax: 203-861-7194

One more note from your friends at Chicken Soup for the Soul: Occasionally, we receive an unsolicited book manuscript from one of our readers, and we would like to respectfully inform you that we do not accept unsolicited manuscripts and we must discard the ones that appear.

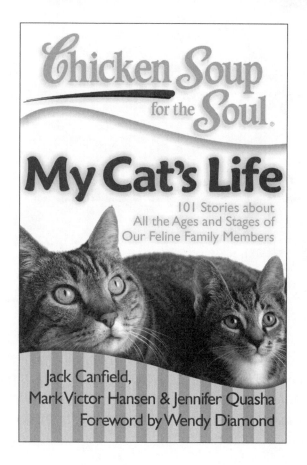

Chicken Soup for the Soul

My Cat's Life

101 Stories about All the Ages and Stages of Our Feline Family Members

Jack Canfield,
Mark Victor Hansen & Jennifer Quasha
Foreword by Wendy Diamond

From kittenhood through the twilight years, our feline companions continually bring joy, love, and laughter to the lives of their "staff." This collection of 101 new stories captures the experience of living through the natural life cycle with our cats — from the laugh-out-loud antics of kittens and tear-your-hair-out escapades of teenage cats to the more mature adult years and final stages of life. Stories cover each age and stage with all the fun, frustrations, special bonds and routines involved. The book also holds a special chapter about grieving and recovery when our feline friends leave us.

978-1-935096-66-5

*C*lassics for **Cat Lovers**

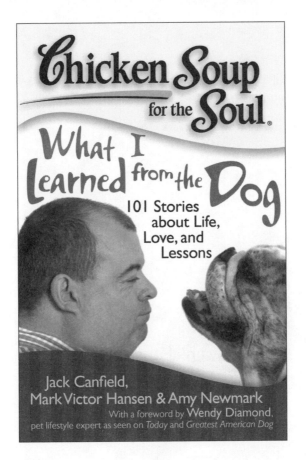

Chicken Soup for the Soul.

What I Learned from the Dog

101 Stories about Life, Love, and Lessons

Jack Canfield,
Mark Victor Hansen & Amy Newmark
With a foreword by Wendy Diamond,
pet lifestyle expert as seen on Today and Greatest American Dog

An old dog might not be able to learn new tricks, but he might teach his owner a thing or two. Dog lovers will recognize themselves, or their dogs, in these 101 new tales from the owners of these lovable canines. Stories of learning how to be kinder, overcome adversity, say goodbye, love unconditionally, stay strong, and tales of loyalty, listening, and family will delight and inspire readers, and also cause some tears and some laughter.

978-1-935096-38-2

Classics for Dog Lovers

Chicken Soup for the Soul

www.chickensoup.com